CaseBase:
Case Studies in
Global Business

ISSN 2160-326X

CaseBase: Case Studies in Global Business

Andrew Ashwin,
General Editor

GALE
CENGAGE Learning

Detroit • New York • San Francisco • New Haven, Conn • Waterville, Maine • London

CaseBase: Case Studies in Global Business

General Editor: Andrew Ashwin

Product Management: Jenai Drouillard

Project Editor: Virgil L. Burton III

Managing Editor: Scott Bragg

Editorial: Miranda Ferrara

Composition and Electronic Prepress: Evi Seoud

Manufacturing: Rita Wimberley

Gale
27500 Drake Rd.
Farmington Hills, MI 48331-3535

ISBN-13: 978-1-4144-8682-6
ISBN-10: 1-4144-8682-0

ISSN 2160-326X

This title is also available as an e-book.
ISBN-13: 978-1-4144-8693-2
ISBN-10: 1-4144-8693-6
Contact your Gale, a part of Cengage Learning sales representative for ordering information.

Printed in the United States of America
2 3 4 5 6   15 14 13 12 11
ED263

Contents

Introduction

This is the first in a series of volumes to complement the publication of case studies as part of Gale's Business Insights: Global (BI:G) online research portal. BI:G is being developed to help equip students to research, analyze, interpret, and understand international business topics. It provides the tools students need to analyze business data, delivered in narratives with an international perspective. BI:G also supports teachers of international business; it presents cases organized around countries, industries, companies, and topics, and extends these case studies and data from the research environment to the learning environment.

BI:G uses case studies to highlight key business issues. As business becomes ever more global, the boundaries between national business interests blur, and students are required to understand perspectives across different cultures. Even though there are many different cultures and ways of conducting business, certain fundamental principles bind businesses together wherever they operate. These principles involve the need to respond to customer demand, focus on cost, increase revenue, and maintain and improve quality. In addition, there is no avoiding the effect of external factors on business operations, including rules, regulations and legislation passed by governments and organizations such as the European Union (EU), the North American Free Trade Association (NAFTA), and the Gulf Cooperation Council (GCC). The perspectives, conduct, and cooperation of diverse peoples involved in carrying out business operations around the globe is another key factor in shaping every venture.

The majority of these case studies have an international focus. They describe business in an international context, providing an overview of key issues in business from a global perspective, free of specific country bias. Considering different perspectives helps to develop a broader understanding of the business environment. It illustrates the fact that there is rarely a right answer in business, but rather a series of decisions often made with incomplete or inaccurate information, and the consequences of these decisions makes business a fascinating and ever-evolving subject to explore and study. These case studies are designed to complement the study of business and business related topics, wherever in the world the student or instructor happens to live.

All the case studies have been presented in a consistent way. Each case is preceded by a series of suggested learning objectives that help the reader to focus on a particular aspect or outcome of the case. The learning objectives relate to general assessment objectives that are common to students and courses regardless of the country in which the learning is taking place. They focus students on a range of skills, from basic knowledge and understanding, to the application of knowledge in different contexts, the analysis and synthesis of knowledge and the ability to evaluate and make judgements, place a value on issues and make recommendations.

The case study concludes with a series of questions, designed to test students' comprehension of the case content and their ability to take new information and apply it in various ways. The questions can generate classroom discussion for students who have read the case as part of their assigned homework. Alternately, the questions might be assigned to students and their answers submitted as part of an assessment or simply by the student who wants to build his or her own understanding of the subject and develop core skills. The case could also be used as the basis for discussion in a class setting; the lecturer setting the case for students to read prior to the next class when discussion will be held on key issues arising out of the case study. The questions provided could form the basis for the discussion or the lecturer might decide on a completely different set of questions.

One of the advantages of case studies is their versatility as learning tools. While the authors in each case here have provided some suggested learning outcomes and associated questions, each case can also be used for different purposes. Instructors might identify topics or issues not covered in a given case and use them to promote further investigation and debate. The case studies offer educational guidance yet are flexible enough to allow room for additional exploration and discovery.

Many people made this book possible. First, I would like to express my thanks to the authors who have contributed to this first volume. Authors have risen to the challenge set by the editors with commendable flexibility and determination. I would like to express my thanks for the hard work that the authors put in to submit their final drafts.

As with any book, there are a large number of people working in the background who make the production a reality but who do not get any direct credit. In particular I would like to thank David Forman, Vice President and Publisher at the Learning and Research Solutions department of Cengage Learning who drove the project forward, Jenai Drouillard for product managing BI:G, Scott Bragg, Michele LaMeau, Virgil Burton, Keith Jones and Miranda Ferrara.

I believe that this first volume of CaseBase sets a baseline on which we can build future volumes. We welcome suggestions from readers as we plan future case studies. If you can contribute a future case study or have comments on how this product may be improved, we would love to hear from you. Our aim is to meet our customers' needs; by evaluating this product and letting us know what you would like to see in future, you can play an important part in helping us to meet those needs.

Andrew Ashwin, General Editor

A Compliance Model of Corporate Social Responsibility: The Example of Manville Trust, Shareholder versus Massey Energy Company

Jean E. Harris • Associate Professor, Accounting, School of Public Administration, Pennsylvania State University, Harrisburg

LEARNING OBJECTIVES

Studying this case should enable students to do the following:

- *Explain how the compliance model of corporate social responsibility (CSR) differs from the exemplary model of CSR*
- *Explain the meaning of a derivative lawsuit*
- *Examine how the assessment of risks can influence CSR*
- *Analyze the relationship between corporate governance and CSR*

This case was prepared for classroom discussion rather than to illustrate either effective or ineffective handling of an administrative, ethical, or legal decision by management. Information was gathered from corporate as well as public sources.

INTRODUCTION

The 2010 lawsuits of a shareholder, The Manville Trust, against the coal company, Massey Energy, seek to establish a concept of corporate social responsibility (CSR) as compliance with laws and regulations. Although these lawsuits were filed at the Kanawha County Court House in Charleston, West Virginia, the emergence of this compliance model of CSR has implications that go beyond state and national borders. In this case study, readers are asked to consider CSR from the perspective of two distinct objectives. From one perspective, a compliance model of CSR directs attention to the achievement of compliance with laws and regulations. From another perspective, an exemplary model of CSR directs attention to the achievement of various expectations that are assumed by senior management to provide social benefit as perceived primarily by investors and potential investors.

This case study has three primary parts. First, the two models of CSR are contrasted. Then the compliance model is illustrated with reference to an example of its development. The compliance model and the exemplary model are not competing models of CSR. Rather, these models of CSR are complementary models with the compliance model directed toward the achievement of certain externally defined, basic expectations of CSR and the exemplary model directed toward the achievement of certain internally defined, additional expectations of CSR. Finally, suggestions are made to extend the applicability of the compliance model of CSR.

The use of a compliance model of CSR can be seen in the adoption of a law in the United States requiring the disclosure of data about mine safety violations for all corporations, domestic and foreign that trade on U.S. exchanges. These disclosures are included in filings intended primarily for investors and potential investors along with the reporting of financial data.

TWO COMPLEMENTARY MODELS OF CSR

The compliance model of CSR is externally driven. It is directed toward reducing corporate social irresponsibility as evidenced by the violations of laws and regulations. Change is motivated largely by penalties ranging from adverse publicity to loss of investment capital and legally imposed sanctions. The measure of success is the minimal baseline achievement of compliance by corporations with laws and regulations. In contrast, the exemplary model is driven internally by dominant shareholders and/or senior managers who seek to demonstrate CSR in ways that are consistent with various organizational objectives. The exemplary model is directed to the voluntary pursuit of practices that are thought to be socially responsible. Change is motivated by various factors, including the incentive of attracting investments by investors who value the pursuit of CSR. Success is measured against organizational objectives.

Figure 1 contrasts the compliance model of CSR and the exemplary model of CSR.

From accounting and auditing perspectives, one can argue that the compliance model is stronger than the exemplary model. The production, collection, and aggregation of data about compliance are guided by the clearly defined and publicly accepted standards of laws and regulations. Often, third parties produce compliance data externally, and these data can be verified by audit. Because the compliance model is grounded in laws and regulations, the means of enforcement are explicit. Although the exemplary model has no explicit means of enforcement, from a managerial perspective, one can argue that the exemplary model that is driven by internally generated motivations is more powerful than the compliance model that is driven by externally imposed

FIGURE I

Attribute	Exemplary Model (EM)	Compliance Model (CM)
Objective	Achievement of socially responsible performance that is exemplary	Avoidance of socially irresponsible behavior by compliance with law and regulations
Standards for judgment of responsible behavior	Various	Compliance with relevant laws and regulations
Source of standards for judgment	Many sources from individual entity to private bodies	Legally constituted representative government
Comparability of entities with respect to CSR	Difficult due to various standards	Moderate to strong if within same industry
Source of evidence with respect to standards	Mainly internal evidence.	Mainly external evidence from third-party regulators.
Internal Enforcement	Means vary	Heavy reliance on internal control systems targeted toward compliance with laws and regulations.
Enforcement	Weak, largely voluntary, and primarily internal.	By government action.
Content of report	Flexible	Specific to compliance
Third-party examination by independent audit	Difficult due to lack of common standards and content	Achievable with compliance auditing

Compliance Model of CSR and Exemplary Model of CSR

controls. By looking at both of these models, one can see two distinct and powerful forces for CSR.

AN ILLUSTRATION

The compliance model is illustrated by using an example of its development. Five aspects of that development are

a. the means
b. the participants
c. the objective
d. the process
e. the results

An Illustration: The Means

Acceptance of the compliance model of CSR can come from (a) attention created by publicity that seeks to change expectations, (b) lawsuits, (c) enforcement actions initiated by governments, and (d) other means. For example, in this case study, the relevant means are a derivative lawsuit and adoption of a new law. The term *derivative* as used in derivative lawsuit has no relationship to financial instruments that are described as derivatives. In a derivative lawsuit, power derives from the existence of a corporation for a shareholder to seek legal remedies to benefit the corporation. A shareholder, acting on behalf of the corporation, can bring such a lawsuit against a third party. Typically, the third party is a corporate officer or a corporate director, whose actions are alleged to have damaged the corporation. Typically, the remedy that is sought is a change in corporate governance or policy.

The shareholder who brings the lawsuit does not benefit directly by receiving damages or other means of direct compensation. Rather, the corporation is viewed as the immediate and direct beneficiary. For example, the corporation can be compelled to improve its governance structure. A *stipulation of settlement* agreement is the name given to an agreement that is submitted for approval and for subsequent enforcement by the court in which the suit is brought. If the parties to the lawsuit come to a mutual resolution of matters that are before the court, such agreement can be submitted for court approval as an alternative to a trial.

Derivative lawsuits can be brought in many countries, including Australia, Canada, France, Japan, Korea, the UK, and the United States. Adoption of the judicial mechanism of a derivative lawsuit has been encouraged for other countries as a tool for achieving reforms relative to corporate governance. For example, Deng argues that China should adopt the derivative lawsuit as a means for shareholders to influence corporate governance. With respect to the compliance model, two relevant aspects of corporate governance are (a) implementing control systems to prevent violation of laws and regulations and (b) instituting reporting systems to provide for public disclosure of data about violations.

An Illustration: Parties to Suits

To illustrate the principle of derivative lawsuits, a particular example focusing on Massey (Massey Energy Company) and The Manville Trust (Manville Personal Injury Settlement Trust), a shareholder in Massey, is used. Massey, which trades on the New York Stock Exchange under the ticker symbol MEE, is the fourth largest coal company in the United States and the largest coal company in the Central Appalachian region of the eastern United States. in this region, absentee corporate ownership of land and of natural resources is as common and as extensive as in many developing counties. With almost $4 billion in total assets, Massey operates both underground mines and surface mines. It is the largest supplier of high volatile coking coal to the Canadian metallurgical markets, and it exports coal to other foreign countries.

Massey has been aggressive in pursuing the environmentally damaging, mountaintop removal method of mining. By using this method of mining, massive amounts of earth are moved from the tops of mountains to fill valleys and cover streams. Additionally, vast quantities of liquid waste, called coal slurry or coal sludge, are stored in enormous dammed reservoirs called impoundments. Sources for information pertaining to Massey are provided in Figure 2.

The Johns Manville Corporation was a U.S. manufacturer of asbestos from 1858 to 1982. Because of a class action suit in 1982 related to asbestos injuries, it became the largest U.S. company at the time to seek bankruptcy protection. As of the early 2000s, the reorganized Johns Manville Corporation is a wholly

FIGURE 2

Coal River (2008) a book by Michael Shnayerson, Editor of Vanity Fair, about the aggressive practices of Massey in mining by mountaintop removal. See also the related documentary film *On Coal River.*

Massey's web page (http://www.masseyenergyco.com/about/index.shtml)
To find Corporate Social Responsibility Report go first to Investor tab and then to Annual Report tab. Starting in 2009, the annual financial report posted on Massey's web page is highly abbreviated. For full annual financial report, see 10-K filed with SEC.

SEC (http://www.sec.gov/edgar/searchedgar/companysearch.html)
Search financial reports filed with U.S. Securities and Exchange Commission (SEC) by using ticket symbol MEE. An annual report is a 10-K and a quarterly report is a 10-Q.

Blogs and articles by Ken Ward, Jr, award winning reporter who covers Massey
(http://www.niemanwatchdog.org/index.cfm?fuseaction=about.viewContributors&bioid=202) for *Charleston Gazette Newspapers* (http://www.wvgazette.com/).

Letter from William Patterson, Executive Director of CtW Investment Group, dated April 29, 2010, asking shareholders to withhold their votes for some members of Board of Directors with explanation of violations of safety and environmental policies.
See: http://wonkroom.thinkprogress.org/wp-content/uploads/2010/04/CtW-Inv-Grp-to-Massey-Shareholders-4-29-10.pdf.

Yahoo Finance (http://finance.yahoo.com/q?s=MEE).

Sources for Information About the Massey Energy Company

---

owned subsidiary of Berkshire Hathaway, a conglomerate holding company with nearly $300 billion in assets invested in both U.S. and foreign operations. The Manville Personal Injury Settlement Trust, a legally separate entity from the Johns Manville Corporation, was established in 1982 as part of the reorganization in bankruptcy of the Johns Manville Corporation. The purpose of The Manville Trust, which in 2009 had over $1 billion in assets, is to compensate asbestos claimants. Approximately 60% of the assets of this trust are held in equity investments.

The Manville Trust, which owns 2,700 shares of Massey, brought two major derivative lawsuits in Kanawha County, West Virginia, against the Board of Directors (the Board) of Massey. The first of these derivative lawsuits, brought in 2007, sought to achieve certain changes in Massey's corporate governance. The second of these derivative lawsuits, brought in 2010, pertains to the deaths of 29 miners on April 5, 2010, at Massey's the Upper Big Branch Mine. This second lawsuit is notable because The Manville Trust was joined by two other institutional shareholders: 1) the California State Teachers' Retirement System (CalSTRS) with 336,000 shares of Massey and $138 billion of total assets and 2) the Amalgamated Bank with 23,740 shares of Massey and $11 billion of assets in its LongView Collective Investment Fund (Burr).

An Illustration: The Objective

In its 2007 derivative lawsuit against Massey, The Manville Trust sought a court-sanctioned stipulation of settlement agreement to alter the corporate governance of Massey. Among the governance reforms that The Manville Trust sought were the implementation of internal control systems to ensure compliance with laws and regulations pertaining to the environment and to safety and public reporting relative to compliance. Of all the corporate governance reforms The Manville Trust might have sought, one can ask, why did The Manville Trust seek 1) internal control systems to promote compliance with law and regulations pertaining to the environment and to safety and 2) reporting about that compliance? Most likely the answer is one word—costs, costs that can arise in the future for the violation of laws and regulations pertaining to workplace safety and/or environmental damage.

Two types of violations that could create significant costs for Massey are environmental violations and safety violations. In 2008, after the Environmental Protection Agency (EPA) in the United States documented over 4,600 cases of pollutants being dumped in waterways, Massey Energy agreed to pay $20 million for violations of a the Clean Water Act, the largest civil penalty ever assessed by the Environmental Protection Agency. Massey owns one reservoir, the Brushy Fork Impoundment, which is designed to hold eight billion gallons (approximately 30 billion liters) of liquid mining waste and is secured by an earthen dam. In 1972, an earthen dam broke at the Buffalo Creek, West Virginia, impoundment owned by Consolidated Coal Company killing 125 people. In 2000, an earthen dam broke at the Massey-owned impoundment in Martin County, Kentucky, spilling 300 million gallons (approximately 1.1 billion liters) of slurry, creating one of the worst environmental disasters ever in the eastern United States.

Although causation remains to be determined, 29 miners were killed in one disaster in a Massey mine in April 2010, the worst single mine disaster in the United States between 1970 and 2010. For the operation where this disaster occurred, MSHA (the U.S. Mine Safety and Health Administration) had issued 557 citations for violations in the year before the explosion and had shut down work in portions of the mine 48 times for noncompliance. Most likely the costs of any disaster involving workplace safety or environmental damage will increase significantly if plaintiffs or prosecutors are able to establish that laws or regulations were violated in a material way that would provide evidence of a negligent disregard for the laws and regulations.

Changes in public attitudes and in enforcement policies have the potential to create other material costs. Four of the largest banks in the United States (Bank of America, Citi, JPMorgan Chase, and Wells Fargo) have announced policies to back away from financing the production of coal via the environmentally damaging mountaintop removal method of extraction. Increasingly, environmental groups are publicizing the actions of the coal mining industry with respect to the alleged contamination of water from mountaintop mining. Although a Massey operation was not involved, on January 13, 2011, in a rare action, the U.S. Environmental Protection Agency reversed a permit that had authorized the Arch Coal Company to operate a mountaintop mining operation. In this environment of violations and potential violations, costs can increase rapidly and in a material way—costs for damages, costs for legal fees, costs for borrowing, and sunk costs for investments in development when permits are denied.

In theory, market-based decisions about compliance and noncompliance with laws involve assessments of risks. A management can view the risks associated with noncompliance as acceptable when costs appear to be minimal. Based on an assessment of minimal risks, noncompliance can offer a means of increasing the value of a firm, especially in the short term. In contrast, shareholders who view themselves as long-term investors, as opposed to short-term speculators, can view the risks of noncompliance as unacceptable because they see potential costs that appear to be significant and a threat to the long-term value of a firm. In the later circumstance, it is the assessment of market risks of noncompliance that can drive shareholders either to seek corporate compliance with laws and regulations or to seek the opportunity to sell a risky investment.

An Illustration: The Process

The strategy of The Manville Trust to achieve changes in the corporate governance of Massey is apparent in Massey's record of derivative lawsuits and related events. Key events are listed in chronological order in Figure 3.

From the observation of its actions, the strategy of The Manville Trust appears to be based on three premises: (a) derivative lawsuits can be used to change corporate governance, (b) changes in corporate governance can be structured to encourage compliance with laws and regulations and in particular with laws and regulations pertaining to safety and environment, and (c) increased compliance can lead to higher levels of CSR and to increased financial return via reduction in potential financial liabilities.

As of late 2010, The Manville Trust was trying to use derivative lawsuits to achieve corporate governance reforms, an aspect of CSR. With this strategy, The Manville Trust was advancing a basic concept of CSR as being minimal compliance with laws and regulations. One of the motivations for the use of this strategy by The Manville Trust is that future financial liabilities arising from noncompliance with laws and regulations pose the risk of eroding the value of its investment in Massey.

FIGURE 3

March 31, 2003, Phillip R. Arlia, a shareholder, brought a derivative lawsuit (Arlia Suit) against the CEO of Massey and others alleging insider trading. This lawsuit was resolved by a Stipulation of Settlement agreement (Arlia Stipulation) that provided for certain modest and tentative corporate governance reforms at Massey.

July 2, 2007, The Manville Trust, a shareholder, brought a derivative lawsuit (Manville Environmental and Safety Suit) against the Board of Massey alleging conscious failure to comply with applicable environmental and worker-safety laws and regulations. The court approved a Stipulation of Settlement agreement (Manville Environmental and Safety Stipulation) that included a Corporate Governance Agreement (CGA). Subsequently, The Manville Trust filed for a court order to show cause as to why the Board of Directors of Massey should not be held in civil contempt for failing to comply with the Stipulation of Settlement agreement. At present, proceedings on this motion are in process.

April 15, 2010, The Manville Trust, a shareholder, brought a derivative suit (Massey Safety Suit) against the Board of Massey alleging the personal accountability of the Board for the Upper Big Branch Mine disaster in which twenty-nine miners died on April 5, 2010 and for mine safety violations. Subsequently, The Manville Trust was joined in this action by two other institutional shareholders: the California State Teachers' Retirement System (CalSTRS) and the Amalgamated Bank (Picardo-Allison, 2010).

May 18, 2010, possibly in response to a campaign by the pension funds of eight states to have shareholders withhold votes for the reelection of three directors, Massey agreed to propose two corporate governance reforms: 1) to de-stagger or declassify terms to enable all directors be elected at same time for terms of one year and 2) to require majority voting for directors, meaning that any director, running unopposed, who receives less than a majority of vote must tender a resignation which the Board then can accept or reject (Coster, 2010).

July 21, 2010 The Dodd-Frank Act was signed into law in the U.S. with Section 1503 requiring the disclosure of mine safety violations along with the disclosure of financial data in pubic reporting to the U.S. Securities and Exchange Commission by domestic and foreign issuers.

January 29, 2011. Alpha Natural Resources, Inc. announced, subject to regulatory approval, it would acquire a majority interest in Massey Energy for $7.1 billion USD.

Chronological Order of Key Events

An Illustration: The Result

One of the results that The Manville Trust achieved was the agreement of Massey to a court-sanctioned stipulation agreement (The Manville Environmental and Safety Stipulation of 2008). This settlement included an eight-page Corporate Governance Agreement (CGA) of changes in policies that Massey agreed to implement. This CGA sets forth a control structure to provide for the design and the implementation of internal control systems to ensure compliance with laws and regulations pertaining to environment and to safety. The Board is designated as having oversight responsibility through a committee of directors; the committee has responsibility for two vice-presidents acting as compliance officers; and each of the two vice-presidents has responsibility for a separate set of subordinate compliance managers. As a part of the oversight process, independent external audits are required every two years of Massey's practices and of internal controls with respect to the environment and to safety. Additionally, Massey's Board is required to report to shareholders annually regarding matters of environment and of safety in a Corporate Social Responsibility Report. The provisions of this CGA are summarized in Figure 4.

As of late 2010, it was anticipated that an explicit concern for internal controls over environmental and safety matters would heighten concern for the quality of controls in litigations. Arguments about legal liability are grounded in notions of reasonable action, of reckless action, and of intent. The quality of control systems speaks to the intent of management. Strong internal controls can provide evidence of reasonable action and suggest an intent of due care. In contrast, weak internal controls can provide evidence of neglect and suggest an intent lacking in due care. Thus, a part of the legal discourse becomes queries and responses about the quality of internal controls. For Massey in particular, the CGA of 2008 is likely to be an agreement that is referenced in future lawsuit because the design and the implementation of the on-going internal control systems for which it provides speak to the past and to the present intent of management in evaluating the nature of due care it exercised.

Although not directly related to the derivative lawsuit or to the CGA of 2008, two other events merit mention: (a) the July 2010 adoption of a law that requires national reporting in the United States of mine safety violations as part of financial reporting and (b) the acquisition in January 2011 of Massey by another company. Section 1503 of a major financial reform law in the United States, known as the Dodd-Frank Act, requires detailed and periodic reporting of mine safety violations by domestic and foreign issuers in publicly accessible documents filed with the U.S. Securities and Exchange Commission (SEC) and used primarily by investors and potential investors to access financial data. A foreign issuer is a foreign company that trades its equity or debt securities on U.S. securities exchanges. As with the filing of financial data, the primary filings are by the consolidated or group reporting entity, and data about safety violations are aggregated by the consolidated or group reporting entity. Although limited in scope to mine safety violations, this law is clear evidence of the beginning of acceptance of a Compliance Model of CSR.

FIGURE 4

Sec.	Provision
A	* Provides for the creation a Safety, Environmental and Public Policy Committee (SEPPC) of the Board. * Requires that a majority of SEPC members be being independent members. (In brief, an independent member is one not involved in management.) * Defines other rules with respect to selection and service of SEPPC members.
B-1	* Requires SEPPC to develop goals for implementing enhancements to the company-wide processes utilized to monitor, count, and report environmental incidents and complaints and sets forth the same requirements for safety incidents and complaints. * Mandates that an internal environmental compliance officer (Section C) and the external environmental compliance auditor will report to SEPPC. * Mandates that an internal safety compliance officer (Section C) and the external safety compliance auditor will report to SEPPC with first external safety audit occurring before June 30, 2009. * Requires SEPPC to report to the Board with respect to Massey's compliance with environmental laws and regulations and mine safety laws and regulations. * With respect to mine safety violations, SEPPC must report incidents by type, the findings of external auditor, and analysis of any causal factors contributing to incidents.
B-2	* Requires Board to report annually to shareholders about environmental and worker safety compliance in a Corporate Social Responsibility Report posted on Massey's website and referenced in SEC filings.
B-3	* Requires SEPPC to review annually Massey's safety training programs and environmental compliance training programs, to recommend enhancements as appropriate for both programs, and to report to Board annually on objectives and progress of both programs. * Requires SEPPC to give consideration to criteria and to measurement protocols to assure all responsible personnel, including contractors, know of all compliance obligations including obligations under EPA Consent Decree.
B-4	* Requires SEPPC to recommend to Board quantitative goals for reducing environmental violations and mine safety incidents and near misses with a high potential for injury. * Requires Board in Corporate Social Responsibility Report to report to shareholders in 2008 with respect to progress on these goals.
B-5	* Requires SEPPC, once every two years, to retain independent auditing firms to conduct comprehensive reviews and assessments with respect to worker safety and environmental compliance, and to report findings to Board.
C	* Establishes two senior positions for compliance: VP for Best Environmental Practices (aka: Environmental Compliance Officer) and VP for Best Safety Practices (aka: Safety Compliance Officer). And, under there senior officers establishes a hierarchical managerial structure of compliance mangers for environmental and safety compliance.
C-1	* Requires compliance officers in consultation with SEPPC to establish means for employees, suppliers, customers, and advisory professionals to report illegal and/or unethical conduct with respect to safety and environmental issues.
C-2	* Requires senior compliance officers to examine and to evaluate internal control procedures with regard to worker safety and environmental compliance and subordinate compliance manager to do same for internal control procedures of resource groups.
C-3	* Requires public reporting on Massey's web site of whistle blowing mechanisms and adoption of procedures for internal reporting of a whistle blower's communications to Massey's general counsel and to its senior compliance officers.
C-4	* Requires senior compliance officers to report to SEPPC and to be present at the meeting of SEPPC.
D	* Requires Massey to establish whistle blowing mechanisms, to adopt policies to protect whistle blowers, and to inform employees annually of mechanisms and of protections.

Summary of Corporate Governance Agreement, 2008

In January 2011, pending regulatory approval, it was announced that Alpha Natural Resources Inc. would acquire a majority interest in Massey Energy. This acquisition would enable Alpha to expand its marketing of coal to new global markets. Aside from Alpha, several international energy companies explored the potential acquisition of Massey. This acquisition raises many questions. Two fundamental theoretical questions are these. Can noncompliance with laws and regulations erode the value of a firm and invite outside acquisition? Is outside acquisition the market response to noncompliance and is it an effective response?

EXTENSION OF COMPLIANCE MODEL

The actions of The Manville Trust and provisions in the Dodd-Frank Act shift thinking toward extension of a compliance model of CSR with the potential to evolve and to gain acceptance by a general constituency. Conceptually, such a compliance model holds that the first objective of CSR is for corporations to comply with the laws and regulations of a society. It is possible that this objective could be adopted across corporate entities and across borders in any country that has adopted laws and regulations that pertain to corporate practices.

When corporations fail and fail systematically in complying with laws and regulations, the risks of costs increases for shareholders and for society. Although derivative lawsuits can be confined to particular legal systems, other means to promote disclosure about compliance are available. The extension of a compliance model of CSR does not depend solely on the availability of derivative lawsuits. It depends on looking from a new perspective at the concepts of CSR, the purpose of data, the needs of users, and the means of disclosure.

Purpose of Data about Compliance

Within representative governments, a socio-political mechanism exists for partially defining CRS. A part of the notion of CSR is compliance with laws and regulations. Thus, a compliance model would be guided by a baseline notion of CSR as compliance with laws and regulations.

Private costs are the costs of production incurred in providing a private good or service. These private costs of production are valid costs for a private business entity to recognize in measuring its net income. One way for a business entity to increase its net income is to shift the private costs of production into being costs that individuals or the public at large bear. Many private costs associate with the operation of coal mines. When safety is neglected to increase production, miners pay the costs in injury and death. When mountainsides are striped of trees to facilitate surface mining, the community bears the costs of rapid runoff causing severe flooding. When heavy coal trucks beat roads into gravel, taxpayers pay the transportation cost of coal as road maintenance.

One reason that investment in nonrenewable energies can appear to be more profitable than investment in renewable energies is that many of the private costs of production that can be traced directly to nonrenewable energies are excluded from recognition in measuring net income. The exclusion of such costs can operate much as a price subsidy by distorting demand, production, and the allocation of capital. Consider the costs of production in coal mining that are not incorporated into the price of coal, such as costs with respect to environmental destruction and to the impairment of health and safety. For a private business, to avoid the recognition of the private costs of production is a way to privatize profit and socialize loss. Many laws and regulations are designed to encourage private business to recognize the private costs of production. Noncompliance with these laws and regulations puts a burden on the public treasury and represents social irresponsibility (Friedman).

User Needs for Data about Compliance

Many types of stakeholders have an interest in the records of corporations with respect to compliance with laws and regulations. There is an interest in data about compliance by investor and potential investors, by public activists, by legislative policy makers, by enforcement agencies, and by regulators. Two distinct motivations can drive the demands of investors and potential investors for data about compliance. The socially concerned investor can prefer to receive financial returns that are achieved by corporations that are at a minimum legally compliant. Additionally, most investors recognize that persistent noncompliance is a risk that can result in consequences that can increase future financial liabilities and thus reduce the value of a company. Activists can be concerned with noncompliance relative to specific legal and regulatory interests. Legislative policy makers can have an interest in information about noncompliance to guide new policies and to modify existing policies. Enforcement agencies can have an interest in such information to direct enforcement to be efficient and effective.

The wide variety of potential users of data about compliance suggests the need to design systems that aggregate information in different ways to meet the needs of different users. For example, legislative policy makers can want information aggregated by industry, enforcement agencies can want information aggregated by legal corporate entity, and investors and potential investors can want information aggregated by the consolidated or group reporting entity.

Socially responsible investing has been directed largely to identifying firms that pursue exemplary behavior. One difficulty with this concept of CSR is the lack of a public consensus about behaviors that constitute CSR. For example, a bank can excel in observing laudable practices with respect to its employees and its premises, but this same bank can engage in egregious lending practices. Is this bank demonstrating CRS? With advances in technology and with a compliance view of social responsibility, a baseline approach to social investing could evolve with information about compliance designed to meet the user needs of investors and others. The end objective in such a baseline approach would be the disclosure of data about compliance along with the reporting of financial data. If disclosure of data about compliance were required, then it would be the decision of the informed user as to whether to take or not to consider those data in making decisions. Consistent with this baseline approach, one can foresee near index funds of equities from which egregiously noncompliant corporations could be removed either by investor choice or by statistical modeling. For a global perspective on socially responsible investing, see the Web site of the Sustainable Investment Research Platform (www.sirp.se).

Disclosure of Data about Compliance

In designing systems for disclosure of information about compliance with laws and regulations, three considerations merit special attention:

a. the dispersion of data sources

b. the disaggregation of data, and

c. the independent reporting of data.

One concern is that sources for data are dispersed. Potential users must seek data about noncompliance from various regulatory agencies. There is no one source for data about noncompliance per legal corporate entity. Another concern is that often data are disaggregated by legal corporate entity. For reporting of financial data, the structure of legal entities was supplanted decades ago by the notion of economic power, by the structure of the consolidated or group reporting entity. Likewise, disclosures about compliance need to be grounded in this same useful notion of economic power, the consolidated or group reporting entity. The final consideration is the independence of the source for the reporting of data.

Financial reports are issued by operating entities because the data are generated internally. But compliance data are available externally from regulatory and enforcement bodies. Reporting might be less subject to manipulation if data were collected directly from enforcement agencies and managed by an independent entity. An alternative might be to require corporations to have internal control systems to enable reliance on the reporting systems that generate compliance data, and to report the compliance data much as financial data are reported. Additionally, the control systems and the compliance reports could be subject to independent audit. For the development of a reporting infrastructure, each of these three matters merits consideration: the purpose of data, the needs of users for data and the means of disclosure of data.

CONCLUSION

The emergence of a compliance model could mark a significant development in the evolution of thinking about CSR. It is significant not merely for shareholders but for a broad base of stakeholders. Increasingly, information about compliance with laws and regulations would seem to be fundamental to societies in seeking to reduce the public cost of corporate social irresponsibility. Most likely, private and public investment will be required to structure information systems that are efficient and effective in supporting a compliance model to meet the needs of various users about the compliance of corporations with law and regulation. Some entities, especially those with managements that want to avoid transparency, can assert that the challenge is too complex and too costly. Others will ask, given the public costs of noncompliance and the significance of public subsidies that go to many corporate entities, how can not making the investment be justified?

QUESTIONS FOR DISCUSSION

1. How does the compliance model of CSR differ from the exemplary model of CSR?
2. Using an example, explain what means are available to citizens and to shareholders in the country in which you are studying to influence the governance of a corporation.
3. Identify a company in the country in which you are studying to use as an example. For the company you selected, analyze some possible risks that could arise from the violation of laws pertaining to workplace safety or destruction of the environment.

4. With regard to the example you used in Question 3, assess the extent to which such risks could lead to financial loss reducing the value of the company.

5. Examine the actions that management might take to mitigate the likelihood and costs of such risks.

6. What is the relationship between corporate governance and CSR? Give an example of a change in policy with respect to corporate governance. How might this change affect the exercise of CSR by a company?

7. Identify a practice that you view as being a part of CSR of a business. How is this practice influenced by corporate governance?

REFERENCES/BIBLIOGRAPHY

Burr, Barry B. "CalSTRS Signs on to Lawsuit against Massey Energy." Pensions & Investments 9 June 2010. Web. 19 Feb. 2011. http://www.pionline.com/article/20100609/DAILYREG/100609873

Costner, Helen. "Corporate Governance Gets Personal: The Mess at Massey Energy." The CSR Blog, Forbes 16 June 2010. Web. 19 Feb. 2011. http://blogs.forbes.com/csr/2010/06/16/corporate-governance-gets-personal-the-mess-at-massey-energy/

Deng, Jiong. "Building an Investor-Friendly Shareholder Derivative Lawsuit System in China." Harvard International Law Journal 46.2 (Summer 2005): 347-85. Print.

Friedman, Thomas L. Hot, Flat, and Crowded 2.0: Why We Need a Green Revolution—and How It Can Renew America. New York: Picador-Farrar, Straus and Giroux, 2009. Print.

Picardo-Allison, Raquel. "CalSTRS Sues Massey Energy over Safety Lapses." Global Pensions 10 June 2010. Web. 19 Feb. 2011. http://www.globalpensions.com/global-pensions/news/1653798/calstrs-sues-massey-energy-safety-lapses

Shnayerson, Michael. Coal River. New York: Farrar, Straus and Giroux, 2008. Print.

Assessing and Managing Risk in the Financial Services Industry in the Middle East

Andrew Ashwin • Content Developer, Biz/ed, Cengage Learning EMEA

LEARNING OBJECTIVES

After reading this case study and completing the questions, students should be able to do the following:

- *Outline the nature and meaning of risk*
- *Outline some advantages of risk management to a business*
- *Outline key steps that need to be taken in managing risk*
- *Discuss the role of regulation in managing risk*
- *Examine the link between high standards of corporate governance and effective risk management*
- *Assess reasons why some firms may not see risk management as being important*

This case was prepared for classroom discussion rather than to illustrate either effective or ineffective handling of an administrative, ethical, or legal decision by management. Information was gathered from corporate as well as public sources.

INTRODUCTION

Any decision involves some element of risk. Crucial in decision-making, therefore, is some attempt to quantify the risk and to understand the probability that the risk will materialize. Risk can manifest itself in many different forms from serious risk such as terrorist attack or natural disaster (such as the Pakistan floods in 2010) through to loss of critical data, malfunction, and simple human error.

INSURANCE FOR RISK

One way of managing risk is to take out some form of insurance against the risk happening so that the business can be put back to what it was before the risk event occurred. In Bahrain, taking risk management seriously ensures protection and signals the rest of the world that it is a place in which to do business. For example, in 2010, Bahrain Financial Exchange (BFX) took out insurance coverage from the New India Assurance Company Limited for security against financial transactions carried out on the exchange. BFX is a multi-asset exchange, and its various members benefit from this protection. BFS protected itself against risks specifically associated with operating sophisticated financial exchanges, including fraud; losses resulting from errors (such as the so-called fat finger errors that can occur when traders press the wrong key); cases in which employees break exchange rules, which can have a damaging effect on the exchange and its business; and cyber-crime.

BFX's protection coverage is relatively complex, which reflects the nature of the business in which it operates. Trades on such exchanges, especially given the fact that they trade in a range of assets, can have a variety of layers of risk, each of which needs to be identified, quantified, and then managed through insurance coverage. Arshad Khan, managing director and chief executive officer of the BFX and its associated clearing house, the BFX Clearing and Depository Corporation (BCDC), said: "multi-layered protections at every stage of transactions, therefore minimizing the risk of default situations which may affect the Exchange." This precaution protects the exchange and builds confidence in it among those who use it, which is crucial for the financial institution's success. Such confidence helps boost its reach and generate increased demand for multi-asset trading in the Middle East.

REGULATORS

In the financial sector, the role of regulators is also important. Given the turmoil across global markets as a result of the financial crisis between 2007 and 2009, the role of regulators has received special attention. This issue was a key agenda item at the third annual Middle East Risk Management Forum in Bahrain, which took place in March 2010. The conference brought together key regulatory authorities in the Middle East, including the Central Bank of Bahrain (CBB). Conference discussions centered on ways to improve the regulatory structure in the region and to manage risk appropriately. The topic of ethics was also discussed. It does not matter how much a business quantifies risk and seeks to manage that risk, if it is not bound by a code of ethics. Putting together a quantitative and ethical approach to risk management is seen by the CBB as an additional step in promoting the region as a trustworthy and reliable place in which to do business.

ROLE OF FINANCIAL INSTITUTIONS: ARAB AFRICAN INTERNATIONAL BANK

As country authorities consider ways to improve the regulatory structure and improve risk management, individual banks and financial institutions also have a part to play in rebuilding trust lost during the financial crisis. The experience of

2007 to 2009 and beyond highlighted how important appropriate and effective risk management is to financial institutions. One of the major criticisms of European and North American banks in the run up to and during the financial crisis was that risk was taken too lightly. Traders bolstered by the prospects of large bonuses and risk-seeking bosses gambled more and more on financial instruments they did not fully understand.

One way in which risk management can be improved is through developing the principle of corporate governance. In August 2010, the Arab African International Bank (AAIB), based in Egypt, took the step of publishing its corporate governance guidelines–something that was not publicly available before–in an attempt to improve transparency.

The AAIB believes that, if it can learn from the mistakes made among European and North American banks before and during the crisis, AAIB will be in a better position to develop new ways of doing finance and improve its risk management resulting the process. Dalia Abdel Kader, head of marketing and communications and deputy general manager at AAIB, has been quoted in *The Daily News Egypt* as saying: "We have been very focused on corporate governance over these years which are integral in the bank's business dealings, defining the control framework that is established to manage various risks."

Corporate governance refers to the way in which the business is run. It includes policies, laws, institutions, customs, and processes to which the business adheres. Stakeholders who interact with a business need to trust that a business will abide by certain widely accepted ways of operating, and assuring that trust is one aspect of risk management. If another bank does business with the AAIB with confidence that the business transactions will be handled appropriately, in accordance with international conventions and rules and within the regulatory framework, then the risk of doing business is reduced.

STANDARDS OF CORPORATE GOVERNANCE

Doing business with those who are known for having high standards of corporate governance is one element in identifying and then quantifying risk management. Clearly, if a bank does business with another institution with weak corporate governance principles, then it must understand the potential risks involved and take steps to manage those risks. However, high standards of corporate governance generate greater confidence in the business but contribute to lower risk. The customer is better placed to quantify the risk if there is a clear understanding of the corporate governance principles. Therefore, AAIB knows that the transparency of its principles helps its stakeholders to assess risk more accurately.

In addition to adding its stakeholders, AAIB wants to find ways of reducing its own risk, and it recognizes that an evaluation of the way it does business contributes to this process. First, it considered ways in which it can rethink its financing strategies and the inherent risks involved. In order act more responsibly, AAIB emphasizes the social and environmental credentials of its potential clients. Measuring these credentials involves using the United Nations (UN) Global Compact principles, which help to guide corporate citizenship in the world economy. The ten principles are:

Human Rights

1. Businesses should support and respect the protection of internationally proclaimed human rights and
2. Make sure that they are not complicit in human rights abuses.

Labor

1. Businesses should uphold the freedom of association and the effective recognition of the right to collective bargaining;
2. The elimination of all forms of forced and compulsory labor;
3. The effective abolition of child labor; and
4. The elimination of discrimination in respect of employment and occupation.

Environment

1. Businesses are asked to support a precautionary approach to environmental challenges;
2. Undertake initiatives to promote greater environmental responsibility; and
3. Encourage the development and diffusion of environmentally friendly technologies.

Anti-corruption

1. Businesses should work against corruption in all its forms, including extortion and bribery.

In addition, AAIB uses the Equator Principles, a financial industry benchmark for determining, assessing, and managing social and environmental risk in project financing. Together these allow AAIB to choose clients partly on the basis of their financial credentials but also the wider criteria given by the ten principles mentioned above. Doing so enables AAIB to establish a standard for managing risk in project financing and to incorporate the extent to which social and environmental risk can be managed. Any loan above $10 million is based on an assessment of these wider criteria.

Abdel Kader points out that the policy adopted by the bank was not universally welcomed, but eventually it was accepted. It proved particularly useful in AAIB's developing business in the green energy and technology industries. In a country where some 90% of companies are classified as small and medium enterprises (SME), AAIB also believes it has a role to play in helping to support this important aspect of the Egyptian economy. AAIB's approach to risk management is especially important given the results of a survey published in August 2010 by Collaborative Management and Control Systems (CMCS).

Collaborative Management and Control Systems Study

CMCS carried out a study of project-based construction firms that often have a higher degree of risk built into them than other businesses. The study compared such firms in the Middle East using the United Kingdom (UK) as the basis for the comparison. The study found that over 40% of Middle East companies in this sector do not have a risk policy, and in almost every category studied, companies in the Middle East compared less well with their counterparts in the UK. The study suggests that attitudes toward risk management may not be as strong as it could be and that managers may not see this as important to the success of their businesses.

The study showed that only 45% of businesses that have risk management policies in place have a risk management officer to enforce and monitor the policy compared to 51% in the UK. Fifty-one per cent start a project without a complete risk register (30.4% in the UK), 61% assess risk against the probability of its occurrence compared to nearly 80% in the UK, and 695 of business managements specify what actions to take in response to high-risk exposures compared to 72.3% in the UK.

Financial institutions across the Middle East are, like AAIB and BXF, coming to see risk management as important. They see improvements in risk management as a vital part of attracting new business to the region and helping to promote economic growth. They agree that poor risk management strategies contribute to project and investment failures, which certainly do not promote confidence. Attitudes toward risk management from leading institutions in the region can be improved and shown to be important. By being role models in the way that both BXF and AAIB have attempted to be, such leadership can help foster improvements in the quality of identifying, quantifying and managing risk.

To emphasize this point even further, the news agency Reuters reports that by 2020 risk management skills in the Middle East will be in high demand. Those with IT-related skills in risk management and the skills in "mining overwhelming amounts of data, protect systems from security threats, manage the risks of growing complexity in new systems, and communicate how technology can increase productivity" will be in a particularly strong position in the labour market.

QUESTIONS FOR DISCUSSION

1. What is risk? Explain your answer in the context of the financial services industry.

2. Explain some of the costs and benefits of risk management to a business?

3. What steps would a business such as a commercial bank have to take to identify and manage the risks inherent in its operations?

4. In the context of the financial services industry, what role can regulators play in helping to manage risk?

5. To what extent is a high standard of corporate governance vital in reducing the risks of carrying out business in the financial services industry? Justify your answer.

REFERENCES/BIBLIOGRAPHY

"BFX Boost Risk Management Provisions" Bahrain Financial Exchange. Press Release. 16 June 2010. Retrieved Jan. 2011 from http://www.bfx.bh/En/MediaCentre/PressReleases/2010/BFXBoostRiskManagementProvisions.aspx

Collett, Stacy. "5 Indispensable IT Skills of the Future." *Reuters.com*. Web. 23 Aug. 2010. Retrieved Feb. 2011 from http://www.reuters.com/article/2010/08/23/urnidgns002570f3005978d8852577880056ba3d-idUS252354228320100823

Ramadan, Amr. "AAIB says Responsible Financing is Key." *Daily News Egypt*. 25 Aug. 2010. Web. Retrieved 17 Feb. 2011 from http://www.thedailynewsegypt.com/banking-a-finance/aaib-says-responsible-financing-is-key-dp2.html

"The Equator Principles." Web. 29 January 2011.http://equator-principles.com/

"The Ten Principals." United Nations Global Compact. Web. 29 January 2011. http://www.unglobalcompact.org/aboutthegc/thetenprinciples/index.html

Business Enterprise in Jordan: Promoting Small Business Start-up and Development

Andrew Ashwin • Content Developer, Biz/ed, Cengage Learning EMEA

LEARNING OBJECTIVES

After reading this case study and completing the questions, students should be able to do the following:

- *Define entrepreneurship and outline its key features*
- *Outline the key features which need to be in place to promote entrepreneurship in a country*

This case was prepared for classroom discussion rather than to illustrate either effective or ineffective handling of an administrative, ethical, or legal decision by management. Information was gathered from corporate as well as public sources.

Entrepreneurship is an important focus for any country wishing to help develop its economy. Encouraging the use of initiative, risk-taking, planning, and organizing in setting up business activity is all one important part; putting the infrastructure in place to enable entrepreneurs to set up and grow new businesses is another part. Jordan is one example of countries in the Middle East in which the approach to enterprise and entrepreneurship is changing. The ongoing economic reforms introduced by King Abdullah include the long-term strategy of focusing more on the role of the private sector in developing the economy and encouraging enterprise at all levels in society. In the early 2000s, there are signs that it is beginning to pay some dividends in terms of reducing unemployment and boosting overall economic growth.

In order to help develop the enterprise culture and provide help to those who are considering setting up new businesses, a number of organizations have sprung up in Jordan. The aim of these organizations is to provide assistance with funding and to help give advice on technical, marketing, and management issues. The government has put in place appropriate legislation to allow new business areas to grow and develop networks so that budding entrepreneurs feel they have support and access to helpful contacts.

ORGANIZATIONS INVOLVED IN SUPPORTING BUSINESS

A number of the organizations were set up in conjunction with Jordanian government departments, including the Jordanian Ministry of Tourism and Antiquities, the Ministry of Energy and Mineral Resources, and the Ministry of the Environment. These government departments have acted in conjunction with various non-governmental organizations (NGOs) such as the Royal Society for the Conservation of Nature, the Jordan Tourism Development Project, the Tatweer Project, the Jordan Renewable Energy Society, the Higher Council for Science and Technology (HCST), Jordan Enterprise, and the Jordan Forum for Business and Professional Women.

These, along with partners from outside Jordan such as the European research community, USAID, and the Business and Export Development Project for Jordan are providing the framework and infrastructure to help entrepreneurs get the support they need to assume the risk of starting businesses. Changes to the law are also a part of the overall strategy, for example, the temporary Renewable Energy Law, passed by the cabinet in early 2010, provides a number of opportunities for enterprises in the field of renewable energy.

Four examples illustrate how the Jordanian government and other agencies are working together to help entrepreneurs: tourism in the Ajloun trail, Tatweer, passage of the temporary Renewable Energy Law, and Alriyadi.net.

TOURISM IN THE AJLOUN TRAIL

The first example involves the Jordan Tourism Development Project (JTDP) and the Ministry of Tourism and Antiquities. The ministry is keen to promote Jordan as a tourist area, and the initiative, launched in March 2010, aims to encourage entrepreneurs to be part of that process. The JTDP and the ministry, along with the Royal Society for Conservation of Nature (RSCN), offers grants to entrepreneurs to help them set up businesses and to support existing small and medium-sized enterprises (SMEs) along a 25 meter trail in Ajloun. This region in the north of Jordan has a number of historical sites, a Bronze-Age necropolis, Byzantine wine presses, forts, water mills and villages, all located amid picturesque hills and valleys. There is also a designated nature reserve and a castle built in 1184 by a general of Salah ad-Dinin to protect the area from invasion by the Franks and to oversee the iron mines there.

The agencies concerned offer grants and technical assistance. A range of enterprises benefit from already-established cooperatives in the Ajloun area, producing crafts and food for eco-tourism businesses. Applicants for grants have to demonstrate that their idea meets the overall tourism strategy for the area, estimate the potential number of jobs they create, and describe their sustainability. It is also hoped that new businesses will help to provide a trickle-down effect on the people and other businesses along the Ajloun trail and thus have a positive impact on communities in the general area. It is hoped that the new businesses will range in type and complexity with some offering services such as traditional Jordanian breakfasts and others setting up new hotels.

TATWEER

The second example is Tatweer, a U.S.-funded development project operating in a number of Middle Eastern countries, including Jordan. In Jordan, Tatweer is managed by the not-for-profit organization Business Development Centre (BDC), of which Jordan Enterprise and the Business and Export Development Centre are part. The main objective is to target SMEs and provide financial assistance to help entrepreneurs improve competitiveness and increase exports from Jordan. According to figures quoted in the Jordan Times, between December 2005 when it was established and late 2010, Tatweer helped to preserve over 4,500 jobs in small businesses, helped to provide employment and training for more than 4,000 graduates from Jordanian universities, supported over 400 SMEs, and gave 560 grants to help these businesses develop marketing, management, and technical skills in relation to entering and exploiting export markets. In some cases, businesses have been helped to obtain ISO certificates, which enabled them to compete as equals with other international sellers.

Tatweer also helped Jordanian women to build their business skills. Eighty-eight businesses owned by women have received technical and financial assistance and facilitated contacts with international buyers. The help included training and education through links with management schools in the United States and provision of mentoring programs with peers overseas. The aim of such programs is to help develop management skills that can then be applied in the recipients' own businesses and cascade to others in their own organizations.

EFFECTS OF PASSING THE TEMPORARY RENEWABLE ENERGY LAW

The temporary Renewable Energy Law, passed in January 2010, provided an impetus for businesses to invest in the energy sector. The law illustrates how greater private sector involvement can help to meet government targets in developing renewable energy. Previously some private sector firms complained that the bureaucracy surrounding the bidding process for energy projects and the lack of technical data hampered possible enterprise initiatives. The law also established a Renewable Energy and Energy Efficiency Fund to provide support for businesses and to encourage private/public initiatives.

The new law allows businesses to negotiate directly with the Ministry of Energy and Mineral Resources. The intention is that Jordan will increase the proportion of renewable energy in relation to its overall needs to 7% by 2015 and 10% by 2020. It is hoped that new renewable energy projects will be able to sell the electricity they produced to the national grid. The National Electric Power Company will have to pay the cost of connecting renewable energy projects to the national grid. With a guaranteed buyer, the incentive for new enterprises increased considerably, and it is hoped that this incentive will provide entrepreneurs with the spur they need to develop and set up new projects.

Support for Research and Development

New enterprises often start when research and development are encouraged. A crucial link needs to be made between the research and the opportunity to turn this research into commercial enterprises. Some believe that Jordan suffers from researchers working in relative isolation without the networks to make the jump from theory to practical commercial realization. Bridging this gap is the aim of a European Union (EU) funded project called Support to Research, Technological Development, Innovation Initiatives and Strategies in Jordan (SRTD).

The SRTD aims to support research and to build links between research facilities and the private sector to encourage innovation—bringing new ideas to market. Researchers in Jordan are able to exploit networking opportunities with each other, and they can develop closer links with the European research community. The €4 million fund is designated to helping the Higher Council for Science and Technology (HCST) work with Jordan Enterprise to encourage research projects that can create added value products; Jordan Enterprise can then provide assistance to entrepreneurs in setting up businesses to market the new products.

Incubators

In addition, the funds can be used to help provide the skills needed by budding entrepreneurs to set up and run businesses successfully. One part is having a good idea with market potential; another part is being able to run a business. To accomplish this second part, business incubators are set up to help increase the likelihood of long-term survival and success for new enterprises. Two of these incubators are part of the Jordan Innovation Centers; one is focused on promoting female entrepreneurs and the other specializes in tourism and salt and minerals from the Dead Sea. Those working in these incubators can advise on strategic and action planning, market research, and promotion.

In the early phases of the project, 30 entrepreneurs received start-up grants to develop their businesses within the incubators. The grants were allocated based on specific criteria and covered a number of business areas, including energy, environment, agriculture, ICT and nanotechnology. One important aspect of the work of the SRTD is clarifying the intellectual property issues that arise from research and innovation. A national Intellectual Property Commercialisation Office is being established with El Hassan Science City. El Hassan Science City is a campus that hosts the HCST, the Royal Scientific Society, and the Princess Sumaya University for Technology. Having sound intellectual property (IP) rules and legislation is essential if researchers are going to be encouraged to share their ideas and bring them to market. The office notes that "it is of urgent importance to create a conducive environment in which Arab scientists, researchers, academics, entrepreneurs and students are given the opportunity to promote a knowledge-based economy by innovating and disseminating their intellectual wealth." This serves to emphasise the importance of IP in allowing research to flourish which in turn begets the development of new business enterprises.

ALRIYADI.NET

The final example of how entrepreneurs in Jordan are receiving help and advice is Alriyadi.net, an online resource dedicated to helping young entrepreneurs set up and run businesses successfully. Sponsored by the Young Entrepreneurs Association (*Alriyadi* means *entrepreneur* in Arabic), it provides consulting services; information about training and educational camps; and advice about registering and licensing a new business, creating business plans, and sourcing finance.

Together these four types of initiatives serve to highlight the emphasis Jordan is now placing on the development of the private sector in the country and how that sector can be built up by SMEs, those in research, and by budding entrepreneurs. Building an enterprise culture is a long-term supply-side initiative that will not result in overnight success. However, for the long-term development of the Jordanian economy in an increasingly global business environment, it is being accepted that Jordan's future prosperity will rely on building a strong and vibrant private sector and that the government and other agencies have a role to play in helping to establish that culture.

QUESTIONS FOR DISCUSSION

1. Give a definition of the term 'entrepreneur' and outline what you think are the key features of entrepreneurship.
2. What is the role of support organisations in helping budding entrepreneurs establish successful businesses?
3. Explain how and why cooperatives can often be an important solution to the development of new business enterprises in countries such as Jordan.
4. To what extent is financial support such as grants or microfinance essential in helping new enterprises become established and to flourish?
5. Discuss the role of the state-developing infrastructure such as research and development facilities, incubators, clear intellectual property rules and legislation in helping encourage entrepreneurship.

REFERENCES/BIBLIOGRAPHY

El Hassan Science City. Queen Rania Center for Entrepreneurship. Web. Retrieved April 2010 from http://www.qrce.org/?q=node/8

Intellectual Property Commercialization Office.http://ipco-jo.org/

Obeidat, Omar. "Tatweer Project Celebrates Four Years of Achievements" *The Jordan Times.* 3 Feb. 2010. Retrieved Apr. 2010 at http://www.jordantimes.com/index.php?news=23688

Chinese Brand Strategies: Li Ning and the Creation of a Global Sportswear Brand

M.L. Cohen • Freelance Writer

LEARNING OBJECTIVES

Students should be able to the following:

- *Discuss China's transition from low-cost manufacturing center to a consumer market, and how this relates to the sportswear sector*
- *Identify early impediments, and continuing obstacles, in the growth of home-grown Chinese footwear brands*
- *Understand the "paper tiger" marketing strategy and discuss its applicability to the Li Ning brand*
- *Recognize key elements in Li Ning's evolution from Chinese sports hero to national sportswear brand*
- *Discuss Li Ning's strategy for competing against major global brands such as Nike and Adidas*

This case was prepared for classroom discussion rather than to illustrate either effective or ineffective handling of an administrative, ethical, or legal decision by management. Information was gathered from corporate as well as public sources.

BACKGROUND

More than two billion people watched Li Ning walk through the sky above Beijing's Olympic Stadium, carrying the final torch to signal the start of the 2008 Summer Games, according to the Nielsen Company. As the most-watched opening ceremony in Olympic history, the event underscored China's emergence as one of the world's economic and cultural powers. Suspended by cables high above the stadium, Li's walk in the sky also served as an introduction of the Li Ning name to a global market. For Li Ning is both the name of one of China's greatest athletes and a leading domestic sportswear brand.

China is the world's fastest-growing market for sportswear, including sport shoes. The sportswear market in China has grown from a standing start in the early 1980s to become second only to the United States. The turn of the twenty-first century witnessed a dramatic acceleration of sportswear sales in the country, topping $7 billion in 2009. By 2012, sales of sports shoes and clothing in China are expected to reach $12 billion and even more, according to an *Economist Intelligence Unit* report titled "Asia Consumer Products: The Dash for Cash."

DRIVING THE BRANDING PHENOMENON

Driving this growth are a number of factors, not least of which are the rising affluence of Chinese consumers and their rush to embrace Western culture and fashion. As in the Europe and North America, sportswear has moved beyond the sports field to become everyday attire. Brand names, particularly such global brands as Nike, Adidas, Puma, and Reebok, have played an important role in this development. Chinese consumers initially sought out high-end brands as a symbol of their own growing economic status. Into early 2000s, however, a growing number of Chinese have also begun to adopt the Western notion of branding as a lifestyle statement.

China itself played an important role in the global branding phenomenon. The Chinese government's economic reform policies from the late 1970s positioned the country as a new force in low-cost manufacturing. At the same time, the clothing and footwear industries in other countries were shifting from a manufacturing model to one based on brand-building and marketing. Leading the way was Nike, which from its beginning focused solely on its footwear designs and, especially, its marketing juggernaut.

By the end of the 1980s, nearly all major sports shoe and sportswear brands had abandoned their roots in manufacturing and turned to low-cost original equipment manufacturers (OEM) producers. China, with its seemingly unlimited supply of cheap labor and less restrictive health, safety, and labor regulations, emerged as the largest supplier to the global sports shoe and sportswear market. Freed from the expense of operating factories and warehouses, sportswear companies directed their resources toward building their global brand image.

BEYOND THE OEM MARKET

The growth of a middle class with more leisure time than ever before spurred a new interest in sports in China. More and more people were participating in sports. Still more people were watching televised sports, especially broadcasts of Western sporting events. Basketball and soccer became hugely popular in the country, introducing Chinese consumers to the sophisticated sports shoe and sportswear designs developed by the global brand name companies. Demand for sportswear rose sharply through the 1990s.

The OEM manufacturers responded by flooding the Chinese market with their own sports shoes and sportswear. While these were often cheaply made, inferior imitations of the global brands, the late 1990s witnessed the emergence of a growing number of Chinese sportswear companies eager to develop their own brand identities. Li Ning, Anta, Xstep, Peak, and even the country's own so-called retro brand, Warrior, began competing for control of the domestic market.

NATIONAL MARKET, GLOBAL RIVALS

These brands enjoyed free reign in China through the 1990s, protected from international competition by high tariffs that placed the global brands beyond the reach of the average consumer. Li Ning grew into the country's largest sportswear company by the end of the 1990s, producing a wide range of sportswear, sports shoes, and sporting equipment. The company, like its competitors, supported its sales through the creation of a vast sales and distribution network. Into 2010, Li Ning's national retail network included more than 7,500 stores. Chief domestic rival Anta had in the meantime opened more than 6,600 stores.

The companies' position changed radically in the early 2000s as China complied with conditions for joining the World Trade Organization. As a result, Li Ning and the others faced the massive entry of far larger and far more experienced sportswear players. Nike and Adidas (as well as Reebok, acquired by Adidas in 2005) quickly grabbed the lead in the Chinese sportswear market. More important, these companies placed conquering the Chinese market at the center of their continuing global growth plans.

Li Ning, Anta, and other Chinese companies found themselves at a distinct disadvantage in this newly emerging market. Conditioned by a relatively young and still limited free-market economy, Chinese companies had built up little experience in modern marketing techniques. As Joe Nocera, writing for the *New York Times*, points out: "For a long time, this was a country of scarcity—it still is in some parts—so there was no need for anything so high-falutin' as branding. Even when that began to change, the primary way Chinese companies competed was on price."

PAPER-TIGER MARKETING STRATEGIES

The focus on price overshadowed other considerations, such as technological innovation, design imperatives, quality standards and brand-building, and other marketing methods. With the entry of higher-priced but higher-quality foreign brands, the price-based marketing strategies of the Chinese brands actually undermined their attempt to hold their ground. This was true despite the fact that most, if not all, of the global brand shoes were produced in China. In the minds of the country's consumers, the Chinese sportswear brands remained inferior copies of the global brands. The more sophisticated and more affluent consumers in first-tier markets such as Beijing and Shanghai quickly switched their allegiance to Nike, Reebok and Adidas.

Few observers considered the Chinese sportswear players as down for the count, however. Indeed, many of the companies had already begun to put into place new strategic initiatives. A central feature of this new effort involved developing what *Business Week* called a "paper tiger" marketing strategy, suggesting that companies sought merely to create the illusion of global brand status in order to attract brand-hungry Chinese consumers. Cracking the international market, however, provided its own share of pitfalls. Unsuccessful efforts by Anta, Peak, and others to expand beyond China quickly forced these companies to return their focus to mainland.

Li Ning, too, set out to establish a global brand identity in order to regain the lead of the Chinese market. More than that, in 2010, the company announced the goal of becoming one of the world's top five sportswear companies by 2018. When Li Ning lighted the flame to start the 2008 Olympic Games—stealing the thunder from Adidas, which had spent $200 million as the official sponsor of the Games—he also signaled the start of his company's pursuit of a place on the global sportswear podium.

Significantly, Li Ning had been preparing for its global launch for the better part of the decade. The second part of this case study examines Li Ning from a historical perspective and details the steps it has taken in its quest to become a global sportswear brand in the twenty-first century.

LI NING: FROM NATIONAL ICON TO NATIONAL BRAND

Born in 1963, Li Ning was a product of the Chinese government's notorious sports program, which drafted many thousands of the nation's children into rigorous training regimes. While this program ultimately failed to produce a generation of world-class athletes, it did discover a small number of genuine talents. Li Ning, however, stood out among all the rest. By the age of 17, Li Ning had joined the Chinese national gymnastics team and, by 1982, had already won gold medals in international competitions.

Li's moment came with the 1984 Summer Olympic Games in Los Angeles. China had not competed in a Summer Olympics since Helsinki in 1952 and had never won an Olympic gold medal. Li Ning changed all that: By the end of the Games, Li had won a total of six medals—three of them gold. As Hannah Beech wrote in *Time International*: "In doing so [Li] became, more than anyone else, the face of an emergent China shaking off three decades of . . . isolation." He also became the hero to an entire generation.

Hailed as China's Michael Jordan, after the popular American basketball star, Li went on to win more than 100 medals and 14 regional and international titles. The parallel with Jordan would run still deeper. Soon after the 1984 Olympics, Nike launched its Air Jordan basketball shoe—credited by many with single-handedly vaulting sports shoes from the athletic field into the world of cutting-edge street fashion. Nike's long-running partnership with Jordan also represented one of the most successful marketing campaigns of all time and played a major role in Nike's rise to dominance over the global sportswear market.

Spotting a Sportswear Opportunity

While the rest of the world had begun clamoring for Nike, Adidas, and other sportswear brands, China had only just begun to shrug off decades of uniformity and generic clothing designs. Li spotted the opportunity to parlay his status as a national icon into the creation of one of the country's first home-grown sportswear brands. In 1988, Li announced his retirement from gymnastics and accepted a position with Guangdong Province-based soft drink company Jianlibao Group Company Limited. One year later, Li was placed in charge of developing a line of sportswear and sports equipment for Jianlibao. Li set out to develop a range of sports shoes and apparel featuring higher quality and a stronger design sense than typically found in China

From the start, Li displayed a flair for entrepreneurship—a rarity in China at the time—and marketing. By naming his sportswear collection after himself, Li became his own brand ambassador. Li scored an early marketing coup when he made a national appeal for help in designing the company's logo. Within a month, the company received more than 20,000 suggestions from across the country. While Li Ning ultimately hired professional designers to develop its logo, which bore a marked resemblance to the famed Nike swoosh, the contest succeeded in introducing the Li Ning line to the national market.

Li Ning launched its first sportswear line in 1990. That year the company scored its first sponsorship, while at the same time becoming the first Chinese company to supply the clothing for China's delegation to that year's Asian Games. During the opening ceremonies, Li Ning himself appeared as a torchbearer, an event watched by nearly all of China. Other sponsorships soon followed. At the same time, Li Ning began touring China incessantly to promote his brand. As Allen Cheng, writing for *Time* suggested: "It's as if Michael Jordan had his own sneaker company instead of being a shoe tree for Nike."

Li Ning's success came as China itself had begun to emerge as the world's manufacturing center. By the middle of the 1990s, China had firmly replaced Taiwan and South Korea as the world's sports shoe and sportswear capital, while outpacing other emerging markets, including Indonesia and Thailand. Li Ning itself initially operated as a manufacturer, producing an extensive range of sports shoes, sportswear, and sports equipment and accessories under its own brand and others. Like other companies at the time, Li Ning competed largely on price, while benefiting from the continued popularity of its famous founder. The company also set up its own retail network, launching a franchise formula in 1993. Two years later, Li Ning laid claim to being China's largest domestic sportswear company.

Emulating Nike

Li Ning took a number of important measures to support the company's corporate development. Perhaps most important among these was his decision to enlist outside consultants to help him develop its strategy for the rest of the decade.

As a result, the Li Ning sportswear division split off from Jianlibao and moved to Beijing in 1993. The company's business strategy also increasingly emulated Nike. Toward the end of the decade, Li Ning switched to outsourcing its manufacturing. The company then focused on its product design and marketing. Much of this work took place at the company's sprawling new headquarters, which borrowed from the so-called campus format favored by Nike and other companies. As Frederik Balfour wrote in *Business Week*: "Li Ning makes no bones about admiring its bigger rivals. Its gleaming corporate campus near Beijing, complete with indoor swimming pool, basketball courts, and a climbing wall, seems like a page out of Nike's playbook."

LAYING THE FOUNDATION IN THE LATE 1990S

Li Ning's business strategy went beyond the surface, however. The company sought to overcome an important hurdle that stood in the way of the growth aspirations of many of China's companies. In the sport shoe sector, technology had long been an important driver of the global market, providing credibility to sports shoe designs even for consumers who rarely, if ever, participated in sports.

The lack of homegrown technology, both in China's sportswear industry and beyond, became an increasing impediment in the country's dreams of becoming a global business center. To overcome the country's technology disadvantage, in 1998, Li Ning founded China's first sportswear design and development center in Foshan, in Guanddong Province.

Li Ning also strengthened its back office, adopting SAP's Athletic Footwear Solution (AFS) platform in 1999. The implementation of an ERP backbone, a first for the Chinese sportswear industry, became a crucial part of the company's national expansion program.

WTO Entry Changes the Game

China's entry into the World Trade Organization in 2001 marked the beginning of a new and more competitive era in the country's sportswear market. The major global brands, spearheaded by Nike, Reebok, and Adidas, rushed into the country. These companies quickly claimed control of the all-important first-tier markets of Beijing, Shanghai, and the country's other larger, more affluent cities. Li Ning and the other Chinese brands found themselves confronted with far more experienced brand strategists. Nike, Adidas, along with others, had spent decades honing their marketing methods in the world's most competitive markets.

In addition, Li Ning faced a number of other issues. Chief among these was the growing consumer preference for the foreign brands. This preference stemmed, on the one hand, from the rise of an affluent middle class and its upwardly mobile aspirations, which embraced the more expensive global brands as a symbol of their rising social status. On the other hand, after years of a price-based sales strategy, Chinese sportswear makers suffered from a loss of confidence among consumers, who identified Chinese-made products with low quality, poor design, and a lack of innovation as compared to their global rivals.

The Compromise Choice

For Li Ning, the turn of the century brought other bad news. By 2002, barely a decade after its launch, the Li Ning brand was already aging badly. This was especially true among the country's younger consumers, and particularly the all-important 15-to-25-year-old segment. Flush with cash from doting parents, Chinese youth barely remembered Li Ning's athletic achievements. As Li told *Time* in 2002, people "used to come by the thousands when I opened outlets. Senior local officials, mayors, even local provincial governors. Today, only a few people show up. I wish I were still as popular as I used to be. But I guess that's a fact of life."

In the meantime, Nike and Adidas surged ahead, capturing the first-tier cities and then the number one and two positions of the national market. The surge in interest in sports, spurred by the excitement surrounding China's hosting of the 2008 Olympic Games, enabled Li Ning to continue to achieve strong revenue growth. The brand, however, had become a lower-priced compromise to the more expensive models from rival Nike and Adidas.

THE LI NING EFFECT: TAKING THE GLOBAL STAGE

If Li Ning's business strategy had enabled it to outpace its domestic rivals, the company needed to establish a new foundation to take on the international brands. The company strengthened its management in 2001, promoting Zhang Zhi Yong, who held a degree in economics from Peking University, as CEO. Li became the company's chairman and head of business development. Both Li and Zhang then completed the Executive MBA program at Peking University's prestigious Guanghua School of Management. The company also began gearing up for a public offering. When it listed its shares on the Hong Kong Stock Exchange in 2004, Li Ning became the first Chinese sportswear company to list on a foreign exchange. The listing provided the company with new credibility for attracting international sponsorship and partners.

Li Ning put into place a multifaceted strategy in order to enhance its all-important design, technology, and marketing capabilities. The company added its first international sponsorship, dressing the French gymnastics team for the 2000 Olympic Games in Sydney. In order to strengthen its design component, in 2001, the company brought in its first international designers, including Italy's Massimiliano Zago and France's Jean-Philippe Pavot.

At the same time, the company raised its advertising spending to $11 million per year—one of the largest advertising budgets in the country. By 2005, the company's total marketing and research budget topped $50 million, representing 17% of its revenues. This placed it on a level with Nike and Adidas.

In 2002, Li Ning had also rolled out its first lifestyle advertisements featuring ordinary people and athletes and its own Nike-style tagline, "Anything

Is Possible." Unfortunately for the company, Adidas soon stole time momentum with its own "Impossible Is Nothing" slogan. As with its logo, Li Ning still struggled with an image of a Western brand imitator.

To help correct this predicament, Li Ning brought in new expertise from outside the company. In 2003, the company hired Abel Wu, a former marketing director at Procter & Gamble (P&G) China. Wu put the nine years he had spent immersed in P&G's American-style marketing culture to work for Li Ning's own marketing effort. As he told *Advertising Age*: "I'm pure P&G and our core belief is the same, to develop and execute a solid brand strategy. Only the products are different." Upgrading the company's product offering became a core element of the new development strategy outlined by Wu. To this end, the company again took a leaf from Nike's own strategy of extensive product development. By 2008, Li Ning was turning out some 600 new products each year.

Li Ning also brought in help to bridge the technology gap between it and the global brands. In 2004, the company hired former Nike research director Ned Frederick and New Hampshire-based Daniel Richard Design in order to enter the professional sports shoe segment, vital for building the brand's credibility. The partnership quickly resulted in Li Ning's first technology breakthrough, dubbed the "Bow," in 2004. Li Ning then rolled out its first high-end, professional quality basketball shoe.

Joining the Sponsorship Race

With a professional shoe in hand, Li Ning joined the all-important race for professional endorsements. The company scored an important marketing coup in 2005 when it formed a strategic partnership with the NBA, which became its official sponsor.

The partnership also helped Li Ning sign up its first NBA players. These included Chuck Hayes of the Houston Rockets, a teammate of Chinese superstar player Yao Ming. In 2006, Li Ning signed on basketball legend Shaquille O'Neal, who became the brand's ambassador in China, with his own signature line (in the United States, O'Neal agreed to wear Li Ning shoes but without the brand's logo). Cleveland Cavaliers guard Damon Jones also joined Li Ning's stable of stars.

Li Ning's endorsement program became more and more varied as the decade progressed. The company signed contracts with several national Chinese teams, including the gymnastics, diving, and table tennis teams. On an international level, Li Ning sponsored the Spanish women's and men's basketball teams, the Sudanese track team, the U.S. table tennis team, and the Swedish Olympic team. Other notable signings were tennis star Ivan Ljubicic, Russian Olympic gold medalist Yelena Isinbayeva, and Indian badminton champions Chetan Anand and Jwala Gutta.

The Li Ning Effect at the Beijing Olympics

Despite its sponsorship successes, critics continued to view Li Ning as a "paper tiger" marketer, seeking to create a false image of itself as a brand with true global reach when only a tiny fraction of its sales came from overseas. The company also remained saddled with an image as an imitator. As Terry Rhoads, head of Zou Marketing, a leading Shanghai-based sports consultancy, told *Business Week* in a May 2008 story, "They just dusted off a Nike marketing plan, took bits and pieces, and said, 'Voila!'"

Li Ning's walk through the sky at the Beijing Olympics' opening ceremony provided the company with its breakthrough moment. The performance, which has become something of a case study for ambush marketing, provided the Li Ning brand with a global audience for the first time. As Rhoads later admitted to the *Daily Telegraph*, the stunt gave Li Ning global brand recognition "five to 10 years ahead of time." The appearance also provided the company with a major sales bump in China. Flushed with renewed national pride, Chinese consumers soon placed the company ahead of Adidas. By decade's end, Li Ning's sales had begun closing in on Nike as well.

Testing the Global Waters

In a new sign in 2008 of its global aspirations, Li Ning opened a research and design facility in Portland, Oregon, the epicenter of the sports shoe design industry—and near Nike's own home base. In this way, the company hoped to take advantage of the city's deep pool of talented shoe designers in order to develop shoe designs to attract Western consumers.

Li Ning next began developing its own large-scale flagship store concept for the international market, an emulation of the Niketown retail concept, which had played an important role in Nike's own marketing program. The first of the new Li Ning stores opened in Singapore early in 2009; by the end of the year, the company had opened a flagship store in Hong Kong as well and had announced plans to add stores in Malaysia, India, Brunei, the Philippines, and Thailand.

Li Ning's early target, however, remained the United States. In May 2010, Li Ning added another symbol of its global ambitions with the opening of a flagship store in Portland's trendy Pearl neighborhood district, nearby the original Niketown. The new store took a direct approach toward confronting the stigma often attached to Chinese-made goods in the United States, featuring a design and selection celebrating China's cultural and athletic heritage. Rather than opening a string of stores, Li Ning continued in its slow and steady approach. The Portland flagship was meant to test the waters, permitting the company to gain an understanding of the U.S. market.

TOP FIVE BY 2018

Li Ning announced plans to complete a wider global rollout of its brand starting from 2014. As part of the preparations for that effort, Li Ning at last took steps to resolve the issues surrounding its logo and slogan. In July 2010, the company unveiled a new, more distinctive logo. While evoking the company's original logo—helping to avoided creating consumer confusion—the new design was both more distinctive and clever: The logo resembled the Chinese character for *people*. Li Ning completed its identity transformation with a new tagline: "Make the Change."

Li Ning's multilevel effort had succeeded in enhancing its design and technology capacity while also building an increasingly global image for its brand. By 2010, Li Ning had regained its momentum, posting revenues of RMB8.4 billion—more than 11 times its sales at the start of the previous decade. Li Ning had emerged as the major challenger for the lead of what had become the world's fastest-growing sportswear market.

Li Ning's ambitions, however, went beyond becoming another of China's paper tigers. As CEO, Zhang told *China Daily*: "By 2018, we expect the company to be one of the top five sports goods companies in the world." Having successfully integrated its Western rivals' marketing and growth strategies at home, Li Ning now intended to take the challenge its rivals on the global playing field.

QUESTIONS FOR DISCUSSION

1. How has China's growth into consumer-driven economy affected the country's sportswear market?
2. What challenges has Li Ning and other Chinese footwear and sportswear companies faced in developing their brands?
3. What is a "paper tiger" marketing strategy and is it applicable to Li Ning?
4. What major steps did Li Ning and the Li Ning company take to become a leading national sportswear brand?
5. What strategies has Li Ning put into place in order to compete with such global brands as Nike and Adidas?

REFERENCES/BIBLIOGRAPHY

"Asia Consumer Products: The Dash for Cash." *Economist Intelligence Unit: Consumer Goods Briefing & Forecasts*. 24 Nov. 2010. Retrieved 31 Jan. 2011 from http://www.eiu.com/index.asp?layout=ib3Article&pubtypeid= 1122462497&article_id=567617241&rf=0

Balfour, Frederick, "Acting Globally but Selling Locally." *Business Week* 12 May 2008: 51.

Beech, Hannah, "Li Ning." *Time International Asia Edition* 13 Nov. 2006: 76.

"Beijing Olympics Opening Ceremony: Over 2 Billion Viewers Tune In." *Nielsen.com*. 14 Aug. 2008. Retrieved 31 Jan. 2011 from http://www. nielsen.com/us/en/insights/press-room/2008/beijing_olympics_ opening.html

Cheng, Allen T., "The Mainland's Sneaker King." *Time International* 5 Aug.2002: 43.

Cheung, Amy, "Li Ning: The Nike of China?" *China Perspective* 24 Jan. 2007.

"China's Li Ning Toe-to-toe Against Nike and Adidas." *Business Week* 1 May 2008.

"Don't Know Li Ning? Ask Shaq." *Bloomberg.com*. Oct. 2007. Retrieved 31 Jan. 2011 from http://www.businessweek.com/globalbiz/content/oct2007/gb2007108_732560.htm

Dyer, Geoff, "Faced with a Steep Learning Curve." *Financial Times* 23 Apr. 2007: 6.

Gilbert, Sarah, "Chinese Sneaker Giant Li Ning Steps onto Nike's Home Court." *Daily Finance* 1 May 2010.

Kwok, Vivian Wai-yin, "Chinese Sports Brand Takes on Nike." *Forbes* 13 Jan. 2010.

Madden, Normandy, "Study: Chinese Youth Aren't Patriotic Purchasers." *Advertising Age* 5 Jan. 2004: 6.

Moore, Malcolm, "Li Ning Stays One Step Ahead of Rivals in Olympic Brand Race." *Daily Telegraph* 15 Aug. 2008.

Nocera, Joe, "China Seeks To Learn the Art of Cachet." *New York Times* 12 Apr. 2008: C1.

"Olympic Ambush Heats Up Li Ning-Adidas Rivalry." *Bloomberg.com*. 12 Aug. 2008. Retrieved 31 Jan. 2011 from http://www.businessweek.com/globalbiz/content/aug2008/gb20080811_303782.htm

Pitt, Leyland, et al., "Event Sponsoring and Ambush Marketing: Lessons from the Beijing Olympics." *Business Horizons* 15 May 2010.

"Revitalization of the LI-NING Brand Takes China's Sports Goods Industry on a Quantum Leap." *Philippines News Agency* 1 July 2010.

"Wu's Aim: Help Li-Ning Vault into Global Sport-Apparel Biz." *Advertising Age* 25 Oct. 2004: 40.

Yu Tianyu, "Li Ning Makes the Change to Catch Up." *China Daily* 1 July 2010.

Clanton Corporation: Resolving Inter-Generational Conflict

Lisa Gueldenzoph Snyder • Associate Professor, School of Business & Economics, North Carolina A&T State University

LEARNING OBJECTIVES

After analyzing this case study, students should be able to do the following:

- *Understand the inter-generational issues than can impact effective communication in the workplace by reviewing the provided resources*
- *Apply their understanding of intergenerational issues to the case study to offer suggestions to solve the case scenario*
- *Analyze the interpersonal and intergenerational issues illustrated in the case and identify appropriate strategies*
- *Evaluate the outcome of the proposed strategies and extrapolate the resolution of each workplace relationship*

This case was prepared for classroom discussion rather than to illustrate either effective or ineffective handling of an administrative, ethical, or legal decision by management. Information was gathered from corporate as well as public sources.

BACKGROUND

Brad Harris graduated the previous May from Harrington University in North Carolina with a bachelor's degree in business administration and concentrations in both marketing and international business. He spent the summer before he graduated as an intern for Clanton Corporation, a fictitious IT consulting company headquartered in Research Triangle Park, North Carolina. During his internship, he worked with the international marketing team that targets new clients, seeks to foster positive relationships with existing international clients, and figures out new strategies for marketing the company's brand to international audiences. Brad enjoyed his internship and worked well with the five-person marketing team, many of whom had been at the company for several years. Brad's primary role was to gather research and summarize information as assigned by other team members. He learned a lot about the various cultures Clanton worked with and felt he played an active role in getting the team's work done.

A few months before graduation, Brad was very pleased when Josh Martin, Clanton's vice president of marketing, called him about an open position on the international marketing team. The company was looking to expand its international market, and several of the team members individually recommended Brad as a possible candidate for the new position. Although Brad had to compete with other applicants for the job, his prior experience with the company was an important factor. He knew the corporate culture at Clanton, understood its clients and services, and had already built positive working relationships with the team. He was offered the job and immediately accepted it.

In his new position as a permanent employee, Brad's role on the team was very different from his internship experience. Rather than merely finding information for other people, Brad was given the lead on project assignments and was asked to delegate to the new intern the research duties he had performed the previous year. He valued the challenge of being in a leadership role but struggled a little with his new responsibilities. Additionally, at team meetings, rather than report information from his research, like he had done as an intern, Brad was expected to analyze marketing strategies, provide recommendations, and collaborate with the team to make effective decisions. At first, Brad was uncomfortable in his new role. When the team was split on a decision, he wasn't sure how to react. He remained quiet at first, listening to everyone's perspectives. When asked what he thought, he often was unsure how he felt about the issue, but even when he did have an opinion, he didn't know how to explain his thoughts without sounding disagreeable. He assumed the experienced team members had better ideas about what to do than he did. After all, at 22 he was by far the youngest member of team. All but one of the other team members were in their late thirties or older.

Brad sought advice from Lana Miller, the only other young member of the team. She had been with Clanton for five years and had also been hired after interning for the company. Lana helped Brad understand that he was an equal member of the team who needed to learn how to assert himself rather than depend on the direction of senior team members. She explained, "They're looking to you as a colleague now, not an intern." Brad agreed with Lana's advice and worked on his confidence, especially in meetings. He also reviewed a PDF of a resource Lana emailed him that she thought might be helpful: "The Multi-Generational Workforce Challenge," published by Next Step, a corporate training company. According to this research, workers Brad's age—the Millennial Generation—often experienced communication problems with older employees and should be more proactive to request specific information. Brad took the initiative to begin asking his colleagues more questions about his assignments and seeking their advice, both during team meetings as well as individually. Brad benefited from their feedback, and his colleagues appreciated his interest in their perspectives. Brad developed solid mentoring relationships that improved both his confidence and assertiveness.

Work was going well for Brad until a few months later when Josh Martin made an announcement at a division meeting. Clanton's initiatives to expand its international market were going so well that the company would be opening new branches soon in Brazil, India, and China. This exciting company news meant significant changes would occur in the main office. Three people from Brad's team were chosen to lead the marketing staff at the new branches and would be replaced with internal candidates from other departments or new external hires. Brad was sorry to see his mentors go but was happy for them in their appointments to leading new teams at new branches in foreign countries.

After several interviews with competitive applicants, the new international marketing team met for the first time. Brad's team now consisted of Harold, a 52-year-old former marketing division head of a GenEd, an educational publishing company that downsized dramatically after a merger with another company; Martha, a 48-year-old independent marketing consultant whose children were finally grown and gone, which gave her the freedom to rejoin the workforce full-time; and Carlos, a 45-year-old marketing manager from Clanton's East-Coast office who had been transferred as the new team leader. In addition to Brad, the following two people remained on the team: Stacy, a 38-year old self-proclaimed Clanton Lifer who had been with the company (and on the same marketing team) for 16 years, and Lana, his 27-year-old friend who helped him find his place on the original team.

The first team meeting went well, even though Stacy monopolized the conversation. Twice when Brad started to say something, she interrupted him with what she thought was a better idea. She had mentioned to Brad and Lana before the meeting that she was disappointed that Clanton transferred Carlos to lead the team. She clearly had more seniority with the company. Brad decided not to take Stacy's interruptions personally; they were probably her attempt to demonstrate her experience to the new members of the team. Brad was impressed with Carlos's leadership during the meeting. He asked questions about how things had been done at the office before and how best to reassign and prioritize the current projects. He set timelines and goals, but maintained a collaborative dialogue by asking for everyone's input. Brad left the meeting energized.

Later that week when Brad stopped by Carlos's office to get his advice about a problem he was having with one of his projects, Brad was shocked at Carlos's reply: "I don't care how you handle it; just get it done. Let me know how it turns out." When Brad repeated his comment to Lana, she told Brad not to worry. "He obviously has faith in your ability to figure it out yourself. If you really want experienced advice, ask one of the other new people. That might be a good way to break the ice with them."

Brad found Martha first. Half-way through explaining his problem, Martha replied: "I'm sorry, Brad. I'm overwhelmed with my new client load. It's been awhile since I've had a full-time gig. How long have you been here, anyway? You look younger than my son who's a college freshman."

Brad smiled and said: "I've got one of those baby faces. I started with the company last year." Brad stretched the truth a little, using his internship as his starting date. He continued: "No need to apologize, though; I understand, Martha. If I can do anything to help you get to know the company, don't hesitate to ask."

Brad then went to Harold, who was on his office phone, but covered the receiver when he saw Brad and said: "Hey, kid. How's it going? Can you fax this stuff for me? And when you bring it back, stop by the supply closet and bring me a ream of paper. I don't know who had this office before me, but they must have never used the printer. Go figure! Thanks!" At that point, Harold immediately went back to his telephone conversation, leaving Brad standing there holding the papers he wanted him to fax. Not knowing what else to do, Brad walked down the hall to the fax machine, feeling like an intern again.

As Brad sent Harold's fax, Stacy walked by and said: "What's wrong, Brad. You look like you just lost your best friend." Brad shrugged, "It's nothing. Just a stressful day." Stacy laughed, "Stress? Really? You're too young to know what real stress is!" Stacy laughed and walked away.

QUESTIONS FOR DISCUSSION

1. Carlos maintained a collaborative dialogue during the first meeting but was quick to dismiss Brad's problem in an individual conversation. Why do you think that is?

2. None of the new team members seems to want to build a mentoring relationship with Brad. What are the pros and cons of (a) convincing one of them to mentor him? (b) asking Stacy or Lana to be his mentor? Or (c) finding a mentor external to the team?

3. What can Brad do to build positive working relationships with his new colleagues? Review the generational communication resources listed below. Identify strategies Brad can use to regain his confidence with his older teammates.

REFERENCES/BIBLIOGRAPHY

Cross Generational Communication: Implications in the Work Environment. Duke University, Office of Institution Equity. Retrieved 5 Feb. 2011 from http://www.duke.edu/web/equity/div_genera~ppt%20III.ppt

Dittmann, Melissa. "Generational Differences at Work." Monitor 36.6 (June 2005): 54. Retrieved 5 Feb. 2011 from http://www.apa.org/monitor/jun05/generational.aspx

Dobbs, Jason, Patrick Healey, Katherine Kane, et al. "The Center on Aging & Work / Workplace Flexibility at Boston College." Retrieved 5 Feb. 2011 from http://agingandwork.bc.edu/documents/FS09_MultiGenWork place_000.pdf

Lieberman, Simma, and Kate Berado. "Communicating Across Generations in the Workplace." Simma Lieberman Associates. Retrieved 5 Feb. 2011 from http://www.simmalieberman.com/articles/commacrossgenerations.html

Next Step. "The Multi-generational Workforce Challenge: A Research Summary." 2009. Retrieved 5 Feb. 2011 from http://www.softwareceo. com/files/white_papers/Next_Step_Multi_Generational_Research.pdf

Coffee Wars: Protecting Starbucks' Name in China

Terence R. Egan • Associate Professor, Central University of Finance and Economics, Beijing, China

LEARNING OBJECTIVES

After considering and discussing this case, students will be able to do the following:

- *Demonstrate an understanding of the scope of the protections provided by trademarks*
- *Outline some of the diverse challenges encountered by trademark owners*
- *Identify and explain the key steps and missteps taken by the trademark owner in this case and how they might apply in other business domains*
- *Offer suggestions for a set of general principles for protecting trademarks across various industries and product categories*
- *Make a judgment on the relative importance of the pursuit of trademark violations across various forms of infringement*

This case was prepared for classroom discussion rather than to illustrate either effective or ineffective handling of an administrative, ethical, or legal decision by management. Information was gathered from corporate as well as public sources.

INTRODUCTION

"We came first...We can't lose the case."

To say that Mao Yibo, outspoken general manager of Shanghai Xingbake (pronounced Shing-Bah-Ker), was confident would be an understatement. His small but thriving coffee chain in Shanghai was facing a trademark infringement case brought by Seattle-based coffee giant Starbucks Corporation. Trademark litigation is rarely as clear-cut as General Manager Mao predicted, however, especially when one of the world's best-known brands deems it necessary to bring action in a Chinese court.

For European and North American companies, China is a long way from home geographically, culturally, and legally. While considerable progress has been made in recent years, courts and administrative authorities often lack the resources, the knowledge, or the determination to combat infringements, especially in areas involving intellectual property (IP). For this reason, many companies are reluctant to take legal action even when confronted with blatant violations.

When Starbucks' customers wrap their hands around a warm cup of their favorite blend, few of them pay any attention to the little green logo that adorns every cup, napkin, and retail item in the store. Yet the Starbucks Corporation holds around 140 patents that protect its rights to logos, trademarks, coffee blends, merchandise, and even the look and feel of their stores. It may be just a little green circle to most people, but for Starbucks it is a symbol of the company that must be protect vigilantly and vigorously. With 16,000 stores worldwide, Starbucks has an astounding 10,000 patent applications. Each market has its unique commercial, cultural, and legal characteristics, so it takes a large team of dedicated trademark attorneys to safeguard Starbucks' rights.

STARBUCKS ENTERS THE CHINESE MARKET

In 1999, Starbucks Corporation set up its first China store in Beijing's China World Trade Centre. The China market presented many new business challenges, including issues connected to local rules and regulations, labor law, management of human resource, marketing, logistics, and contract negotiations. Intellectual Property was just another of the issues with which the international management team had to contend.

China is regarded by many multinational firms as a challenging business environment. In the early 2000s, many business laws have been introduced or expanded. In the case of IP and trademark legislation, a severe shortage of adequately trained people has led to a deficit in monitoring and enforcement. As if the differences in legal, cultural, and business environments were not enough, Starbucks also discovered that the Chinese language adds another dimension to trademark protection.

THE CHINA MARKET

Traditionally, China is a nation of tea-drinkers. It was only in the late 1980s that the current generation was introduced to coffee through a simple slogan from Nestlé: "Tastes great!" Nestlé's high-recognition campaign marked the beginning of Chinese consumers trying coffee products. By the late 1990s, the youth market was beginning to accept coffee as a popular beverage, but they were not about to settle for instant types. This increasingly affluent and highly status-conscience segment of the market was spending money on luxury and specialty items as a means to establish themselves as part of their new social group. They were keen to experience these new gourmet coffee blends.

Starbucks cleverly positioned itself in China as providing its customers' so-called third space, the place to meet beyond work and home. For Starbucks, the China market represented its greatest potential for long-term growth.

THE NAME GAME

China's seven major languages and 80 regional dialects, all of them using the same written character system, present a particular problem in choosing business and brand names. Most international business names, trademarks, and brand names have a Chinese equivalent. These *sino-fied* names usually represent one of the following:

1. Direct translation (e.g., General Electric; 通用电气; tōng yòng diàn qì or ING Group; ING集团; ING jítuán)
2. Semantic, that is, a product promise (e.g., Pampers baby diapers; 帮宝适; bāng bǎo shì; helps baby comfort)
3. Phonetic equivalent (e.g., Coca Cola; 可口可乐; kě kǒu kělè; or McDonald's; 马蛋糕 mǎ dàng āo)
4. Phono-semantic, that is, incorporating a phonetic equivalent and a product promise (e.g., Tide washing powder; 汰渍; tài zì; select, soak)

A specific challenge arises from the fact that the same Chinese syllable can have different characters and meanings. This provides ample opportunity for the Chinese fondness for amusing wordplay. Several famous brand names, including Coca Cola and Peugeot, made serious blunders in the translation of their names for the China market resulting in embarrassing, urgent, and expensive modifications.

Starbucks' Chinese equivalent is 星巴克 (*Xīng bā kè*; approximately pronounced Shing-Bah-Ker). In this case, *Xīng* means *star* and *bā kè* is the Chinese phonetic equivalent of *bucks*. Before entering the China mainland market, Starbucks had the benefit of several years of trading in Taiwan, which also uses the Chinese writing system. In fact, the name *Xīng bā kè* had evolved through popular consumer usage in Taiwan rather than through a deliberate branding strategy. The Chinese version of the Starbucks name was already well-known before it arrived on the mainland.

While Starbucks was well prepared, having registered more than 200 trademarks in China, within three years the company found itself fighting to protect its name on two fronts: Both its English name and its Chinese name were in dispute.

STARBUCKS VERSUS STAR SBUCK

The coastal city of Qingdao, located halfway between Beijing and Shanghai, is probably best-known for its Tsingtao brand beer, now an international brand. The color and excitement of Qingdao's annual beer festival rivals, according to local claim, the Munich Beer Festival. It is ironic, then, that Qingdao became an early battleground over a beverage of a different flavor.

In 2003, a large red banner with white lettering proudly announced the opening of a new store in the center of town: Qingdao Star Sbuck Coffee. The logo was a circle surrounded by stars (the same as the Starbucks logo), but in place of the Starbucks mermaid, the central design element was a coffee cup. The Star Sbuck coffee menu included Starbucks' trademarked offerings such as Frappuccino and Yukon Blend. The packaging of coffee beans was identical to that used by Starbucks and was boldly labeled Starbucks Coffee. The Starbucks trade dress, which includes its colors, interior design and decor, exterior design and signage, also appeared to have been closely imitated. The store used the Chinese name in its complete and accurate derivation.

In its court defense, the Qingdao company claimed that, although Starbucks had registered *Xīng bā kè* in China, the company had never used the name. Accordingly, they argued, they should be free to use the term *Xīng bā kè* as its business name. In relation to the Star Sbuck English appellation, they contended that, since this was a business name and not a trademark, they had no case to answer.

THE CASE THAT COULDN'T BE LOST

Further south, the case of Shanghai *Xīng bā kè*, owned by the ebullient and self-assured Mao Yibo, was coming to a conclusion. General Manager Mao's claim to the *Xīng bā kè* name hung largely on the fact that that his company name was approved on 20 October 1999, a clear 67 days before Starbucks registered its Xingbake trade mark. Mao declared that it was just a coincidence that his company's name and green-and-white circular logo so closely matched that of his U.S. competitor. "The logo was designed by our own staff," he was quoted as saying. "To be frank, I hadn't heard of Starbucks at the time, so how could I imitate its brand or logo?"

It should be mentioned that Starbucks had not used the Chinese appellation *Xīng bā kè* (or 星巴克) up to that time, although the Chinese public had already popularized the name as being synonymous with the U.S. company. Accordingly, the Shanghai No.2 Intermediate Court found that trademarks such as Starbucks and *Xīng bā kè* "spread rapidly and [were already] well-known by the public in the mainland" and thus "should be regarded as well-known trademarks." Although the defendant had a prior registration, theirs was a business name and, as such, the court found that the critical date should be the commencement of operations rather than the date of registration. As it happened, Shanghai *Xīng bā kè* did not open for business until several weeks after the registration of Starbucks' trademark.

The court held that the registration of Shanghai *Xīng bā kè* was a bad-faith attempt by the defendant to take advantage of the Starbucks name, reputation, and logo.

Back in Qingdao some two years later, the finding on Qingdao Star SBuck Coffee was even more clear cut. The local court found that the defendant had deliberately copied Starbucks' entire trademark system, including the Starbucks' logo and its trade dress, thereby creating confusion among customers as to the identity of the owners.

Both cases were awarded to Starbucks and the defendants were ordered to change their names and their logos. Shanghai *Xīng bā kè* was ordered to pay economic damages to Starbucks in the amount of US$62,000 and to issue an apology in a local newspaper. While the defendant conceded on the use of the Starbucks English language trademarks, the company appealed on the issues of using the *Xīng bā kè* name, the Star Sbuck name, and the logo, as well as on various procedural grounds. On 20 December 2006, the High Court rejected the appeal and upheld the decision of the first action.

LESSONS LEARNED

These were landmark cases in China. Conventional wisdom at that time held that China's courts would not uphold the rights of foreign companies. The outcome of these cases appeared to confirm that China was finally making progress in the protection of international trademarks and provided further proof to the theory that rule of law follows closely behind economic progress.

Starbucks' experiences in China demonstrate that western companies operating in any unfamiliar environment must remain vigilant and proactive in protecting their trademark rights. While it is true that the legal system in China and other developing markets often lack the resources to effectively combat infringements, it would be a mistake not to seek the protections for which local laws provide. Firms should also pay careful attention to the local derivations of their names and should register those names regardless of their intention to use them.

Successful products are often copied, so international firms need to defend their rights vigorously and early. The Starbucks Corporation prides itself in taking swift action against any firm or individual that it considers to be infringing its trademark rights. However, Starbucks argues that doing so is not being heavy-handed or opportunistic in its approach. "Our first step is to send cease and desist letters," says Batur Oktay, Starbucks Director and corporate counsel. "About 95% of enforcement matters are resolved after the first letter" (McDermott).

An ounce of prevention, as they say, is worth a pound of the cure.

QUESTIONS FOR DISCUSSION

1. Search the Web for different types of trademark disputes that Starbucks has pursued around the world. Specifically, you should be able to find action taken against cartoonists, satirists, and Internet bloggers. How strongly should each of these types of infringement be pursued by trademark owners, in your opinion? Consider how the circumstances or the parties involved might affect your judgment and how the law might accommodate these variables.

2. What were the particular challenges faced by Starbucks in the China market? If you were an executive at Starbucks engaged in entering the Chinese market, how might you have faced these challenges?

3. Even a company as famous as Starbucks may not be well-known in a new market. Should the fame of the company and/or its logo be taken into account in trademark litigation?

4. In which countries would you expect Starbucks to be engaged in most trademark litigation? Why?

5. You work for a government trade agency in your country. If you were to prepare a set of general principles to assist companies to protect their trademark rights, what would you include?

REFERENCES/BIBLIOGRAPHY

北京市工商局, Beijing Administration for Industry and Commerce, n.d. Web. 17 Web. 2011. http://www.baic.gov.cn/

China International Electronic Commerce Center. Intellectual Property Protection in China. http://www.chinaipr.gov.cn/cases/trademark/247066.shtml (accessed April 18th. 2009

International IP update, Winter 2005-06, Freshfields Bruckhaus Deringer, London UK.

Lehman, Lee, and Xu. "Starbucks Coffee Chain Sues Shanghai Competitor Over Use of Chinese Name." *China Intellectual Property Law Newsletter* 5.1 (9 Mar. 2004). Web. 17 Feb. 2011. http://www.lehmanlaw.com/resource-centre/newsletter/intellectual-property/vol5-no01.html.

McDermott, Eileen. "Interview: Batur Oktay, Starbucks." *Managing Intellectual Property: The Global IP Resource.* Web. 19 May 2009. http://www.managingip.com/Article/2206188/Interview-Batur-Oktay-Starbucks.html

Michael, David C., et al. "Beyond the Great Wall: Intellectual Property Strategies for Chinese Companies." Boston: Boston Consulting Group, 2007. Web. 17 Feb. 2011. http://www.bcg.com/documents/file14932.pdf

"Starbucks Corporation vs. Shanghai Starbucks Cafe Co. Ltd. for Trademark Infringement and Unfair Competition." 中国知识产权司法保护网, China Intellectual Property Rights Judicial Protection Network, n.d. Web. 17 Feb. 2011. http://www.chinaiprlaw.cn/file/2007081611833.html

Crying Over Spilt Milk: Danone's Joint Venture in China

Terence R. Egan • Associate Professor, Central University of Finance and Economics, Beijing, China

LEARNING OBJECTIVES

After discussion on the various aspects of this case, students should be able to do the following:

- *Analyze the concerns of two disputing parties and make judgments on the key issues raised in the case together with supporting explanations*
- *Outline principles that will help to avoid partnership problems of this nature or to bring disputes between partners to a speedy and mutually satisfactory conclusion*
- *Understand some of the difficulties facing companies in cross-cultural partnerships*

This case was prepared for classroom discussion rather than to illustrate either effective or ineffective handling of an administrative, ethical, or legal decision by management. Information was gathered from corporate as well as public sources.

INTRODUCTION

The feud between Groupe Danone SA of France and China's Hangzhou Wahaha Group (WHH Group) shows how easy it is for a high-profile joint venture to fall apart. It highlights the contrasting styles of Chinese and European partners and the consequent difficulties in establishing successful cross-cultural partnerships.

The dispute has raised the allegation that WHH Group was secretly using the Danone brand on products manufactured and sold outside the joint venture. "We found out [Mr. Zong] had been developing businesses which are directly competing with our business," said Danone Asia Pacific president Emmanuel Faber, in a *Chinabusinessservices.com* article. "He had significant interests, and sometimes management interests, in those companies."

Zong Qinghou is the founder and president of WHH Group and one of China's wealthiest people. He is a hard-driving, charismatic, hands-on leader whose personality pervades every aspect of the organization. Zong's response to Danone's allegations was blunt: "I told them the Chinese have stood up and the era of invasions by eight-country armies is long gone," he said, referring to the invasion of Beijing in 1900. "Chinese people have their own national character, you are always trying to threaten us, bully us, this is only making us angry" (AFP Shanghai). The battle lines had been drawn.

Disputes of this nature are exceedingly complicated. Many details remain private, partners' strategic purposes are often unknown or uncertain, and news reports and analyses can be heavily biased. This is exemplified by the diverse reportage of this dispute by media outlets and business commentators.

BACKGROUND TO THE JOINT VENTURE

Hangzhou Wahaha Group Company Limited (WHH Group) was founded in 1987 as a beverage sales company for a local government business in the province of Hangzhou. Zong Qinghou led the company from its humble beginnings as a three-person business—selling drinks to school children—into one of China's most successful beverage makers with 70 factories, sales of around US$2 billion, and a 23% share of China's bottled water market.

In 1995, with a capital injection required for their expansion plans, WHH Group entered a joint venture arrangement with the French company Groupe Danone SA, a multinational food conglomerate employing 90,000 people in 120 countries. Danone manufactures Danone brand dairy products, Lu biscuits, and is the bottler of Evian and Volvic waters. Danone has several joint ventures in China, including a 49% stake in China's biggest milk producer, China Mengniu Dairy Company, and 92% ownership of beverage company Guangdong Robust Group.

SCOPE AND OPERATION

The joint venture agreement, signed on 28 March 1996, folded major parts of the WHH Group business into the Wahaha-Danone Joint Venture (WHH JV). Zong retained his position as managing director of WHH Group, became chairman of WHH JV, and also became a significant minority shareholder in the newly privatized company. Danone obtained a 41% stake in five joint venture companies along with two positions on the board. Danone's partner, Peregrine Investments Holdings, held 10% of the shares and one board position. WHH Group retained 49% of WHH JV and held three board positions.

WHH Group licensed its name and other trademarks to the joint venture. While Danone had little influence on day-to-day operations, key decisions still required ratification by the board. At the same time, Danone felt that it was important to give Mr. Zong the space to exercise his proven entrepreneurial flair. Early in the relationship, their faith in the chairman's ability appeared to be justified. From the commencement of the joint venture operations in 1996 until 2010, the business grew from five joint venture entities to 39. Annual revenues soared from US$120 million to around US$2 billion, contributing US$120 million to Danone's annual operating profit and more than 5% of their global net profit.

OWNERSHIP CHANGE

In April 1998, due to the collapse of Peregrine (Danone's partner in the deal), a vacancy opened up on the board. Danone quickly filled the position without consultation with Zong Qinghou. The new appointment gave Danone equal voting rights and, with the transfer of their partner's shares, majority ownership of 51%. Because the foreign investment was set up through an investment vehicle registered in Singapore, the China government's authorization of the share transfer was not required.

Chairman Zong felt that WHH Group was losing control of the joint venture in what he later described as a takeover by stealth.

DANONE MAKES AN OFFER

As the businesses expanded, Danone made several attempts to buy WHH Group's stake in the JV; however, these overtures were always rejected by Zong and WHH Group.

In 2005 Danone noticed a sudden and unexplained slowdown in sales at WHH JV. The company's investigations eventually revealed that Wahaha products were being produced secretly at factories owned and managed by Mr. Zong's family. Holding companies had been set up in the names of Zong Qinghou's wife and daughter and, in some cases, were even located within the WHH JV facilities.

In a conciliatory move, Danone made an offer—reported to be for US$566 million—for 51% of these non-JV enterprises. This arrangement would have brought all of the Wahaha-branded products back under WHH JV control. Zong accepted the offer, signed the agreement, but subsequently reneged on the deal. He claimed that the businesses were undervalued by as much as US $240 million; consequently, he was unable to persuade his co-investors to accept the deal.

Zong Qinghou then set about creating even more parallel companies, including his own separate sales division. Danone immediately filed a lawsuit in California against a company registered in the Virgin Islands and controlled by Zong's relatives. (Zong family members list California as their state of residence.) Danone also began several proceedings—mostly related to legal technicalities—in California, Sweden, and other jurisdictions.

Zong responded by initiating arbitration proceedings in Hangzhou, arbitration being a Chinese legislative requirement prior to proceeding to a full court hearing. He resigned as chairman of the joint venture saying that he would not continue under the harassment of "Danone's smear campaign" against him and his family.

CLAIM AND COUNTER-CLAIM

On 3 April 2007, recriminations and accusations spilled into the public arena, first with an article appearing on a leading Chinese Internet news portal, Xinghua News Service, headlined: "Wahaha victim of low-ball buyout by Danone." The article was based on a leaked internal document and had all the hallmarks of an attempt to garner the support of political leaders.

The following is a summary of the key claims and counter-claims of both parties.[1]

Parallel Networks

Danone: WHH Group's parallel companies began operations as early as 2001 and expanded aggressively from 2005. Some of the products were secretly fed into the joint venture's legitimate sales network, while others were sold through separate distributors. These parallel or mirror companies took full advantage of the joint venture's marketing in a clear breach of the agreement.

Mr. Zong: Until the conflict became public, Zong was allowed to pursue his own commercial ventures in areas of activity in which Danone was uninterested. Zong claimed this had the personal authorization of Danone president, Emmanuel Faber.

Danone: In 2003, or thereabouts, Danone allowed Mr. Zong to become a minority partner with some independent contractors who made Wahaha products under license. These were not part of the joint venture agreement. This, Danone said, was simply an expedient and efficient way to work with local governments that had preferred to partner Mr. Zong.

Mr. Zong: Although it is his duty to support the China government's efforts to develop the European region, Danone would not allow him to invest there. As a direct consequence, Mr. Zong claims that he set up 61 separate companies under the Wahaha name with the express purpose to invest in China's interior.

Danone: Between 2001 and 2006 Mr. Zong established more than 80 unauthorized companies that used the Wahaha brand name. The scale of these mirror operations was so large and so intertwined with the legitimate WHH JV operations that it was difficult to unravel ownership. Danone claims that, by 2007, the revenues of Mr. Zong's mirror operations were almost as high as those of WHH JV.

Mr. Zong: Danone officials were made aware of these outside companies from the beginning. "To put it seriously," Zong said, "they were trying to bribe me to infringe the interest of small shareholders to achieve the goal of a cheap acquisition" (China Briefing).

Danone: Zong asked distributors to use new bank accounts with different names to sell products from the mirror factories.

Mr. Zong: Danone has separate joint ventures in China making juice and milk under other brand names that compete with Wahaha-branded products. Danone's other sizeable stakes include China Huiyuan Juice Group, Shenzhen Health Food, Bright Dairy & Food, Shanghai Aquarius Drinking Water Ltd., Mengniu (China's largest milk supplier in which they had 49% ownership) and Wahaha's largest competitor, Guangdong Robust Group (which is a 92%-owned subsidiary of Groupe Danone). Zong claimed that these investments were made after the WHH JV commenced operations and had a negative impact on the joint venture's revenues. He said that the acquisition of Guangdong Robust Group in 2001 had cost WHH JV US $10.5 million in the following year alone.

"So these terms are unfair and need to be revised. Either you call off the restrictions on us, or I add restrictions on you," Zong declared (China Law Blog).

Trademark Rights

Danone: The joint venture agreement gave Danone exclusive rights of production, distribution, and sales of products under the Wahaha brand.

Zong: WHH Group would continue to own the trademark since the Chinese government had already rejected the transfer application on the grounds of safeguarding national assets. Zong claims that he fell into a trap that was set by Danone and had consequently caused trouble for the Wahaha brand. For this reason, he decided not to pursue the recordation of the agreement with the appropriate government department.

WAR ON ANOTHER FRONT

While claim and counter-claim continued through Chinese and international courts, the partners also found themselves in a very public PR battle. In April 2007 Zong accused Danone of engineering a hostile takeover. He was also rallying strong community support with appeals to national pride.

Danone responded by issuing a media release stating that Zong had breached the agreement and outlined details of the parallel companies. Zong responded with a media release that made a modest conciliatory gesture with the proviso that Danone stop investing in Chinese beverage companies, apologize for damaging the joint venture, and drop its claim on Wahaha's brand name. It was a gesture that was not designed to succeed.

After Zong Qinghou resigned as chairman of the joint venture company, Danone replaced him with its Asia region CEO, Emmanuel Faber. Subsequently, the management and staff of Wahaha rose up against Danone, issuing public statements denouncing the French company and the new leader. Wahaha released a series of employee letters that attacked Danone managers for bullying behavior. Another statement criticized Danone's appointments of two directors. An open letter published widely in the Chinese media claimed to be from the WHH JV sales team and stated: "We formally warn Danone and the traitors they hire, we will punish your sins. We only want Chairman Zong ... Please get out of Wahaha!"(Financial Times Chinese Version).

Danone then released a statement that said, in part: "We think that it is inappropriate for anyone to seek to leverage employees, business partners and the public to support their goal of maximizing their own personal wealth, while endangering the business continuity of the company" (Barboza and Kanter).

By this time, however, the situation was clearly out of control. Many managers had left or were threatening to leave, distributors were choosing sides, and staff members of some distribution partners were refusing to sell Danone products. The entire organization in China had lost focus as employees were consumed by the turmoil and uncertainty surrounding the JV dispute.

Danone continued to present a positive face. "At the end of the day, we want a fair share of the pie," said Emmanuel Faber. "We don't want to destroy the pie" (Barboza and Kanter). In the second half of 2007, Danone suspended sales from the joint venture. Revenues plunged by more than 30% in the Asian market.

PRESIDENTIAL INTERVENTION

With more than 21 actions instigated in courts around the world, this conflict had become one of the biggest disputes in China's history. Danone's lawsuits were meeting with little success in China. The Hangzhou Arbitration Commission agreed with Zong that ownership of the Wahaha trademark had never been transferred to the joint venture.

Zong also initiated proceedings against Danone-nominated JV directors for breaching their obligations under the non-compete clause. The directors were also serving on the boards of companies that, Zong claimed, competed in some of Wahaha's product categories. Qin Peng, a founding director of WHH JV, was cited as holding directorships in approximately 20 competing companies without board approval.

Billions of dollars—and perhaps the pride of two nations—were at stake. In November 2007 the dispute had escalated to being an agenda item for a meeting between Chinese president Hu Jintao and French president Nicolas Sarkozy. Immediately following the French president's visit, Danone and

Wahaha released a joint statement: "Both parties agree to temporarily suspend all lawsuits and arbitrations, stop all aggressive and hostile statements, and create a friendly environment for peace talks" (Perkowski).

After extensive meetings held over the next three months, Danone proposed to merge the China assets of the two companies' and float 20% of the new joint venture's shares. WHH Group rejected the proposal.

Zong's Nationalistic Fervor under Scrutiny

A newspaper report in *Morning China* by Eric Mu revealed that Zong Qinghou had held a United States permanent resident card since 1999, which caused great controversy since Zong had been elected as a representative to People's Congress in 2002 and 2007. While there is no a law preventing Chinese citizens with U.S. green cards from becoming People's representatives, many Chinese were displeased that a so-called American was representing them in government proceedings.

Zong's highly successful PR campaign was further damaged by revelations that his wife also had a U.S. green card and that their daughter had full U.S. citizenship. The public's faith in their hero, Zong Qinghou, was severely tested.

Another report accused Zong of tax evasion involving up to US$40 million in taxes on undeclared overseas income. Danone's only major legal success was to have assets linked to Wahaha frozen in the tax havens of Samoa and the British Virgin Islands. This issue was destined to haunt Zong Qinghou.

A SO-CALLED AMICABLE SETTLEMENT

In January 2008, Danone Asia Pacific president Emmanuel Faber resigned from his position, in an action widely seen as one last attempt to resolve the dispute. However, relations seemed to be irretrievable and no reciprocity was forthcoming from the WHH Group.

Danone then abandoned its legal actions in China, and both parties agreed to refrain from making hostile public statements. For the next two years, the dispute was largely off the media's radar providing a more stable environment for constructive dialogue to proceed.

In early 2009, WHH Group rejected Danone's offer to sell its stake in WHH JV. Then in May 2010 the companies announced that an "amicable settlement" had been reached. Danone agreed to sell its 51% stake in the joint venture to WHH for a reported US$438 million (Deloitte U.S. Chinese Service Group). This is less than one-fifth of Danone's offer valuation in 2009. Danone and Wahaha agreed to conclude their joint venture relationship. All legal proceedings related to the dispute would be ended.

As of late 2010, the agreement was still subject to approval from the Chinese government; however, this appeared to be a formality given that the governments of both China and France reportedly played an integral role in reaching this latest agreement.

Despite the end of the joint venture, Danone emphasized its continuing commitment to the China market and announced that it would seek to accelerate its growth in the country.

QUESTIONS FOR DISCUSSION

1. It is said that three different agendas or strategic objectives exist at the commencement of any joint venture: (a) the agenda of Party A; (b) the agenda of Party B; and (c) the agenda of the joint venture. How would you describe those three agendas in the Wahaha-Danone case? In your opinion, could these different agendas have been managed successfully?

2. What were the other reasons for the breakdown of this relationship? What part did trust play? What could or should Danone have done differently, in your opinion?

3. Danone was the main litigant in this dispute. What would you advise the company to do differently from the time the dispute first arose?

4. Is it reasonable that Zong Qinghou be allowed to create a parallel set of companies?

5. What are some of the challenges facing companies when they enter into cross-cultural partnerships?

6. Drawing your conclusions from this case, outline some general principles for companies entering new markets, especially where those markets have starkly different cultures, laws, and business practices to their own.

NOTES

1. For the purpose of ensuring that a complicated series of events is no more complex than is necessary, all statements in this section have been attributed to Mr. Zong although some of the assertions were made by the WHH Group or on behalf of the WHH Group by Mr. Zong or the Group's lawyers.

REFERENCES/BIBLIOGRAPHY

AFP Shanghai. "The Self-made Chinese Entrepreneur who Refuses to Back Down." *Taipei Times* 8 July 2007: 12. Web. 15 Feb. 2011.http://www.taipeitimes.com/News/bizfocus/archives/2007/07/08/2003368682

Bao, Wanxian. "Danone's Legal Pursuit of Wahaha a Sign of the Times." *China Daily* 16 Mar. 2009: 11. Web. 15 Feb. 2011. http://www.chinadaily.com.cn/bw/2009-03/16/content_7580766.htm

Barboza, David, and James Kanter. (2007, June 12). "Brawl Threatens Huge Investment by Danone in China." *New York Times* 12 June 2007.

Web. 15 Feb. 2011. http://www.nytimes.com/2007/06/12/business/worldbusiness/12iht-danone.3.6110611.html?_r=1

Callick, Rowan. (2007, June 25). "Danone under Pressure to Quit China Venture." *The Australian* 25 June 2007. Web. 15 Feb. 2011. http://www.theaustralian.com.au/business/danone-under-pressure-to-quit-china-venture/story-e6frg8zx-1111113815854

"The Danone-Wahaha Brouhaha." *China Briefing* 13 June 2007. Web. 15 Feb. 2011. http://www.china-briefing.com/news/2007/06/13/the-danone-wahaha-brouhaha.html

Deloitte U.S. Chinese Service Group. *China M&A Digest.* 26 Sept. 2009–2 Oct. 2009. Web. 15 Feb. 2011. http://www.deloitte.com/assets/Dcom-UnitedStates/Local%20Assets/Documents/us_csg_ChinaMADigest_100609.pdf

Dickie, M. (2007, December 23). "Danone and Wahaha Agree to Truce." *Financial Times* 23 Dec. 2007. http://www.ft.com/cms/d96380f2-ac42-11dc-82f0-0000779fd2ac.html

Dyer, G. "Blow to Danone in China Brand Dispute." *Financial Times* 10 Dec. 2007. http://www.ft.com/cms/s/bd3551ee-a747-11dc-a25a-0000779fd2ac.html

Financial Times Chinese version, (2007, June 18). Still waters run deep in dispute at Wahaha. Retrieved from http://www.ftchinese.com/story/001012101/ce

Gordon, Jeremy. "Another MNC in Hot Water." *China Business Services* 12 Apr. 2007. Web. 15 Feb. 2011. http://www.chinabusinessservices.com/blog/?p=474

Harris, Dan. "Danone v. Wahaha—Which of us is the Most China Rookie." *China Law Blog.* 17 Jan. 2007. Web. Retrieved 15 Feb. 2011 from http://www.chinalawblog.com/2007/04/danone_v_wahaha_which_of_us_is.html

Jing, J. "Danone Regional Head Quits to Heal Wahaha Row." *China International* 18 Jan. 2008. Web. 15 Feb. 2011. http://en.ec.com.cn/article/newsroom/newsroomindustry/200801/706734_1.html

Kurtenbach, E. "Wahaha-Danone Brand Name Feud Highlights Pitfalls." *thestar* 27 June 2007. Web. 15 Feb. 2011. http://thestar.com.my/news/story.asp?file=/2007/6/28/apworld/20070628113413&sec=apworld

Laurent, Lionel. "Danone Denied in Wahaha Ruling." *Forbes.com.* 11 Dec. 2007. Web. 15 Feb. 2011. http://www.forbes.com/2007/12/11/danone-wahaha-china-markets-equity-cx_ll_1211markets08.html

McGregor, James. *One Billion Customers: Lessons from the Front Lines of Doing Business in China.* New York: Simon & Schuster, 2007. Print.

Mu, Eric. "Wahaha Chairman Revealed to Hold Green Card." *Morning China* 24 June 2007. Web. 15 Feb. 2011. http://www.wsichina.org/morning-china/article.asp?id=3169

Perkowski, Jack. *Managing the Dragon: How I'm Building a Billion-Dollar Business in China.* London: Bantam, 2008. Print.

Tao, Jingzhou, and Edward Hillier. "A Tale of Two Companies." *China Business Review* May-June 2008. Web. 15 Feb. 2011. http://www.chinabusinessreview.com/public/0805/commentary.html

Xiao Yu. "Danone, Wahaha Reach a Settlement in Beverage Dispute." *China Daily* 5 Oct. 2009. Web. 15 Feb. 2011. http://www.chinadaily.com.cn/china/2009-10/05/content_8763937.htm

The Development of Microfinance in Syria: Issues in Innovation and Change

Andrew Ashwin • Content Developer, Biz/ed, Cengage Learning EMEA

LEARNING OBJECTIVES

After reading this case study and completing the questions, students should be able to do the following:

- *Explain the meaning of the term* innovation
- *Analyze and assess the importance of microfinance in supporting small businesses*
- *Comment on the importance of infrastructure in facilitating cash-flow*
- *Examine how innovation can be compromised by resistance to change*
- *Evaluate factors that need to be in place to encourage and support innovation*

This case was prepared for classroom discussion rather than to illustrate either effective or ineffective handling of an administrative, ethical, or legal decision by management. Information was gathered from corporate as well as public sources.

INTRODUCTION

One of the keys to maintaining a strategic advantage in business is innovation. Innovation can take a number of forms, but whatever form it takes, it presents options for businesses to exploit and gain important footholds to improve the business. This case study looks at two examples where external changes have provided opportunities for businesses to be able to make significant changes to the way they work and so be able to make plans to implement strategic change.

The lifeblood of business is cash. In order to operate effectively businesses need to have cash flow under control and also access to credit lines to help alleviate cash flow problems. This means that countries have to have a developed financial system to be able to service the needs of businesses and some countries in the Middle East are recognising this and putting into place structures to help ease the flow of credit and give businesses the life-blood they need to survive and grow.

SYRIA'S FARMERS AND CASH FLOW

As of 2010, Syria was in the process of developing and improving its financial and banking services. Of special interest was microfinance, which refers to the provision of loans and credit for small businesses. Microfinance is particularly important in Syria where there are many small businesses, especially in rural areas. Many of these businesses failed in the early 2000s. According to a United Nations report, over 800,000 Syrian farmers have had to leave the industry between 2006 and 2010 due to ongoing drought and other climate problems. Such natural disasters can cause revenue to fall dramatically as crops fail to grow. For people facing such losses, microfinance can play an important role. A thriving microfinance sector would provide one way for farmers to get temporary cash to see them through difficult times.

New Banks in Syria

Between 1960 and 2000, Syria had four state-owned banks and its central bank. In 2000, reform of the banking system began with a series of legislative changes that led to the establishment of 14 new private banks. Of these, six are state-owned and three based on Islamic banking practices. These private banks have all witnessed significant growth and helped establish the basis for the expansion of banking practices throughout the country, thus supporting business development. In April 2010, bank deposits in these private banks reached SYP1.1 trillion (LE135.2 billion, $21.6 billion).

The establishment of these new commercial banks operating in the private sector led to over SYP298.42 billion (LE 34.8 billion, $6.4 billion) of credit being distributed in 2008. Much of this money, however, found its way to larger business enterprises, and smaller businesses continued to need a way to benefit from credit lines. The first lady, Asma Al Assad, was instrumental in setting up a microfinance initiative in the form of the Fund for Integrated Rural Development of Syria (FIRDS). This initiative led in 2007 to the government passing a new law regarding microfinance. Law No. 15 established systems to enable banking institutions to set up operations with a social finance emphasis. These social finance banking institutions (SFBIs) can be charitable institutions or profit-making ones. The aim of SFBIs is to "help families create opportunities for owning and increasing the accumulation of assets." (Syrian Legislative Decree)

NEW BANKING INSTITUTIONS

The new law allows various institutions to be developed, focusing on different business areas but sharing the same goal—helping families financially. The First MicroFinance Institution Syria (FMFI-S) was the first to be licensed under the new legislation. It lends small amounts of money to rural businesses and small enterprises. These loans can be a little as $100, and between 2004 and 2010, it handled over $82 million in loans to approximately 60,000 businesses. The United Nations Development Program (UNDP) set up a microfinance initiative in the Aleppo region to help small businesses in agriculture. The initiative requires the community to contribute; members pay a small fee that gives them access to loans. The average loan under this initiative is approximately SYP25,725 (LE3,000, USD550). The *sunduq* scheme follows Islamic banking practice and charges a fixed fee of 5% for borrowing.

Interest on loans has been problematic for SFBIs. In order to set up and survive, institutions need to raise sufficient funds from borrowers to pay for operating costs. Some SFBIs are non-profit making, but that arrangement is not always good for an institution's long-term sustainability. Some have tried to operate without charging interest but have found it difficult to survive, and while the 1% interest charge of FMFI-S loans sounds good for borrowers, it does not always allow sufficient robustness to enable the institution to grow and develop and thus reach more borrowers. Both the *sunduq* scheme and the FMFI-S have received financial support from outside Syria and its government: the former from UN grants and the latter from a German development bank and from the Syrian government.

Finance Legislation and Costs

Though new legislation has made microfinance development possible in Syria, there are still plenty of challenges facing the government and the industry. Interest rates remain problematic. As of 2010, the government set a cap of 9% on interest rates charged by non-profit organizations, but this cap may have to be removed. The reason is that when interest rates are capped, the number of institutions that can afford to operate under such constraints is limited. This fact may help to explain why the demand for microfinance continues to exceed supply.

The cost of operating microfinance is relatively high compared to other forms of business finance. Microfinance involves many small transactions and the operating costs of setting up and managing these is high. Thus, institutions that charge low interest rates may not be able to survive in the long term. The Microfinance Information Exchange puts the break-even interest rate at around 20% and quotes an average across the sector of almost 26.5%. Plus, people need to be educated about the benefits of using microfinance institutions, given that many small businesses traditionally rely heavily on friends, family, or local money lenders. As the program develops, this situation should change. The potential for the market to expand is clear; a 2009 Arab Microfinance Analysis and Benchmarking Report estimates the microfinance market in Syria to be worth around USD15.3 million. As of 2010, the demand for microfinance was not being met, and the government recognized that meeting this need is essential if businesses are to become more independent and sustainable. As with any innovation, the initial stages of development can be slow, and there are plenty of hurdles to overcome, but as the initiative gains momentum, the benefits to all concerned are anticipated to be significant.

NANOTECHNOLOGY

Another area of innovation associated with small business is nanotechnology. As of 2010, the Middle East was starting to build interest in this area, and the implications for businesses were thought to be significant. *Nanotechnology* refers to operating with materials at a nano level, *nano* referring to structures that are 100 nanometers or smaller where a nano is one-billionth of a meter. Working at this molecular level and beyond is innovative. Considering how people use materials and how these materials and processes work is new, and few can conceptualize the extraordinary potential the technology possesses. Applications of nanotechnology being developed in the late 2000s include socks and shirts that repel sweat and stay fresh; lightweight, high-strength materials for boat and jet-ski construction, among other vehicles; memory chips for computers, mobiles, and MP3 players; cleaning materials; waterproof and dirt proof textiles; materials for bicycle frame construction and other sports equipment such as golf clubs; and materials to be used as wound dressings, adhesives, coatings, and toothpastes and anti-bacterial products of all kinds.

SabryCorp

Egypt is one of the Middle East countries that embrace nanotechnology. There are government program to boost involvement in the sector, including the launching of a post-graduate program in nanotechnology at the Nile University. SabryCorp, one of the first regional companies to specialize in nanotechnology consultation, was established in 2005. SabryCorp advises businesses regarding how nanotechnology can be used and how it can provide solutions to existing problems. The company focuses on small scale uses of nanotechnology where the risk is small. Given that the industry in the Middle East is still not well known, the company's expansion depends on educating others about the scope and importance of nanotechnology. Attention also is given to potentially significant ethical issues that may arise as a result of developments in the technology.

Globally the interest in nanotechnology is growing. In 2007, global investment stood at LE810 billion (USD148 billion) and is expected to grow by over 16 times to LE14.2 trillion (USD2.6 trillion) by 2014. In addition to Egypt, Saudi Arabia recognizes the potential of the technology, especially in relation to the oil industry. Reports say that the Saudi government will allocate LE33 billion (USD6 billion) between 2010 and 2015 to nanotechnology.

SabryCorp stresses its role in providing education and awareness to the public in general about the ramifications of nanotechnology. Existing technologies are likely to become redundant as nanotechnology develops.

These changes can be difficult for people to accept, and SabryCorp is intent on highlighting the benefits. It wants to focus attention on the way the technology can be used to solve problems regarding pollution, renewable energy, medicine, computers, transportation, and the production of materials such as steel, cement, and textiles, all areas that have significance in Egypt and the wider Middle East. SabryCorp recognizes that misconceptions about the technology can create a barrier to the company's progress. Ordinary people tend not to understand the technology, and they may fear its potentially negative applications, for example, for military uses.

Textbooks may present innovation as positive for both business and the wider community. However, as these two examples show, innovation can also be associated with ignorance and that can be a barrier to the speed with which innovation can take hold and generate benefits. Breaking social norms and traditions, as shown in the case of microfinance, is one barrier to its growth. People need to be comfortable with initiatives and trust that changes will have positive effects.

The more complex the innovation, the more difficult it is to create this receptive and trusting mindset in the public. Such is the case with nanotechnology. Fortunately, for the Middle East, certain companies are more interested in ground-breaking developments in the region than in relying on businesses from other parts of the world. Innovation requires firms to take the initiative and governments to recognise the potential for such innovation.

The Syrian government has demonstrated how legislation can empower business. As is the case with microfinance, there is room for further changes in the regulatory process to encourage the growth of fledgling industries. Government can take the lead in supporting business involved in developing cutting-edge technology. This sends out signals to business and the wider community that support will be forthcoming and that investment by business in innovation can generate returns that justify it. The $6 billion budget earmarked by the Saudi government for nanotechnology signals the market that innovation is valued and will be supported.

QUESTIONS FOR DISCUSSION

1. Explain how *innovation* differs from *invention*.
2. Evaluate the importance of cash flow to the success of a small business and discuss the role of microfinance in helping to ease cash flow problems.
3. Discuss the importance of a sound financial infrastructure in a country to the ability of small businesses to manage their cash flow effectively.
4. Explain why and how can innovation be the source of considerable resistance to change.
5. Using an example from the case study or one with which you are familiar, assess the factors that need to be in place to encourage and support successful innovation.

REFERENCES/BIBLIOGRAPHY

2009 Arab Microfinance Analysis and Benchmarking Report. Microfinance Information Exchange. May 2010. Web. http://www.cgap.org/gm/document-1.9.43821/2009_Arab_Microfinance_Analysis_Benchmarking%20Report.pdf

Syrian Arab Republic. *Syrian Legislative Decree No. 15*. 15 Feb. 2007. Web. Retrieved on 17 Feb. 2011 from http://www.banquecentrale.gov.sy/ban-sup/Legislative%20Decree%20No.%2015%20for%202007%20%20on%20micro-finance%20institutions.pdf

United Nations. *Syria Drought Response Plan: 2009-2010 Mid-term Review*. February 2010. Web. http://ochadms.unog.ch/quickplace/cap/main.nsf/h_Index/2010_Syria_DroughtResponsePlan/$FILE/2010_Syria_DroughtResponsePlan_SCREEN.pdf?OpenElement

Does it Pay to Be Proactive? Considering an IT Change Management System at Gainer, Donnelly & Desroches

Patricia Long • IT Department Manager, Houston, TX, Gainer, Donnelly & Desroches

Jamison V. Kovach • Assistant Professor, Department of Information and Logistics Technology, University of Houston, Houston, TX

LEARNING OBJECTIVES

After completing this case study, students should be able to do the following:

- *Formulate arguments to support a particular course of action*
- *Assess methods used to investigate/solve problems and develop alternative approaches*
- *Compare and contrast various improvement ideas*
- *Defend the selection of a particular improvement idea*

This case was prepared for classroom discussion rather than to illustrate either effective or ineffective handling of an administrative, ethical, or legal decision by management. Information was gathered from corporate as well as public sources.

BACKGROUND

It was 8 a.m. on Monday morning, and the first help desk ticket of the day was just being logged as Ann Edwards walked into the office. Ann was the information technology (IT) manager for Gainer, Donnelly & Desroches, a large public accounting firm in Houston, Texas, and in this position, she was responsible for ensuring that all software applications and IT equipment functioned properly so that others within the firm could complete the necessary work for their clients. As Ann started her work that day, she could already feel the stress level in the building beginning to rise. It was April 15, which meant all their clients' taxes were due that day. Ann especially hoped all the firm's IT systems worked smoothly on this particular day. In an effort to be proactive and try to keep all systems under control, the first thing Ann did was check the status of open help desk tickets in the system. She saw that only one new ticket had been submitted so far that day and that Mark Stafford, one of her network administrators, was already investigating the problem.

Just minutes before Ann saw the new help desk ticket, Mark noticed it in the system and went ahead and assigned it to his case load, since he knew that the senior network administrator, Jonny Liu, would be a little late that day. As Mark reviewed the ticket, he saw that the issue involved a user who could not access the data she needed to do her work. He began to think about some of the possible causes of this problem. He wondered if it was just a problem with her computer. Perhaps she was not connected to the network. Maybe she forgot where her data are located. To begin investigating this problem, Mark looked at the configuration of her computer through the system. It appeared to be correctly connected to the network, and the user was looking for her data in the correct location. From Mark's perspective, everything looked fine, except the user could not find her data, which meant the work for her client would be delayed. Mark instantly worried that perhaps her work was tax related. Then, Mark noticed a second help desk ticket appear in the system: Another user also reported being unable to access his data. Mark now concluded that the issue must be some type of network problem since it was affecting multiple users. He wondered if the server was down. He wondered if the server got rebooted and did not come back up properly. Mark looked at the server, and it seemed to be running as it should. Mark quickly realized he was in over his head, and since Jonny wasn't in yet, he headed to Ann's office for some help.

For almost an hour Ann and Mark worked together in his office to try to identify the location of the missing data, but they still did not understand how this problem occurred. While in the system, Ann and Mark noticed a third help desk ticket. This one was unrelated to the current issue. Instead, it was a user who reported being unable to access the network. Ann told Mark to continue working on the first problem and that she'd quickly take care of this new ticket. Back in her office, Ann realized that the user could not access the network because his account had been disabled. She wasn't sure who had done this or why, but it was a quick fix—just reinstate the account and then get back to helping Mark. But before she did, she had a nagging feeling that she should check with Human Resources (HR), just to be sure.

As it turned out, the user who submitted the help desk ticket had been dismissed from the company the previous Friday, and HR had called the IT department to request that his account be disabled. Ann knew Mark or Jonny must have done the work, but because it was a verbal request she didn't have a help desk ticket for the job. Ann closed the ticket she was working on and headed back to Mark's office to continue helping him with the other issue. Knowing that there was a lot of work the firm needed to complete that day, she was concerned that if they didn't find an answer to Mark's problem soon, the phone would start ringing off the hook with anxious users or worse from partners, demanding to know how much longer they would have to wait to get back to work.

When Ann returned to his office, she saw Mark had made no progress. But she was curious, so she asked him if he had disabled an account for HR on Friday. Mark acknowledged that he had, so she reminded him that when HR called in requests, he still needed to create a help desk ticket in the system and email the IT staff members to let them know the job was complete. And that's when they began wondering if Jonny had changed something in the system over the weekend and forgotten to tell them about it. Mark had already been through all his new emails and knew he didn't receive an email from Jonny about this problem. So Ann went back to her office to check her email. She hadn't had a chance to read all her new emails before going to help Mark. In fact, there was an email from Jonny to let her know that he had moved the data to a different server the previous night. The problem was he hadn't copied Mark on the email. Ann quickly forwarded the email to Mark, knowing that this information would quickly resolve the current problem.

After a long sigh of relief, Ann began to think about how often things like this happen and how much frustration they caused for her and her staff. It was simple really. Someone just forgot to create a help desk ticket or someone else forgot to tell others about a change they made, but the effect was often significant. For some time, Ann had tried to develop a way for her department to communicate IT system changes more effectively. It was clear, however, that their biweekly department meetings and manual email notifications to communicate changes were not working. After the events of the morning, Ann was convinced she needed to find a better solution and the sooner the better.

COMPANY OPERATIONS

Gainer, Donnelly & Desroches is a mid-size certified public accounting firm that specializes in serving individuals and private entrepreneurs. In 2009, this firm was listed as the eighth largest public accounting firm in the Houston area (Ferweda). As of 2010, Gainer, Donnelly & Desroches employed more than 60 certified professional accountants (CPAs) in Texas and had been in business for over 60 years. The firm offers professional services, including audit, tax, bookkeeping, and risk services, in a variety of industries, such as real estate, energy, and manufacturing. It also provides services to high net worth individuals and non-profit organizations.

The IT department within Gainer, Donnelly & Desroches is relatively small and consists of the IT manager, two IT staff, and one external consultant. The SIPOC (Suppliers, Inputs, Process, Outputs, Customers) diagram in Figure 1 provides a brief overview of the operations within the IT department. These include tasks such as handling help desk tickets and requests for changes, which

FIGURE 1

Suppliers	Inputs	Process Steps	Outputs	Customers
Help Desk Staff	User Issues	Received Request via Email/Phone	Problem Resolved	Company
IT Manager	Staff Experience	Gather Customer Information	Standard Operating Procedure	Employees
Training Department	Staff Training	Classify Issue	Ticket Closed & Logged Documentation	Company
External Consultants	Staff Availability	Analyze Issue	Resolution Added to FAQ Database	External Consultants
Vendors	FAQ Database	Solve Problem	New Configurations Versions	
HR Department	User Availability	Manage Request Changes	New Hardware/ Software Installed	
Users	Hardware/Software	Install New Hardware Software		
Staff	New/Terminated Users	Perform System Maintenance		

IT Department Operations at Gainer, Donnelly & Desroches

directly affect company employees (i.e., users) and IT staff and consultants and indirectly affects clients. The help desk staff, IT manager, company employees, the Training and HR Departments, as well as external consultants and vendors, supply the inputs to this process, which include user issues, staff experience, and staff training. The outputs of this work include problem resolutions, ticket documentation, and new configurations.

As of 2010, the IT department used an informal method for managing IT system changes that was not very effective. This process consisted mainly of communicating changes verbally at biweekly department meetings and/or through email, which was causing several problems for the IT department. These problems often included failure to communicate changes, changes communicated via email are not acknowledged by others, and lack of documentation about changes, which meant there was no way to easily identify what changes had occurred recently that might be responsible for new problems encountered by the IT staff.

PROBLEM AND SIGNIFICANCE

Change management is the process responsible for controlling and managing requests to change aspects of the IT infrastructure or service, which is a central IT control that is required to support the business operations of any organization. Many IT changes occur on a daily basis within organizations, including daily activities (such as installing, moving, adding and and/or changing hardware/ software), new projects, enhancement projects, and maintenance activities. The number of change requests can range from 300/month for a small company to 10,000/month for a Fortune 500 company (Brittain). Problems that result from poor IT change management include unplanned downtime and frustration for IT department staff.

In IT systems, downtime occurs when a system is unavailable, which prevents users from doing their work. There two types of downtime: planned and unplanned. Planned downtime occurs when a system is shut down at a predetermined time, which is scheduled and communicated to users so as to minimize negative effects on user productivity caused by system unavailability. IT departments use planned downtime for hardware upgrades and repairs, operating system patches, and software application upgrades. By contrast, unplanned downtime is caused by failures that render the system unavailable to users; hence, user productivity is negatively affected. Unplanned downtime is, therefore, more expensive than planned downtime and can have a significant financial impact on organizations (Microsoft Corporation, "Understanding Downtime").

Unplanned downtime generally consists of 10% or less of all downtime, yet mid-size organizations typically experience at least six hours of unplanned downtime per month (IBM). Research suggests that 80% of most production outages can be tied back to a change (Peregrine Systems, Inc.), with approximately 40% of that being caused by application failures and an additional 40% of which is caused by operator errors, both of which could be improved through an effective IT change management process (Scott). For example, an error in changing an Internet protocol (IP) address could result in a server being unable to connect to the network, users being unable to access the network, and/or the failure of a company's disaster recovery plan.

Because companies are increasingly reliant on IT services, the potential failure of these services represents increased financial risk for many organizations (Microsoft Corporation, "Increased Risk of IT Failure). In fact, 40% of companies that suffer a critical IT system failure go out of business within one year of the event (Phoenix). According to Haider, Mohammed & Networks First Limited, other consequences of IT system failures are:

- A decrease in work productivity because employees cannot access the systems needed to do their work
- A decrease in customer service because employees cannot interact with customers and because customers are unable to access information

Costs associated with unplanned downtime include lost revenue and reduced cash flow (if billing cannot go out on time) and/or overtime costs (for both employees and IT staff) (Microsoft Corporation, 2005).

Unmanaged changes also cause frustration for the IT department. Without an effective system for managing changes, IT staff members often spend more time troubleshooting issues, thus incurring additional overtime costs and creating unnecessary stress. Research shows that the attribute of the work environment most valued by service employees is being able to achieve results for their customers (Heskett, Jones, Loveman, Sasser, & Schlesinger). IT workers who face little to no impediment in carrying out their job duties are more satisfied, and satisfied employees create more value for the customers they serve. Thus, having the necessary knowledge and tools available to do their jobs will result in more productive IT staff members and more satisfied customers.

IMPROVEMENT IDEAS

After the events of April 15, Ann was committed to implementing some type of change management system that would approve, document, and communicate changes in order to raise awareness about system changes among IT staff members. As the IT manager, Ann had many options for how to follow through on this initiative. She could choose an off-the-shelf software option and direct her staff to begin using the new system. This approach would be quick; however, Ann wondered if her staff would truly embrace the new system and use it or just continue doing things the old way. An alternative would be for Ann to identify several off-the-shelf software options that might work and have her staff members vote on which system they should implement. This option would also be relatively fast; however, Ann worried that a predetermined software system selected in haste might not fulfill all their needs.

Ann thought that perhaps she and her staff could work with the help desk staff to create a proprietary change management system. She seemed fairly certain that adoption by her staff would be high for a system that they had a hand in developing, but she believed that this option would take a long time to implement. Also, it may be expensive to create a customized system because the current help desk staff did not have the skills needed to develop this type of system, so external consultants would have to be hired.

Finally, Ann considered using a structured methodology such as Design for Six Sigma (DFSS) to create a change management system that would address the specific needs of her department. Ann had recently participated in a DFSS training seminar at a conference, and this approach appealed to her because she felt it was a way to get everyone who would eventually use the new system involved in helping to develop it.

Since the goal of DFSS is to translate users' needs/expectations into design requirements and then evaluate and choose the best design alternative (Stahl, Schultz, & Pexton), Ann thought that this approach might be a way to ensure that the new change management system would meet the needs of the work environment for which it was designed. In addition, she felt that involving her staff in identifying the department's needs that a change management system should fulfill and getting their input about potential design ideas might go a long way toward increasing their buy-in for the new system. Ann also recognized that the system they would develop might end up being a composite of one or more off-the-shelf software options, but she thought that the DFSS approach would be a more informed way to select these components. Although this process would take some time, Ann was optimistic about spending the time upfront to create a system that would meet their needs, as opposed to choosing an off-the-shelf option and then hoping for the best, because she knew that the latter often meant a lot of troubleshooting and firefighting down the line, which she wanted to avoid if possible.

CONCLUSION

As the IT manager, Ann has several good ideas about how to address her department's need for creating and implementing an effective change management system. Some of these options would provide fast and easy solutions, while others would require more work up front, but they also may save more time and cause fewer problems and less frustration in the long run. Ann has confidence in her staff members and knows that whatever she decides to do, they'll make it work. She just wonders if a proactive attempt to put in a little extra effort up front will really provide the benefits needed to overcome the costs associated with some of her options.

QUESTIONS FOR DISCUSSION

1. Discuss why you think developing and implementing a change management system is or is not a worthwhile initiative for Ann and her department to undertake.

2. Evaluate the approach used by Ann and her department to identify improvement ideas. What, if anything, should Ann or others have done differently?

3. Identify Ann's improvement ideas and describe the advantages and disadvantages of each.

4. Select the improvement idea that you believe Ann should implement and explain the reasoning behind your selection.

REFERENCES/BIBLIOGRAPHY

Brittain, K. *Common Questions Regarding IT Change Management*. Gartner, 2007. Print.

Ferweda, N. "Largest Houston-Area Public Accounting Firms." *Houston Business Journal* 28 May 2009: 18A.

Haider, Mohammed, and Networks First Limited. *The Impact of Network Downtime on Business Today*. Networks First: Market Insight Paper. 2007. http://www.networksfirst.com/uploads/file/The%20Cost%20of%20 Downtime%20Report%20May%202007%20QD%20-%2005%20May% 202007.pdf

Heskett, J. L., T. O. Jones, G. W. Loveman, et al. "Putting the Service-Profit Chain to Work." *Harvard Business Review* 2008: 118-29.

IBM. *Disaster Recovery: An Iron Shield to Business*. 2009. Retrieved 11 Oct. 2009 from http://mediaproducts.gartner.com/gc/webletter/ibm_stg/ issue5/index.html

Microsoft Corporation. "Understanding Downtime." *Microsoft Technet*. 20 May 2005. Retrieved 21 Sept. 2009 from: http://technet.microsoft.com/ en-us/library/aa998704(EXCHG.65).aspx

Microsoft Corporation. *Microsoft TechNet*. "Increased Risk of IT Failure." Retrieved 26 Sept. 2009 from http://technet.microsoft.com/en-us/ library/cc546670.aspx

Peregrine Systems, Inc. *Evolution Model for Service Management*. Peregrine Systems, Inc., 2005.

Phoenix, Helia. "Hidden Threats to Enterprise: Will Your Business Continuity Go according to Plan?" *The Magazine* 4 (2009). Retrieved 5 Feb 2011 from http://www.usfst.com/article/Hidden-threats-to-enterprise-will-your-business-continuity-go-according-to-plan/

Scott, D. "Making Smart Investments to Reduce Unplanned Downtime." GartnerGroup, 1999. Retrieved 5 Feb. 2011 from www.maoz.com/dmm/complexity_and_the_?internet/downtime.pdf

Stahl, R., B. Schultz, and C. Pexton. "Healthcare's Horizon from Incremental Improvement to Designing the Future." *Six Sigma Forum Magazine* (Feb. 2003): 17–26.

Economic Development in Dubai: Are the Benefits Greater than the Costs?

Andrew Ashwin • Content Developer, Biz/ed, Cengage Learning EMEA

LEARNING OBJECTIVES

After reading this case study and completing the questions, students should be able to do the following:

- *Explain the meaning of the term economic growth*
- *Identify and outline the main sources of economic growth*
- *Analyze and evaluate the external costs and benefits of economic growth*

This case was prepared for classroom discussion rather than to illustrate either effective or ineffective handling of an administrative, ethical, or legal decision by management. Information was gathered from corporate as well as public sources.

BACKGROUND

In the United Kingdom (U.K.), there has been a protracted debate about the need for and development of a third runway at its main airport, London Heathrow. The growth in the demand for air travel and the increasing number of passengers that the airport has to handle has led to the owner BAA saying that a third runway is essential if the airport is to maintain its role as a primary hub and to meet the expected increase in demand for air travel between 2010 and 2040. In early 2009, a decision was made to allow the runway to be built, which set in motion legal challenges and delay tactics by those opposed to the new runway because of its environmental impact.

In Dubai there seems to be no such protracted debate on the need for or benefits of a new runway. In fact, Dubai is happily planning to construct six of them in the coming years. Work is progressing at pace on a second major airport fewer than 30 miles away from the existing Dubai International Airport. The growth of Dubai as a commercial and tourist center was extensive between the mid-1990s and 2010. The population has more than doubled since 1995, economic growth has been near double digit figures,, and sometimes above between 2000 and 2010, and there has been a proactive move by the rulers of Dubai to promote the city as a business center.

The number of new developments and complexes such as Knowledge Village and Internet City has provided western businesses with opportunities to expand their operations into the city to gain the benefits of a number of economic initiatives set up by the government, including no foreign exchange controls, no barriers to trade, and no corporate profit or personal income taxes. The existence of a skilled and relatively cheap labor force and competitive energy and real estate costs has also been an attractive draw to major corporations around the world.

THE EXPANDING DUBAI AIRPORT CAPACITY

Dubai's development owes some debt of gratitude to the existence of oil, but as of 2010, oil exports only made up 6% of Dubai's gross domestic product (GDP). Tourism accounts for around 30% and real estate and construction just over 20%. The rulers of Dubai believe that to maintain Dubai's growth the emphasis needs to be on developing an economy that is not reliant on oil. The rapid expansion of the city has led to the growth of the main airport, Dubai International Airport (DAI). As of 2010, the airport accounted for over 260,000 flights a year and handles over 34 million passengers. Compared to the 9.7 million passengers who passed through the airport in 1998, the growth of the airport has been significant.

The development of new aircraft and the desire of the ruling Al Maktoum family to continue to promote Dubai's status as an international hub and commercial and tourist center have prompted a decision to plan for the future by expanding the airport's capacity. The result is the new Al Maktoum International Airport at Jebel Ali, part of the development of the Dubai World Central (DWC) complex.

DWC is a 54-square-mile (140-sq-km) complex that will include shops, housing, golf courses, offices and entertainment that will make up a city within a city. The DWC is also home to the Al Maktoum International airport. The airport will eventually have six parallel runways each approximately 2.8 miles (4.5 km) in length. (The proposed third runway at Heathrow is anticipated to be 1.36 miles [2.18 km] long.) There will be three passenger terminals and extensive links to the main city of Dubai through the completion of a new high-speed rail system and the new metro system, which is due for completion in 2009. The new airport will be able to handle the new A380 super jumbo, and designers envision the airport catering to future aviation developments. The first of the six runways has been completed and in early 2009 was undergoing testing and certification. The developments at Al Maktoum International are expected to be completed by 2017, and the eventual capacity of the airport is projected to be 120 million passengers. It is predicted that capacity will reach 70 million by 2015.

SOCIAL CONCERNS REGARDING RAPID GROWTH

The development of Dubai has sparked concerns about the social efficiency of such rapid growth. Visitors to Dubai can be forgiven for forgetting that the city is located in a desert. For the ever-growing population in a city where the average rainfall is around 5 inches (12.7 cm) a year, desalination plants are the main source of freshwater. The building and development projects in Dubai are said to engage 24% of the world's construction cranes. Human rights groups are concerned that the workers employed in building these massive developments are subject to abuse and virtual enslavement. There are reports that the conditions of migrant workers in so-called ghetto camps at places such as Mousafah located between Dubai and Abu Dhabi are extremely poor and that wages are only around $111 (DHS450; UKP70) per month.

In addition to the concerns about human rights of workers, there is also considerable unease about the effect that Dubai developments are having on the environment. In the U.K., protestors against the third runway at Heathrow refer to the contribution that air travel has to climate change. The planned developments at DWC seem to dwarf those of London. The seemingly insatiable desire to expand Dubai is placing an increasing burden on the infrastructure and resources of the region and the environmental effects of developments such as DWC have been heavily criticized by environmental groups.

There is a balance that exists between the benefits and costs of economic development and the positive and negative externalities that arise from economic decisions such as the construction of new airports. The attempt to reduce the reliance on oil as the major source of income for the region may be laudable, but the costs of what is created to replace that income source may be considered by some to be simply too great to make economic sense.

QUESTIONS FOR DISCUSSION

1. Outline the main sources of economic growth in a country like Dubai.
2. Consider the key benefits arising for a country like Dubai of faster economic growth.
3. Examine some of the external costs of economic growth.
4. Discuss the view that Dubai ought to focus more on other aspects of society rather than expansion of its airport capacity.
5. Discuss the factors that a country's leaders would have to consider in seeking to drive economic growth. You may choose to base your answer on a country with which you are familiar or use the example of Dubai.

Economies of Scale: Exploiting Size and Location in the Middle East

Andrew Ashwin • Content Developer, Biz/ed, Cengage Learning EMEA

LEARNING OBJECTIVES

After reading this case study and completing the questions, students should be able to do the following:

- *Define economies of scale*
- *Identify and explain at least two sources of economies of scale*
- *Distinguish between internal and external economies of scale*
- *Explain and apply the concept of the principle of multiples*
- *Assess the role of partnerships and joint ventures in helping to exploit economies of scale*
- *Assess the extent to which economies of scale can be exploited*

This case was prepared for classroom discussion rather than to illustrate either effective or ineffective handling of an administrative, ethical, or legal decision by management. Information was gathered from corporate as well as public sources.

INTRODUCTION

With a number of countries in the Middle East at different stages of development, the benefits of economies of scale are there to be exploited. Certain industries and markets lend themselves specifically to the reduction in unit costs that are associated with the growth of firms which can contribute to improved returns on invested capital. For firms in these markets, there is an incentive to invest and to expand the scale of operations because the returns justify them. In order to benefit from economies of scale, markets have to be large or potentially large so that investment in plant means fixed costs can be spread over a large range of output, thus driving down unit costs.

INTERNAL ECONOMIES OF SCALE: MOBILE TELEPHONY

One example of a market that satisfies these criteria is the mobile telephony market. This market is in the growth phase and so has the capacity to expand prior to maturity. As such, investment in this market is initially expensive, but the potential for large volume unit sales along with relatively low marginal costs of selling additional units makes it perfect for exploiting economies of scale.

Qatar Telecom

The sources of economies of scale lie in various processes and procedures. The Qatar Telecom (Q-tel) group, based in Qatar, has to provide overall network equipment in order to allow mobile users to access services. Investment in equipment to set up such networks requires considerable sums of money, but changes to procurement systems have enabled Q-tel to be able to cut costs by 10-15%. It has done so by centralizing its procurement of network equipment. This is an example of a commercial economy of scale. Central procurement—the focus on securing equipment at appropriate contracts and the capacity to share information within the centralized team—is what helps to drive down costs.

Crucially, it was only after Q-tel expanded the scale of its operations internationally that it made financial sense to centralize its procurement. If a business operates in just a few countries, for example, procurement may be more efficient by employing country-based teams to focus on a domestic market. Once the scale of operation grows to and beyond a critical mass, then centralizing is a powerful and cost effective move. The success of centralized procurement of network equipment has led Q-tel to extend the principle to buying other technologies associated with its operations such as roaming and wholesale access to services, both of which add value for its customers.

Centralization has also enabled Q-tel to develop expertize in particular areas, which it can then further exploit. For example, by being a large-scale operator, Q-tel has the capacity to expand into new technologies more easily, illustrated by its expansion into Wi-tribe and WiMAX services. (*Wi-tribe* is a platform that allows wireless broadband to be brought to communities across the Middle East, and *WiMAX* is a technology that provides fixed and mobile Internet access as an alternative to cable and DSL.) These enable Q-tel to provide Internet access and broadband services to customers not covered by traditional networks.

Etisalat

Other companies are similarly in a position to exploit the benefits of scale operations to improve their efficiency. Etisalat is one such example. Etisalat, with its headquarters in the United Arab Emirates (UAE), is one of the largest telecommunications companies in the world. It operates in 18 countries across the Middle East, Asia, and Africa. It has in excess of 100 million customers and generates net revenues in excess of AED30 billion. Rather than having key functions such as back-office operations, manufacture, and data clearance (removing sensitive data from computers and mobile phones, for example, prior to recycling) spread across different plants, Etisalat has centralized these functions and as a result has been able to reduce inputs while increasing output. The result has been lower unit costs. It has also been able to set up a call center in Egypt to handle customer service enquiries from its subscribers in the UAE, which is cheaper than if it located this function in the UAE itself, primarily because of the lower labor costs in Egypt.

EXTERNAL ECONOMIES OF SCALE: OIL, GAS, AND POWER RELATED

The above examples illustrate internal economies of scale—the benefits that arise as a result of the expansion of the firm itself. External economies of scale refer to the advantages that arise because the industry has grown and is localized in a particular region or area. Abu Dhabi, the UAE capital, is a case in point with its heavy concentration of a developed oil, gas, and power industry. This localization provides firms with the opportunities to exploit the success of these concentrated industries by providing services required by firms in the industry at lower cost than could be incurred by the firms themselves. For example, plant and equipment in the oil, gas, and power industries require regular maintenance and servicing. Such work invariably requires specialized plant and equipment such as cranes and heavy lifting gear. It is not cost effective for the firm itself to invest in these machines partly because of the degree of expertize required to develop and use them and the high fixed costs involved. Most firms in the industry would prefer, as a result, to hire specialists to help with this work as and when they need them rather than investing in the equipment themselves.

Abnormal Load Engineering

Abnormal Load Engineering (ALE) is one such firm providing transport for outsize loads and the supply of specialist lifting equipment. The British ALE has extensive operations based in the Middle East. It recognized the demand for the sort of services it provides from the oil, gas, and power industry in Abu Dhabi and elsewhere in the region. It located a full scale operation in UAE to respond to the needs of the industry. The benefits to both the industry and to firms such as ALE are significant. The specific types of work required by the industry necessitate the design of particular types of equipment to handle complex jobs. For firms such as ALE there would be little point in investing in such complex and demanding machinery if the demand was limited. However, the growth of the industry in Abu Dhabi has made it worthwhile for ALE to invest in research and development (R&D) and work closely with the industry to ensure needs are satisfied.

Such needs include lifting bulky pieces of equipment weighing up to 5,000 tonnes, lifting to ever bigger heights and accessing longer outreaches. ALE can take these factors into consideration in its R&D, ever mindful customer needs in different areas. Doing so means equipment has to be mobile and capable of getting to different jobs in different countries quickly, easily, and at minimal cost. To meet specific customer need, ALE developed the Sliding Krane (SK) range. This equipment matches the demands of the work required in the oil industry in places such as Abu Dhabi and Saudi Arabia and is mobile. Component parts of the system are capable of being packaged or loaded onto standardized ISO containers making for greater flexibility in moving equipment from one location to another.

Exxon Mobile

To fully exploit the benefits of economies of scale, individual firms in the Middle East are increasingly considering building partnerships or entering into joint venture agreements to enable them to retain control of the business and exploit local knowledge while benefiting from the expertize of much larger companies from in other countries. Qatar Petroleum has entered into such agreements with Exxon Mobile. The partnership enables Qatar Petroleum to be in a better position to exploit the economies of scale that arise from the development of oil and gas fields. The investment in fixed capital required to carry out these sorts of operations is extensive, but the high costs can be spread over many millions of unit sales, thus reducing unit costs.

In addition, these partnerships mean that managerial and risk-bearing economies of scale and benefits are derived from experience economies. Firms such as Exxon Mobile have an experience curve that brings economies of scale in learning. These partnerships help to prevent a business from learning as it goes along, thus helping it to avoid the expense of dealing with mistakes and solving problems that arise from inexperience. Using the experience of a firm that has learned by doing means that mistakes can be kept to a minimum and problems avoided, all of which help to lower unit costs as efficiency increases.

Qatar Petroleum is also able to take advantage of technical economies of scale, specifically invoking the principle of multiples. This principle states that if, for example, a ship used to transport gas around the world had its carrying capacity dimensions doubled, the volume it could carry would rise by eight times. The costs of building such ships would obviously rise but not by eight times. It would not cost eight times as much in fuel, need eight times the staff to operate the ship, or eight times the cost to ensure, and so the cost per unit carried would fall. Qatar Petroleum and Exxon Mobile have developed new Q-Max ships that can carry 80% more liquefied natural gas (LNG) than conventional-sized ships at lower unit cost. They have also applied similar principles to the transport of LNG by train.

There are many opportunities for firms in the Middle East to exploit economies of scale because of the region's growth and development of markets and industry. Unlike other more developed economies of the world, the Middle East sill has the capacity to expand scale and thus to allow returns which justify the significant investments that are required to benefit from economies of scale in the longer term.

QUESTIONS FOR DISCUSSION

1. Using appropriate examples, explain the difference between a *fall in costs* and a *fall in unit costs.*

2. Give two examples of how a firm might benefit from economies of scale and explain how these economies of scale arise in the examples you have chosen.

3. Using examples, explain the difference between internal and external economies of scale.

4. Explain the principle of multiples and outline two examples in which this principle might apply and help a firm reduce unit costs.

5. Consider the role of joint ventures in helping firms to achieve economies of scale. Are there limitations to the scale benefits that arise for the parties to a joint venture? Explain your answer.

Exploring a Joint Venture between a Chinese State-Owned Enterprise and a Foreign Multinational Enterprise

Terence R. Egan • Associate Professor, Central University of Finance and Economics, Beijing, China

LEARNING OBJECTIVES

After completing this case, students will understand the following:

- *Strategies and pitfalls of establishing international partnerships*
- *Ways to synthesize complex and broad-ranging issues in order to develop effective plans and solutions*
- *How external factors affect implementation of an international joint venture*
- *How deeply imbedded cultural values and ideologies affect business practices and ethical orientations*
- *Understand the compromises and trade-offs that may be required to achieve a strategic objective*
- *Discuss the importance of cultural awareness and sensitivity during cross-cultural negotiations*

This case was prepared for classroom discussion rather than to illustrate either effective or ineffective handling of an administrative, ethical, or legal decision by management. Information was gathered from corporate as well as public sources.

INTRODUCTION

In the late 1990s and early 2000s, tens of thousands of North American and European enterprises in all sizes, forms, and levels of preparation, sought to do business with companies in China. Western media, business magazines, and academic journals documented the paradigm-changing events of China's dynamic market. However, China remained a difficult market for North American and European enterprises to enter. Pervasive differences in culture, law, economics, politics, and workplace environments confounded even the world's largest organizations.

This fictional case involves a cross-cultural partnership between two enterprises: Wuming Group (China) and Zadcor International (a Western multinational). While the organizations and actors are fictional, the circumstances and incidents depict authentic concerns faced by multinational companies in China. Historical, cultural, economic and business perspectives are faithfully represented, thereby providing deep insights and a rich platform for wide-ranging discussion.

Zadcor International is a multinational enterprise (MNE) whose cost-driven strategy requires it to locate a joint venture partner in a low-cost environment. Zadcor International consolidated its position as a market leader in the 1960s, parlaying its reputation, technology, and know-how into successful international expansion.

Wuming Steel is a Chinese state-owned enterprise (SOE), which ultimately became the low-cost producer and strategic partner. Wuming Steel (a wholly owned subsidiary of Wuming Group) held an important position within the value-added segment of the steel industry, primarily due to political patronage rather than financial performance or market leadership.

Both companies were involved in the value-added segment of the steel industry producing specialized industrial products for manufacturing and heavy machinery.

CHINA'S BUSINESS ENVIRONMENT

The People's Republic of China was founded in 1949 by the Chinese Communist Party (CCP) under the leadership of Chairman Mao Zedong. In line with communist ideology, the party nationalized businesses, depriving companies of their independence. The profit motive was subordinated to managers' desire to assiduously follow government policy and to provide for the livelihoods of their employees.

State-owned enterprises (SOEs) were the backbone of the economy; however, they were run-down, inefficient, and poorly managed. Due to the emphasis on central planning, the role of managers was administrative rather than decision-making in nature. Most managers were untrained and unfamiliar with key functions of a modern firm, such as marketing and advertising, finance and accounting, and effective management of human resources.

SOEs lacked market-orientation. Jobs were allocated by the state, so there was no labor market as such. Employees were not free to move between companies or between provinces. The *iron rice bowl* was the term used for the *jobs-for-life* model that fostered generations of unrewarded, unproductive, and unskilled public sector employees in China. For three decades after the founding of the Republic, various policy misadventures left China in ruin.

After the death of Mao Zedong in 1976 and a short and tumultuous period of political instability, Deng Xiao Ping was installed as president and immediately set about promoting an agenda of economic reform. For the first time, terms such as efficiency, equity, flexibility, competition, accountability, and profit were used in relation to China's SOEs. It would be many years, however, before Deng's ideals began to seep into the foundations of the state sector or into the mindsets of company leaders.

WUMING GROUP HISTORY

Wuming Steel Company was established in Beijing in 1950, soon after the foundation of New China. As a SOE, Wuming Steel Company was one of several state-run companies set up to produce steel ribbing for arcon casings. Each of these companies was strategically positioned to serve domestic demand throughout the country. All but Wuming Steel were located on or close to the east coast. Wuming's inland location was of no concern at the time, however, since there were no international markets and no competition between domestic organizations.

In the late 1980s, under the direction of the central government, many of China's SOEs embarked upon a program of rapid expansion. Wuming Steel quickly grew to be a sprawling conglomerate involved in a diverse range of activities, including finance, construction, transport, and other unrelated manufacturing enterprises. In 1985, the organization was restructured and renamed Wuming Group with Wuming Steel reverting to its original product focus in the value-added sector of the steel industry as a wholly owned subsidiary of the Wuming Group.

In 1994, with more than 300,000 employees, the Wuming Group earned the title of Excellent Enterprise due to its emphasis on and adherence to standardized management routines that were the government's policy focus. In spite of this recognition—and like most of China's SOEs at that time—low productivity and poor management practices negatively affected every business unit and division in the Wuming Group. Group president Li Zhabin (1977–1995) had built a strong, bureaucratic organization that followed government policy to the letter. His consistent record of business expansion and his rapid adoption of the latest government protocols and models placed him—and Wuming Group—in a position of privilege within the CCP.

During Li's presidency, financial records were far from adequate; however, it should also be remembered that China's SOEs existed solely to serve the state. While the profit motive was first stressed in the early 1980s, it only became general practice in the early 2000s. The Group's pattern of sharply fluctuating results, from impressive profits one year to stunning losses in the next, was common across the public sector. Wuming's business units, including Wuming Steel, followed this trend in accordance with the annual dictates of the Group.

Zhang Zhaowei took over as president of Wuming Group in 1995 after "an outstanding career in provincial government" (as it says in his official profile). During his first three years at the helm (1995–1998), President Zhang laid off 50,000 employees in accordance with the directives set out in the government's Ninth Five-Year Plan. Zhang was lauded as a beacon of light in the government's drive for efficiency and was honoured and feted by the CCP, just as his predecessor had been. Unfortunately, the benefits that were anticipated to flow from this initiative—most importantly, improved financial performance—failed to materialize. The costs of generous redundancy payments and ongoing welfare obligations to retrenched employees placed even more financial pressure on the underperforming group.

Government Policy Forces Change

While China's economic development during the 1980s and 1990s was unparalleled, modernization of the state sector remained a major hurdle. More than half of China's state-owned enterprises continued to operate at a loss. In 1996, China's Ninth Five-Year Plan decreed that the majority of SOEs would be sold, merged, or closed. In 2003, China's premier, Zhu Rongji, announced further rationalization and restructuring of many industries. The message to the perennially underperforming state sector was clear: Companies had to make "consistent profits or face government-directed merger or extinction." To ensure that the whole community understood the monumental nature of these changes and the likely short-term ramifications, Premier Zhu famously declared that "the Iron Rice Bowl is broken forever." In order for China's SOEs to become globally competitive, antiquated principles such as the Iron Rice Bowl had to be eradicated.

Zhu's plan for the steel industry was equally uncompromising, calling for more than 2000 steel mills to merge into fewer than twenty mega-organizations. With its long record of unprofitable operations, Wuming Group faced an uncertain future. Wuming Steel was particularly vulnerable, political connections notwithstanding. Its inland location was a liability in the newly competitive, international environment. In addition—or perhaps as a consequence—the company lagged far behind its competitors in both reported revenues and profits.

As had always been the case in response to government policy changes, the so-called organization machine immediately swung into action. With strong connections to state-owned banks, which were always willing to lend, Wuming Group embarked on a dynamic program of acquisitions that saw its rapid entry into diverse industries, including food, machinery manufacture, electronics, travel, financial services, and even the new Internet arena. Wuming Group soon stood as one of China's largest conglomerates with an estimated 400,000 employees.

Wuming Group's executive elite remained elusive, primarily acting as master planner and maintaining tight control over budgets, capital allocation, and reporting. However, the corporation was also known to arbitrarily impose services and infrastructure on its business units and to become directly involved in operational issues such as hiring, compensation policies, and career advancement decisions.

To outsiders, the Wuming Group's strategic purpose was obscure, its structure was increasingly complex, and its constant intervention in subsidiaries' functional decisions idiosyncratic at best. However, none of this really mattered until the early 2000s.

Wuming Steel in the Early 2000s

While Wuming Steel was far from being the most important of the group's companies in terms of strategic position, size, or results, it held a special status within the group as its founding organization. Through the 1990s, Wuming Steel had increasing difficulty sustaining revenues, not to mention its unjustifiably low margins and illusory profits. Since it had been thrust into the global market, cheaper and more sophisticated technologies had changed the entire industry. Given low capital investment over many years, Wuming Steel's equipment and machinery were poorly maintained and outdated. If it were not for the entrenched culture of gratuities provided to machinery inspectors, the plant would have been shut down for safety reasons many years earlier.

International Joint Venture Mooted

In early 2006, Group president Zhang's political connections came to the fore. Zhang was alerted to a joint venture opportunity with a foreign company called Zadcor International, which, it was said, had expressed considerable interest in Wuming Steel. This welcome news was critically important, not only to Wuming Steel, but also to the Wuming Group and to President Zhang himself. Zhang had harbored the desire to turn Wuming into a multinational organization listed on a foreign stock exchange. The Chinese government was about to approve a series of IPOs to be launched in Hong Kong, and, while Hong Kong was no longer foreign soil, in President Zhang's view, the stars appeared to be aligning at just the right time.

ZADCOR INTERNATIONAL HISTORY

Zadcor International was a multinational organization operating in the same industrial market as Wuming Steel. Zadcor was founded in 1946 at the commencement of the global post–World War II reconstruction phase. Through a series of acquisitions in the 1960s and 1970s, Zadcor achieved a dominant position in its market. In the late 1970s, the company began expanding into foreign markets, becoming one of the Big Three international players in its segment.

Zadcor's leading-edge technologies and its highly skilled workforce allowed the company to maintain its position into the 1990s. However, as that decade progressed, Zadcor found itself under increasing competitive pressure. An explosion of cheaper production technologies, the emergence of low-cost competitors in developing economies, and off-shoring by its domestic rivals rapidly eroded Zadcor's competitive advantage both at home and abroad. Whether Zadcor's slow response to changing market conditions was due to hubris or a misreading of industry dynamics, the company found itself out-of-step with the market and vulnerable to decline.

Off-shoring Strategy Rejected

In 1999, concerned with a sharp drop in forward orders, Zadcor's CEO, Tal Burman, called for a comprehensive review of the company's strategic direction. In June 2000, Burman faced the Board with a plan to relocate Zadcor's manufacturing facilities off-shore. He saw reducing the cost base by 40% as necessary for Zadcor to continue into the "If we don't reduce our cost base by at least 40%, Zadcor will cease to exist within the next decade." Burman's presentation was forceful and direct. He knew that it would take a situation of crisis proportions to stir some of the board members into action. Most of them had held their positions for more than a decade and had become—in Burman's opinion—comfortable and negligent. Their response was not unexpected.

The lay-offs that would result from Burman's proposal would be "unconscionable," said one non-executive director, a former trade-union representative. Another board member feared that if word of the discussion leaked, the share price would fall. For almost an hour, heated debate and personal attacks took over, all directed at the only person who seemed willing to confront the company's dangerous situation. While some of those present remained silent throughout the proceedings, no one supported the proposal.

Burman knew that this would be the beginning of the end for him; he knew it before he even entered the room. At the final board meeting of the year, he resigned due to "unresolved differences with the Board." The share price plunged.

New CEO and New Strategy

It was a bad start to 2001. While a sudden change of key personnel is often accompanied by the selling-down of a company's stock, pessimistic earnings forecasts also were not helping. The declining orders that Burman predicted were beginning to bite. The share price continued to fall to a level that had not been seen since the stock market crash of 1987.

Meanwhile, the company's cost base became a recurring topic in private discussions between various board members. Eventually, it also became an ongoing agenda item at Board meetings, although the word "offshoring" and the name "Tal Burman" were studiously avoided. Sales continued to decline and the Board continued to fulminate on a long-term strategy.

In June 2003 the new CEO, James Gellard, outlined his plan to partner with a low-cost producer in China. Burman's proposal—albeit, dressed in a new coat and tie—was finally being ratified more than two years after Burman resigned from the company. This time, there was no word of opposition from the Board.

In essence, Gellard's strategy was to move low-end production offshore while continuing to serve the high-end market from the domestic plant. This solution was considered strategically sound for three reasons. It would (a) protect Zadcor's intellectual property (IP) used in the production of its high-end product and considered to be at risk if taken abroad; (b) leverage the competencies and local knowledge of an offshore manufacturer; and (c) minimize negative publicity by reframing the downsizing of the domestic operation.

IN SEARCH OF THE IDEAL PARTNER

The strategy team appointed to research the China market soon realized that its partnership options were limited. The company would have had first choice of the Chinese manufacturers had it moved five years earlier. But the industry landscape had changed. Most of the company's international competitors had already moved their operations to China and had formed partnerships with the strongest local manufacturers. Zadcor briefly considered converting a manufacturer in a related steel components business; however, due to the unique nature of their products and manufacturing processes, doing so was never considered a viable proposition.

For the next twelve months, the Zadcor team worked at its task. Reliable market data were difficult to locate as, in many cases, the most basic information did not appear to exist. In spite of the obstacles, a report and a Letter of Intent (LOI) from a potential partner—Wayjing Corporation—were presented to the Board in October 2005. The Board immediately and unanimously authorized the joint venture team to proceed to the next step.

Since time was a critical aspect of Zadcor's strategy implementation, the company was delighted that the negotiation of the detailed terms was smooth and relatively quick. This came as quite a surprise given the problems that other MNEs had experienced in China. In February 2006, Zadcor International announced to the New York Stock Exchange and to the media that it signed a Memorandum of Understanding to enter a joint venture partnership with Wayjing Corporation of China. While completion of the deal was "subject to due diligence and normal China government approvals," the Zadcor Board was excited and relieved that a strategy was finally in place. The share price spiked.

An Uncertain Beginning

Four months later, the joint venture was in tatters. The MOU was unexpectedly rejected by the government regulating agency. China's National Development and Reform Commission (NDRC) gave no explanation. Instead, Zadcor was politely advised—by Chinese officials unconnected to the Commission—to seek a partnership with Wuming Steel, a company that the Zadcor team had screened out of contention early in its investigations. Wuming's inland location and the consequent effect on cost-efficient access to overseas markets had ruled out Wuming Steel.

Stock market officials censured Zadcor for its premature announcement, and, once again, the company was deserted by its shareholders. Zadcor was at a critical juncture. Should they withdraw altogether, abandoning all the work and time expended in the China market? Could they afford to begin again and look elsewhere, perhaps India or Vietnam? Should they explore prospects in China again? That did not seem like a wise move given the government's expressed enthusiasm for Wuming Steel. With worldwide sales continuing to decline and no better option available, the Board felt compelled to pursue a partnership with Wuming Steel.

The passage of the new MOU—substantially the same as the one negotiated with Wayjing Corporation—moved swiftly through the China government approval process. It should be noted that this constituted an "in-principle" approval to negotiate terms. In other words, as long as the two parties can negotiate mutually satisfactory terms, they would face no political or bureaucratic barriers. In March 2007, Zadcor and Wuming began their final negotiations in conjunction with Zadcor's due diligence.

Unlike the speedy passage of both MOUs, negotiation of the final terms was long and arduous. While he was rarely seen, Group president Zhang Zhaowei cast a heavy shadow over every detail. On each and every discussion point, the Wuming team was obligated to refer decisions to another department or individual, even on seemingly minor and inconsequential points. Often, when the Zadcor team understood that agreement had already been reached on a particular issue, it would suddenly return to the table for another round of discussion.

The Zadcor team had a litany of complaints about Wuming's tactics, including "its constant, irrational objections," "exaggerated expectations," "selective" use of information, and "double standards." The leader of the Zadcor negotiating team, Roger Janosy, eventually reported that the two companies were not on equal footing from the start. He stated that Zadcor offered concessions to avoid impasse, but Wuming offered nothing in return. Terms were negotiated, then they were renegotiated, and then they were renegotiated again.

Janosy found Wuming's behavior paradoxical and unfathomable. He noted the contradiction between Wuming's hospitality and its aloof, intransigent meeting-room style. "Don't get me wrong," he recounted, "they were great hosts. They wined and dined us to exhaustion at times. It was all backslapping and highly convivial. But back in the meeting rooms, they immediately reverted to their usual aloof, impersonal, and intransigent style."

Due diligence was almost impossible. From its Wayjing Corporation investigations, the Zadcor team already knew that much of the standard market information was either nonexistent or unobtainable. But Wuming Steel's financial records were another challenge entirely. They were riddled with inconsistencies, the legacy of changes to accounting standards and official reporting policies in the 1980s and 1990s. In line with the common practice of the day, standards from the China Accounting Standards for Business Enterprises (ASBE) and other sector-based accounting rules had been applied opportunistically according to the needs of each division at any particular time. This problem was exacerbated by what the Zadcor team saw as a lack of cooperation from Wuming's executive and financial teams.

While the Wuming side understood that time was critical for Zadcor, the Chinese were not to be hurried. Months went by, then a year. The Zadcor team began to show its frustration openly; however, it seemed to make no impression on its associates from Wuming Steel. It did not augur well for a successful partnership.

Shareholders had lost confidence in the company's joint venture strategy much earlier. Debate on the wisdom and ethics of sending jobs off-shore had run its course in the media and was no longer news. The stock price languished and a shareholder revolt brewed. The age and average length of tenure of the Board members was a growing topic of conversation in the financial press and in high-traffic investment blogs. With institutional investors also threatening to withdraw support, the Board demanded swift finalization of the joint venture contract. The Board's message to CEO James Gellard was to conclude the agreement immediately: "Get it done before the AGM. Whatever it takes, just get it done."

As judiciously as they were able to in the circumstances—Chinese executives read investment media too—the contract team negotiated the remaining issues. Concessions were made (almost exclusively by Zadcor) and negotiations were quickly concluded. The announcement of the signing of the Joint Venture agreement was the highlight of the Annual General Meeting of 2008.

Joint Venture Structure

On the surface, the Zadcor-Wuming joint venture was a reasonable strategic fit. Zadcor needed a low-cost manufacturing base for its domestic and global markets, and Wuming Steel needed to modernize its plant and processes in order to become globally competitive. Wuming Steel became the joint venture vehicle with Wuming Group retaining 51% ownership, also providing assets (land, buildings, machinery, equipment, and a going concern), local market knowledge, government and trade connections, and local staffing.

Zadcor's 49% ownership came with equal board voting rights. Zadcor would provide technology transfer, other technical know-how, management expertize, staff development and support, and access to international markets. Zadcor was also to provide a substantial cash injection for the modernization of the Wuming plant.

The JV contract period was five years with an option to extend for an additional five years upon mutual agreement. The JV would continue to trade as Wuming Steel with Zhao Jiangyu, a university classmate of the Wuming Group's president, retaining the leadership. Chinese management would also be retained while expatriate managers from Zadcor would act in an advisory and support capacity. Only one executive position would be filled by a foreign manager: Director of Human Resource, Ric Benoit.

The JV Is Launched

After considerable shuffling of people between Wuming Steel and Wuming Group—without consultation with Zadcor—the joint venture began operations in October 2008 with around 20,000 employees.

As James Gellard put it, "The partner wasn't ideal. The location wasn't ideal. The deal wasn't ideal. But what choice did we have?"

QUESTIONS FOR DISCUSSION

1. Without reference to any particular market, make a list of the actions that should be taken when implementing a successful international cross-cultural joint venture strategy, based upon the example of the joint venture between Zadcor and Wuming Steel.

2. Why do good companies make bad decisions? Discuss using the Zadcor International/Wuming Group joint venture as your example.

3. Do you feel that Zadcor made the right decision to press on after the collapse of the Wayjing Corporation deal and to accept the China government's proposition to partner Wuming Steel? Did they have alternatives? Explain your reasoning.

4. How would you characterize the negotiation styles and tactics of both parties? In your opinion, were their styles effective or ineffective? Can you identify mistakes that were made by either or both parties?

5. Identify the external factors that have had an impact on the establishment and success of this joint venture.

REFERENCES/BIBLIOGRAPHY

Baskin, K. "Ever the Twain Shall Meet." *Chinese Management Studies* 1.1 (2007): 57-68. Print.

Cardon, P. W., and J. C. Scott. Chinese Business Face: Communication Behaviors and Teaching Approaches. *Business Communication Quarterly* 66 (2003): 9-22. Print.

Ding, D. Z., and M. Warner. "China's Labor-Management System Reforms: Breaking the 'Three Old Irons' (1978–1999)." *Asia Pacic Journal of Management* 18 (2001): 315–334. Print.

Kenevan, P. A., and Xi Pei. "China Partners." *McKinsey Quarterly* 3 (2003).

Kenevan, P., and J. R. Woetzel. "Restructuring Alliances in China." *McKinsey Quarterly* 9 (Autumn 2003). Web. 21 Feb. 2011. http://corporatefinance. mckinsey.com/knowledge/knowledgemanagement/mof.htm

Kivela, J., and L. F. Leung. "Doing Business in the People's Republic of China." *Cornell Hotel and Restaurant Administration Quarterly* 46.2 (2005): 125-52. Print.

Lee, K. H. "Moral Consideration and Strategic Management Moves: The Chinese Case." *Management Decision* 34.9 (1996): 65-70. Print.

Li, J., K. Lam, and J. W. Moy. "Ownership Reform among State Firms in China and Its Implications." *Management Decision* 43.4 (2005): 568-88. Print.

Luo, Y. D. "Partnering with Foreign Firms: How Do Chinese Managers View the Governance and Importance of Contracts?" *Asia Pacic Journal of Management* 19 (2002): 127-51. Print.

Miles, M. "Negotiating with the Chinese: Lessons from the Field." *Journal of Applied Behavioral Science* 39.4 (2003): 453-72. Print.

Redding, G. "The Capitalist Business System of China and Its Rationale." *Asia Pacic Journal of Management* 19 (2002): 221-49. Print.

Sachs, T., R. Tiong, and S. Q. Wang. "Analysis of Political Risks and Opportunities in Public Private Partnerships (PPP) in China and Selected Asian Countries." *Chinese Management Studies* 1.2 (2007): 126-48. Print.

Sun, J. M. "Organization Development and Change in Chinese State-owned Enterprises: A Human Resource Perspective." *Leadership & Organization Development Journal* 21.8 (2000): 379-89. Print.

Yang, B.Y., W. Zheng, and M. Li. "Confucian View of Learning and Implications for Developing Human Resources." *Advances in Developing Human Resources* 8.3 (2006): 346-54. Print.

Yang J. CFO Asia 27 Oct. 2003. Print.

Zhao, J. J. "The Chinese Approach to International Business Negotiation." *Journal of Business Communication* 37 (2000): 209-36. Print.

Zhu, Z. C. "Reform without a Theory: Why Does it Work in China?" *Organization Studies* 28.10 (2007): 1503-22. Print.

French Cooperatives Mean Business: Evolving Strategies for the Global Food Marketplace

M.L. Cohen • Freelance Writer

LEARNING OBJECTIVES

Students should be able to do the following:

* *Demonstrate an understanding of farm cooperatives and their role in the French and European agricultural industry*
* *Provide insight into the challenges faced by cooperatives on the local, European, and global levels*
* *Identify and compare and contrast the adaptive strategies of three leading French cooperatives*
* *Discuss the differences and similarities between farm cooperatives and private corporations*

This case was prepared for classroom discussion rather than to illustrate either effective or ineffective handling of an administrative, ethical, or legal decision by management. Information was gathered from corporate as well as public sources.

INTRODUCTION

Cooperatives have held a central position in France's agricultural sector since the formation of the first farmers' trade unions in the late nineteenth century. In the early 2000s, the cooperative model continues to dominate the country's agricultural market: more than 90% of France's 660,000 farmers belong to one of more than 3,500 cooperatives (Coop de France). Many of these cooperatives have grown from small, highly localized and often informal partnerships to become national and even global companies capable of competing with the world's leading multinational agro-industrial and food corporations.

By consistently responding to changes in the agricultural, food, and retailing industries, as well as to changes in European Union legislation, France's cooperatives form a framework for the survival of the country's largely family-based farming tradition. With the advent of the globalization of the agricultural and food industries at the beginning of the twenty-first century, cooperatives have become more important to the French farmer than ever before.

The anticipated reform of the European Union's Common Agricultural Policy (CAP), slated to take effect as early as 2013, promises a new and dramatic shift in the French and European agricultural markets (Expansion). The end of farming and export subsidies and the lowering and even elimination of import tariffs will expose France's farmers to direct competition from low-cost producer nations such as Brazil, New Zealand, China, and others for the first time. This case study discusses the strategies of three leading French cooperatives as they confront the globalization of the agro-food sector.

FARMING COOPERATIVES IN FRENCH SOCIETY

France is Europe's agricultural leader, accounting for more than 20% of the European Union's total agricultural production. French farms tend to be quite small compared to those in other parts of the world, with an average of just 104 acres (42 ha) per farm as of 2000. In the United States, by comparison, the average farm reaches nearly 495 acres (200 ha; Ménard, Klein). Brazilian farms reach an average size of 4,950 acres (2,000 ha) and can grow to as large as 74,132 acres (30,000 ha). Other measurements tell a similar story: The average French herd size, for example, is just 50 head. This compares to herd sizes as large as 20,000 in Brazil (Expansion). As a result, French farmers face a distinct disadvantage in terms of economies of scale.

Competing in a Global Market

French farming has never been easy. From the threat of blight and other crop and livestock diseases to the globalization of the trade in grains, sugar, and other agricultural products, French farmers find themselves in a perennially precarious financial position. The rise of large-scale retailers and their control over pricing, coupled with the concentration of the trading, storage, seed, fertilizer, and related sectors into a small group of multinationals have only exacerbated farmers' vulnerability in the early 2000s to an increasingly competitive market.

Farmers have also been confronted with the dramatic changes in French food consumption habits. The rise of the food processing industry, the growing emphasis on high-valued-added prepared foods and high-margin brand names, and the domination of the food market by such globally operating companies as Kraft, Nestle, RJR Nabisco, Phillip Morris, and Unilever also help place the French farmer at a disadvantage. Whereas farmers remain tied to their land, the industrial food processors have developed global supply networks. This provides a high degree of flexibility for purchasing their ingredients and raw materials. When prices are high in Europe, the industrials turn to low-cost markets for their purchasing. As of late 1990s, the industrial food groups have also begun to shift their food production to low-wage markets, further hampering farmers' ability to compete (Seipel, Heffernan).

As a result French farmers in the early 2000s find themselves in a more precarious position than ever before. In 2009, for example, French farm revenues dropped an average of 32%—and more than 50% for dairy producers and cereal growers—compared to the previous year. In the dairy sector, this situation led to massive demonstrations, including the dumping and giving away of large quantities of milk in protest at the steady drop in milk prices. As one farmer explained to *Le Figaro*: "This year I'll make a net loss of 30,000 euros, and things won't be improving next year, since they'll be eliminating part of our European subsidy."

The Cooperative Response

The history of France's agricultural cooperatives reflects the movement's ongoing response to the many factors affecting the French farming community. This response, particularly in the second half of the twentieth century, can be broadly traced into several distinct phases.

First, cooperatives have always provided farmers with solutions to the many problems they faced. At the beginning of the twentieth century, for example, an oversupply of milk led to the creation of the first butter cooperatives. Wheat farmers joined together to face the economic crisis of the 1930s. During the German occupation in World War Two, farmers grouped together to ensure their seed supply. In the post-war era, French farm cooperatives were granted tax-free status, on the principal that their farmer-members, who already pay professional taxes, should not be taxed twice. This tax-free status in turn helped fuel cooperatives' growth.

Cooperatives allow farmers to maintain the individual status of their farms, while providing them with the advantages of being part of a larger organization. In this way, cooperatives continue to play an important role in underpinning the smaller-scale and generally family-owned farming model favored in Europe. For the most part, early cooperatives remained small and highly localized, often created by the farmers themselves or by local officials seeking to improve farmers' lives and working conditions. Access to cooperatives was generally determined by a farmer's own agricultural focus. Wheat farmers joined with other wheat farmers, corn growers with corn growers, and generally within a specific region or local community.

The small-scale nature of the early cooperatives began to change in the post-World War Two era. Faced with severe food shortages, the French government launched a new policy of actively encouraging the industrialization of France's agricultural sector. This was carried out on a large-scale, and by the end of the twentieth century France had grown into the world's second-largest agricultural producer, behind the United States (State Department, 2009). In response, France's farm cooperatives expanded their own range of services, including financing farmers' acquisition of tractors, harvesters, and other equipment; aiding in the conversion of large swathes of land to intensive agricultural techniques; and promoting the planting of corn, soybean, and other grains and cereals.

Second, the 1960s brought a first wave of consolidation among cooperatives as they confronted the growth of the supermarket sector. Mergers among cooperatives allowed them to expand their range of operations, whether geographically or by developing a more diverse range of products. Many cooperatives also launched their first basic food processing operations, such as vegetable canning and milling, and created their own brand names.

The arrival of the EEC quota system in the 1980s, followed by the creation of the European Union itself in the 1990s, prompted new responses from France's cooperatives. Many cooperatives began expanding beyond the agricultural sector to acquire already established food processing companies. As a result, many French cooperatives came to resemble their private sector counterparts, operating on one hand as an agricultural cooperative while developing on the other hand their food processing activities as non-cooperative corporations on the other. Between 1995 and 2005, the number of non-cooperative companies owned by the cooperatives nearly tripled (Agreste 2009).

Third, the profits from these businesses can be used to help compensate farmers for the shrinking margins generated by their own farm production. As Philippe Duval, architect of Tereos' expansion into the world's second-largest sugar producer, explained to *Les Echos*, the combination of cooperative and corporate models allows "the farmer to complete his income with the margins generated by processing and distribution." A new round of consolidation at the turn of the twenty-first century has also helped created a number of large-scale cooperatives capable of competing with the national and multi-national leaders. This development has prompted complaints from the private sector, who charge that the cooperatives' tax-free status gives them an unfair advantage.

Fourth, a growing number of France's cooperatives have begun to respond to the increasingly global food industry by developing their own international operations. In this way, these cooperatives have succeeded in establishing themselves as major players in the global market. Indeed, the adoption of more generic names such as Euralis, Laita, Tereos is indicative of the cooperatives' evolutionary focus from local associations to multinational businesses.

EURALIS: FROM WHEAT TO MEAT

Expansion into food processing characterizes Euralis's approach to changes in the global agro-food sector. Founded in 1936 by a group of wheat farmers in the Bearn region, Euralis has grown into one of France's top 20 cooperative groups. Euralis claims the world's leading position as a producer of foie gras and is Europe's leading corn producer. Between the mid-1990s and 2010, Euralis more than tripled its annual revenues, which neared $1.8 billion (€1.3 billion) in 2009. Much of this growth has come through Euralis's diversification into food processing, on the one hand, and international expansion, on the other. Into 2010, the group's agricultural production, including seeds, represented less than 50% of its total turnover.

Euralis's development can be seen as a model for the evolving nature of France's agricultural cooperative movement. The group expanded into other cereals, most notably corn, following the Second World War, changing its name to Coopérative de Céréales du Bassin de l'Adour in 1951. The coop expanded its range of support services, developing its own seed production unit and, in the 1960s, began constructing its first corn silos. Through the merger and acquisition of other cooperatives and corn producers, the group expanded its operations to include much of the southwestern region. By the mid-1970s, the group had become France's largest corn collector.

Euralis also responded to the growth of the supermarket sector, taking its first steps in food processing in the mid-1970s. This came with a sweet-corn supply agreement for the Green Giant brand in 1975. The cooperative quickly extended this business into the broader vegetables market, adding green beans, sweet peas, and broccoli. In the 1980s, the cooperative began developing its first non-cooperative operations, including the creation of a vegetable processing joint-venture, Sud-Ouest Legumes, with Bonduelle, France's leading producer of canned and frozen vegetables. in 1985, the cooperative adopted a new name, Coop de Pau, reflecting its diversified nature.

Coop de Pau joined in the consolidation wave of the cooperative sector into the early 2000s, which permitted the group to diversify and extend its geographic range. The integration, for example, of Coopéval in 2007 established the group in two other important French agricultural regions, Vendée and Brittany. To reflect its growing diversification, Coop de Pau also changed its name to Euralis during this time.

The choice of this more generic name, and especially the absence of the word *cooperative* reflects the shift in Euralis's strategy as of 2000. While Euralis remains firmly committed to its status as a cooperative, it has become less and less defined by its agricultural production.

This change in the group's focus became evident starting from the middle of the 1990s. Euralis had already begun to develop new business lines, including poultry production and a business focused on the production of ham and other processed pork products. Then, in 1995, the company made its first major acquisition in the private sector, buying up Grimaud Montfort Distribution (GMD), which, through its Montfort brand, was France's second-largest producer of foie gras. Euralis then invested $5,032 million (€8 million) in order to expand Montfort's production capacity.

The 2000 purchase of Rougié Bizac International, a major supplier of foie gras to the institutional sector, gave Euralis the position as France's foie gras leader. The acquisition led Euralis to carry out a reorganization, in which the cooperative established a new, corporate-style divisional structure. Euralis also adopted a new strategy focused on three core areas: seeds, agricultural products and distribution, and gastronomy. This last division served as the umbrella for the company's foie gras and other largely private-sector food processing businesses. By 2005, when the reorganization was completed, the gastronomy division already accounted for 41% of the cooperative's total revenues of €831 million.

Faced with the impending CAP reform, and the threat of a new level of international competition, Euralis responded by carrying out its own international expansion through the end of the decade. This began with the purchases of stake in foie gras producers in Bulgaria and Canada in 2005. In 2008, the company moved into China, buying up a Yangquing duck farm in order to produce foie gras there.

By then, however, Euralis had already made the leap to expand its range of prepared foods, now targeting the high-margin ready-made meal market. The cooperative's first step in this direction came in 2005, when it acquired 80% of Papillote, based in northern France. The following year, Euralis acquired a 20% stake in Jean Stalaven, a leading Brittany-based producer of delicatessen foods and fresh salads. The family-owned company had launched its own expansion into the ready-made meals segment at the beginning of the twenty-first century. Backed by Euralis, Stalaven became one of France's fastest-growing deli products groups by 2010.

In 2009, Euralis raised its stake in Stalaven to 65%. Stalaven now formed the core of Euralis's new Fresh Deli Products division. By the beginning of 2010, this division had already grown to more than 12% of Euralis's total revenues. At the same time, the group's non-cooperative and non-agriculture businesses represented more than 50% of its activity. By investing in high-margin foods sectors, Euralis successfully reduced its reliance on its agricultural products operations, preparing itself and its more than 15,000 farmer-members for both the 2013 CAP reform and the increasingly global food market.

LAITA: THE MARKETING RESPONSE

Laita, France's third-largest dairy products group, represents another strategy by which the French cooperative movement has met the challenges of the global market. Laita's origins reach back to the 1960s, as France's dairy cooperatives reacted to the rise of the supermarket sector by developing their first branded products. Among the first of these was the Regilait powdered milk brand, established by the France Lait cooperative in the late 1950s. At the end of the 1960s, Coopagri Bretagne, one of the leading and most diversified cooperatives in the Brittany region, introduced its own butter brand, Paysan Breton (Brittany Farmer).

The success of the Paysan Breton brand led Coopagri Bretagne to expand its dairy products operations, through a series of mergers with other regional dairy cooperatives. Doing so led to the formation in 1977 of a production partnership with Cooperative Agricole La Noëlle Ancenis (CANA, later part of Terrena), another major Brittany region cooperative group. CANA opened its own butter production facility for the Paysan Breton brand that year. The following year, the two cooperatives extended their partnership to include a joint-venture Swiss cheese factory. These permitted the cooperatives to resist the rising strength of the private dairy-products companies.

The 1980s brought a new crisis for the French dairy industry. The country's industrialization policies, as in other parts of Europe, had led to massive increases in productivity. By the early 1980s, the EEC found itself faced with an enormous oversupply problem, and by the middle of the decade, milk storage accounted for approximately one-third of the EEC's total budget. The EEC responded with draconian measures, including the installation of strict production quotas from 1984. The Brittany region found itself especially hard-hit by the quotas, facing production cuts of 15% over the next decade.

Despite protests from the dairy industry, which pointed out the oversupply had been caused by the government's own industrialization imperatives, the French government held firm. Dairy farmers were now expected to conform to the demands of the free market system, replacing previous productivity-oriented strategies with a focus on sales.

Coopagri Bretagne provided a two-fold response to its members. On one hand, the cooperative sought to expand its range of dairy-products manufacturing operations, reducing its reliance on raw milk. First, the cooperative targeted the development of a dedicated and more sophisticated marketing operation. Coopagri Bretagne accomplished the first of these through new mergers and acquisitions, including a 50% stake in the Regilait brand, and the acquisition of Laiterie Nouvelle de l'Arguenon (LNA), a family-owned company that produced cheeses as well as milk proteins and other dairy-based food additives. This acquisition also enabled Coopagri Bretagne to double the amount of milk it was allowed to collect under the quota system.

The second objective was accomplished in 1990, with the founding of Laita as a joint-marketing company by Coopagri and CANA. Laita took over the sales and marketing operations for the Paysan Breton brand, as well as the Regilait brand and LNA's King Frais and other brands. Laita's position as a marketing hub for the Brittany region dairy industry was reinforced when CANA acquired a 50% stake in LNA in 1992. The following year, another major Brittany dairy cooperative, Even, joined the Laita partnership as well.

Laita's role began to change, however, into the early 2000s. The movement toward reform of the CAP promised to eliminate much of the dairy industry's all-important subsidies. At the same time, Brittany's dairy cooperatives readied themselves for the soon-to-come international competition. Yet Europe's dairy market remained at a distinct advantage to such high-volume, low-cost dairy producers as New Zealand. The CAP had long protected France's dairy farmers from an increasingly glaring global reality. Butter prices served to illustrate the French farmers' predicament. In 2006, butter sold for $3,633 (€2,650) per metric ton within the European Union, twice as high as the global market price.

Laita's operations increasingly influenced the industrial developments of its cooperative parents into the turn of the century. Nonetheless, Coopagri Bretagne, Terrena, and Even remained responsible for financing their parts of these industrial investments. The partners took a first step toward resolving the inefficiency of this arrangement in 2006, when they agreed to a joint investment, of nearly $14 million (€10 million), to expand two of the factories under Laita's management.

At last, in 2008, Coopagri Bretagne, Terrena, and Even agreed to merge all of their industrial dairy operations into a single, jointly held company, called Laita S.A.S. By retaining the Laita name, the new company also maintained Laita's strong reputation as a leading French dairy products marketing. At the same time, Laita emerged as a new French dairy products powerhouse, processing more than 1.5 billion liters of milk per year and generating revenues of more than $1.5 billion (€1.1 billion). By providing a value-added outlet for its milk production, Laita provided its dairy farmer suppliers—who remained attached to their original cooperatives—with a more solid foundation for meeting the new challenges of the European dairy industry.

TEREOS: THE SUGAR KING

Tereos provides of a third example of how French cooperative have responded to the global market. Tereos is Europe's second-largest sugar producer, spanning the beet, cane, and cereals (glucose) based sugar categories, as well as one of the leading European starch producers. At the same time, Tereos has gone global, becoming the fourth-largest sugar producer in Brazil and governing an industrial network spanning 34 factories in Europe, South America, and Africa. Each year, Tereos processes nearly 2.5 million acres (1 million ha) of farm land, producing 3.8 million metric tons of sugar, 1.8 million metric tons of starch, and 1.8 million cubic meters of bioethanol and alcohol. Together these operations generated revenues of $4.6 billion (€3.3 billion) in 2009 for the cooperative's 12,000 sugar beet farmer-members.

Tereos' roots lay in the 1930s, with the creation of a small distillery cooperative in Origny-Saint-Benoite by a group of Picardy-region sugar beet farmers. Originally focused on the production of alcohol, the Origny cooperative built its first sugar factory in 1951. Led by Jean Duval, the cooperative developed a policy of returning one-third of its profits to its members while investing the rest in its expansion. In 1970, Duval was joined by his son, Philippe Duval, who took over as head of the Origny cooperative in 1984.

The younger Duval became the architect of the future Tereos, leading the Origny cooperative into a series of mergers with other sugar beet farm cooperatives. The first of these came in 1990, creating Sucreries et Distilleries de l'Asne (SDA), which became one of the largest sugar beet producers and processors in France. The cooperative adopted a new name, Union SDA, after merging with Sucrerie-Distillerie d'Artenay in 1999. In 2006, the cooperative merged with Sucreries et Distilleries des Hauts de France, expanding its reach into the Nord-Pas-de-Calais region.

By then, the cooperative had already changed its name, becoming Tereos in 2002. This new generic-sounding name evoked both the group's new global ambitions and its extension beyond its original sugar and distillery functions. The enormous growth of the food processing industry had brought about a surge in demand for food additives. Rather than enter the processed foods market, Duval targeted a diversification into production of additives.

The cooperative's first investment in this area came in 1987, with the launch of a liquid sugar production unit, and the opening of a rectification facility. In 1996, Tereos began producing glucose, forming a subsidiary Syral. This company was situated next to a starch production joint-venture, Staral, created that year with Austria's Jugbunzlauer. Tereos later acquired full control of Staral, which was merged into Syral in 2003. Tereos's industrial wing branched out the following year, acquiring synthetic alcohol producer Sodes, then forming a wheat ethanol-production joint venture with a wheat-farming cooperative.

In this way, Tereos's strategy contrasted sharply with the diversification drive of many of its cooperative counterparts. Tereos's operations remained comparatively focused, with sugar and its derivatives remaining its core area of operation. Instead, as it moved to confront the global market at the turn of the century, Tereos put into place its own globalization strategy.

Duval became determined to extend Tereos's operations into cane sugar, which had become highly competitive against beet sugar, notably through the use of sugar cane waste byproducts as a fuel source. In 2000, Duval formed its first cane sugar joint venture, with Cosan, a leading sugarcane processor in Brazil. The company next turned to the island of Réunion, buying up the sugar cane operations of the Bourbon Group there in 2001.

One year later, Tereos bought up the sugar factories of Beghin-Say, one of the world's leading sugar refiners. The Beghin-Say purchase brought Tereos a major prize: Guarani, one of Brazil's leading sugarcane processors. From this foothold, Tereos expanded rapidly in the Brazilian market, building a network of 16 factories in that country.

Through Syral, Tereos also became a European leader in the starch and glucose market, buying up five factories from Tate & Lyle in 2007. The company also expanded its African operations, buying up Quartier Francais in 2010. In this way, Tereos became the only sugar cane processor in Réunion. By then, Tereos had also become the second-largest sugar in Europe and one of the leading players in the sugar market worldwide.

Tereos marked a new milestone in 2010. In that year, Tereos regrouped all of its non-sugar beet operations into a new company, based in Brazil and called Tereos Internacional. This company then went public, listing its shares on the Brazilian and Paris stock exchanges. Tereos Internacional then announced it had reached a partnership agreement with Petrobras to develop bioethanol production. The venture was expected to double Tereos's revenues by 2015. Tereos' 14,000 farmer-members had become shareholders in one of the world's fastest-growing sugar companies.

On an individual basis, France's farmers have never appeared more vulnerable than at the beginning of the twenty-first century. Faced with the arrival of cheaper imports starting in 2013 and already caught within a system dominated by giant multinational corporations, the French farmer's survival has come to depend on the ability of the cooperatives to adapt to changes in both the agricultural and foods sectors.

France's cooperatives have succeeded in developing a variety of responses to increasingly global foods market. These responses range from building volume through mergers and acquisitions, to developing value-added outlets for members' production, to expansion to an international and even global level. By purchasing their farmer-members' products and by supplementing their incomes with profits generated through an increasingly diverse array of operations, France's cooperatives are anticipated to continue playing an essential role in the country's farm industry in the new century.

QUESTIONS FOR DISCUSSION

1. What role do cooperatives play in the French and European agricultural sector?
2. What are the various challenges facing French farmers and their cooperatives from a local perspective, a European perspective, and a global perspective?
3. Identify the main lines of the adaptive strategies developed by Euralis, Laita and Tereos. How do they differ? How do they compare?
4. Private food companies have complained that French cooperatives' tax-free status gives them an unfair competitive advantage. Discuss the three cooperatives cited in this entry in terms of their similarity to or distinctiveness from private corporations. Is this criticism justifiable?

REFERENCES/BIBLIOGRAPHY

"Agricultural Cooperation in France." Coop de France, 2005

"Background Note: France." U.S. State Department. 10 Dec. 2009. Retrieved 31 Jan. 2011 from http://www.state.gov/r/pa/ei/bgn/3842.htm.

Bauer, Anne, "Tereos: L'Empire Discret du Sucre." *Les Echos* 1 June 2010.

"Coopagri Bretagne." *International Directory of Company Histories*. Detroit: St. James Press, 2008. Print.

Cohen, M.L., La&iulm;ta S.A.S. in Grant, Tina, ed., *International Directory of Company Histories*. Vol. 113. Detroit: St. James Press, 2010. p200-204.

Common Agricultural Policy Explained, European Commission Agriculture and Rural Development, Directorate-General for Agriculture and Rural Development. Web site. Available from: http://ec.europa.eu/agriculture/

Damave, Marie-Cecile. "France's New-found Need to Nibble." *AgExporter* Apr. 1998: 15.

De la Chesnais, Eric. "Chute historique du revenu des agriculteurs en 2009." *Le Figaro* 14 Dec. 2009.

Duriez, Francis. "French Eating Habits: New Habits." *RunGis.com*. n.d. Retrieved 31 Jan. 2011 from http://www.rungismarket.com/en/bleu/enquetesrungisactu/ModesAlimentaires634.asp

Gentleman, Amelia. "France Gives in to TV Dinners." *Guardian* 8 Oct. 2004: 17.

"Groupe Euralis." *International Directory of Company Histories*. Detroit: St. James Press, 2007.

"Les groupes coopératifs poursuivent leur développement." *Agreste Primeur.* Dec. 2009.

Ménard, Claude, and Klein, Peter G., "Organizational Issues in the Agrifood Sector: Toward a Comparative Approach." *American Journal of Agricultural Economics* 7 Jan. 2004.

Neumann, Benjamin, Stéphanie Benz, Chloé Hoorman, and Franck Dedieu. "L'Agriculture Française Condamnée à l'Excellence." *L'Expansion* 1 Feb. 2006.

"La petite coopération agricole poursuit sa reorganization." *Agreste Primeur* Oct. 2007.

"Les Coopératives Européennes Réclament une Adaptation des Règles de Concurrence." 13 May 2010. Retrieved 31 Jan. 2011 from http://www.agraalimentation.fr/reagir-sur-les-cooperatives-europeennes-reclament-une-adaptation-des-regles-de-concurrence-com271713-1.html

Seipel, Michael F., and William D. Heffernan. "Cooperatives in a Changing Global Food System." FIBS Research Report 157. U.S. Department of Agriculture Rural Business-Cooperative Service. Oct. 1997.

Tereos Group. Web site. Available from: http//www.tereos.com/

Global Regulation of Herbal Products

Tamra S. Davis • Clinical Assistant Professor, University of Oklahoma College of Pharmacy

Miki Finnin • CEO/Pharmacist, Medication Advisors, PLLC

LEARNING OBJECTIVES

This case study prepares the reader to do the following:

- *Explain the economic and non-economic reasons for the growth in sales of herbal products globally*

- *Justify the regulation or non-regulation of sales of herbal products via the Internet or mail-order*

- *Justify why standardization of herbal product regulations may or may not be needed globally*

- *Explain the economic and non-economic impact of global herbal product regulation on consumers and the pharmaceutical industry*

- *Justify whether a pharmaceutical company should or should not be able to sell an herbal product if the product is restricted or banned in the country of origin (i.e., a U.S.-based pharmaceutical company selling an herbal product that is banned in the United States to other countries)*

- *Explain how a consumer may be protected from products that originate in one country and are sold via the Internet or mail-order in a different country*

- *Evaluate the regulations of one country concerning the manufacture and sale of herbal products*

- *Recommend improvements to the regulations of one country concerning the manufacture and sale of herbal products*

- *Discuss ethical considerations involving the manufacture of herbal products*

This case was prepared for classroom discussion rather than to illustrate either effective or ineffective handling of an administrative, ethical, or legal decision by management. Information was gathered from corporate as well as public sources.

BACKGROUND

Complementary and alternative medicine "is a group of diverse medical and health care systems, practices, and products that are not generally considered to be part of conventional medicine" (National Institute for Health 1). The World Health Organization (WHO) (2002) further defines CAM as "a broad set of healthcare practices that are not part of that country's own tradition and are not integrated into the dominant health care system. They have not usually been tested in specified clinical indications by an objective scientific discipline" (41). Complementary medicine is typically used with conventional medicine as a complement to the treatment. Alternative medicine replaces conventional medicine in patient care. In a study conducted by Barnes, Powell-Griner, McFann, and Nahin, 62% of adults in the United States incorporated some type of CAM into their healthcare practices. Mills (2001) indicated that CAM in the United Kingdom grew rapidly between 1980 and 2000, evidenced by study results (1999) that identified approximately 50,000 CAM practitioners and 5 million patients that have consulted with a CAM practitioner in the previous year. Madsen and colleagues reviewed multiple studies indicating a growth in worldwide use of CAM. This worldwide growth is also evident in that 141 countries (74%) of the 191 member states of the World Health Organization (WHO) responded to a global survey inquiring about policy and regulations for traditional medicine and CAM therapy (2005). Of the 141 respondents, 45 states (32%) reported having active policies, and 51 (56%) of the states that did not have a current policy reported that one was under development. Additionally, 75 countries (53%) reported having a national office that controls traditional medicine and CAM.

HERBAL THERAPY

One avenue of CAM therapy, herbal products, has been widely described in the literature. Winslow and Kroll identified several reasons that people use herbal medicines, stating that a sense of control is a primary reason along with the belief that since herbal products are not synthesized in laboratories, but rather grown from seed to plant, they are therefore natural products and safe. In addition, people who suffer from chronic diseases such as hypertension, diabetes, cancer, or arthritis often use herbals as they perceive that conventional medicine has failed to cure their condition. Other situations in which herbal treatment may be sought include acute, self-limiting conditions such as insect stings, colds, and sunburns, where professional care is either too expensive or not readily available.

Ethnicity and cultural factors may also play a role in the use of herbals. For example, in a study conducted by Dole et al., the investigators found that when comparing herbal medicinal consumption in Hispanic populations to non-Hispanic whites (NHW), Hispanics use herbal remedies more often than NHW ($p < 0.0001$) and more often had a parent that also used herbal remedies ($p < 0.0001$). The National Institute of Health (NIH) (2010) reported herbal and CAM therapies are also common among American Indians and Alaskan

Native Indians. In the United States in 2007, 50% of this population reported using herbal and CAM therapy. This particular population has been using herbal remedies for medicinal purposes for thousands of years and has passed down their knowledge and beliefs from one generation to the next (Cichoke). Finally, traditional Chinese medicine (TCM), which focuses heavily on herbal medicinal use along with other modalities, has been practiced for over 5,000 years (WHO n.d.). TCM is supported globally through the WHO development of Collaborating Centres for Traditional Medicine, which includes countries such as Sudan, United Arab Emirates, Italy, Norway, Australia, China, the United States, Japan, Korea, and Viet Nam (WHO 2011).

In numerous countries throughout the world, herbal products continue to be available to the general public with varying degrees of regulations enforced that ensure safety and efficacy of products. In New Zealand, for instance, where the aboriginal Maori people have been using herbal medicine for thousands of years (Tourism New Zealand), herbal products are regulated through a combination of both the Medicines Act 1981 and Dietary Supplements Regulations 1985, and they are sold as prescription and over-the-counter products (Ministry of Health; Taylor). For herbs considered dietary supplements, there is no pre-market approval process addressing safety or quality, and no therapeutic claims may be made. By contrast, in Australia herbal products have been regulated under the Therapeutic Goods Act since 1989, which contains some of the same regulations used in evaluating pharmaceuticals (Taylor). In Australia, herbal products are sold as over-the-counter medications and medical, health, nutrient content, and structure/function claims may be made on these products. In the People's Republic of China, herbal medicine has been used for thousands of years and continues to be the mainstay of health care in the country alongside Western medicine. Herbal products have been regulated in some fashion since 1963 and as of 2010 were regulated as prescription and over-the-counter medications, self-medications, dietary supplements, health foods and functional foods, and claims may be made regarding medical, health, and nutrient content (Taylor). Although it is reported that in China safety assessment for herbals is similar to that of pharmaceuticals with the addition of gathered information on the traditional use without harmful effects, specifics about how this regulation is enforced are not available (Taylor). In the United States, herbal products are marketed as dietary supplements and are considered to be food products; therefore, they are not subject to the pre-marketing approval process. Dietary supplements cannot make specific health claims as any product making a health claim falls under the jurisdiction of the Food and Drug Administration (FDA). Specific legislation related to supplements is the Dietary Supplement and Health Education Act (DSHEA) of 1994. "The DSHEA requires that supplements not promise a specific cure on the label, [however] they may claim effect" (Winslow & Kroll 2194). Additionally, the burden of proof falls onto the FDA in determining that a product is unsafe.

As is shown above with the varying degrees of regulation, many countries classify herbal products as dietary supplements or foods with no pre-market approval process. A direct result of no pre-market approval process is that products are only removed from market after consumers have suffered harm

(Ministry of Health). Calixto summarized the regulations of herbal products for multiple countries. In Argentina, the Argentinean National Pharmacopea controls most herbal products, but there is a lack of control over the raw materials used. Australia requires that claims for herbal products be justified by literature references. Brazilian law demands documentation for efficacy, safety, and well-defined quality control, but due to corporate resistance, as of late 2010, the law had not been enforced. In Canada, the Canadian Health Protection Branch (HPB) classified herbal drugs as folk medicine. The HPB regulations are consistent with the Good Manufacturing Practice (GMP) guidelines established by the World Health Organization (WHO). Chile requires registration with the *Unidad de Medicina Tradicional* of herbal products before marketing can take place. In France, licensing approval is generally required for all drugs, but plant-derived drugs and preparations have an abridged application for licensing. The German Commission E, an independent division of the German Federal Health Agency, collects and evaluates information on the safety and efficacy of herbal medicines. The commission releases a monograph that either approves or disapproves of the product for over-the-counter use. Some herbal medicines are only available through a physician's prescription, such as artichoke extract used for high blood pressure and high cholesterol (WHO 2005) and ginkgo biloba extract for short-term memory loss and depression (Murray).

The herbal supplement market is growing exponentially. "Most large multinational companies are interested in commercializing herbal drugs" (Calixto 181), and this interest is due in large part to the annual sales of herbal products. In the U.S. market, sales grew from $3.2 billion in 1996 (Calixto 2000) to $4.4 billion in 2005 (Blumenthal et al.). China reported sales of herbal products as $14 billion in 2005 (WHO 2008). Additionally, up to 80% of the population in some Asian and African countries depends upon traditional medicine, and 70 to 80% of the population in many developed countries used traditional or alternative therapies (WHO 2008). The WHO (2005) published data from nine WHO member states regarding the growth in annual sales of herbal products. The reporting countries include Bhutan, Canada, Czech Republic, Islamic Republic of Iran, Madagascar, Malaysia, Pakistan, Sudan, and Sweden. Sales in 1999 equaled $706.45 million. This amount increased to $1,005.68 million in 2001; an increase of $299.23 million. U.S. sales have risen from the $3.2 billion in 1996 to $4.8 billion in 2008 (Cavaliere et al.). Subsequent analysis showed that the herbal supplements and remedies market globally is forecasted to reach over $93 billion by 2015. The research found that in the United States from 2007 to 2008 sales increased over 10%. Also predicted is that the Asia-Pacific market will lead global growth with a compounded annual growth rate of 10.7% through 2015 (Vocus).

AREAS FOR CONCERN

The World Health Organization (2002) listed eight challenges that face pharmacovigilance (the monitoring of medicines for safety and efficacy): globalization, Web-based sales and information, broader safety concerns, public health versus pharmaceutical industry economic growth, monitoring of established products, developing and emerging countries, attitudes and perceptions to benefit and harm, and outcomes and impact. In 2005, WHO went further to identify five challenges specific to regulation of traditional, CAM, and herbal medicines (WHO, 2005). The challenges are: regulatory status, assessment of safety and efficacy, quality control, safety monitoring, and lack of knowledge about traditional medicine and CAM therapy within nation drug regulatory authorities.

One significant concern is that the disparities in regulations affect public health through international access to products. For example, a product available by prescription only in one country may be obtained from a health food store in another country or, more commonly, may be available via mail order or online sales, which are often unregulated (WHO 2002). As indicated, herbal products are often regulated as food products, not medicines. Globally, the differences between food and medicine are ambiguous. Additionally, the regulations concerning herbals vary significantly between countries, evinced by less than 70 WHO member countries regulating herbal medicines in 2002 (WHO 2002). Although this number increased to 92 WHO member countries in 2005, the number of countries without regulation remained significant with 49 of the responding nations reporting no regulation (WHO 2005). Other variations in regulations can be found in the marketing approval and distribution processes. As pointed out earlier, China and Australia have regulations that enforce proof of safety prior to marketing, whereas New Zealand and the United States do not. With regards to distribution regulation differences, herbal products can be sold over-the-counter in New Zealand and in the United States, but many must be accompanied by a prescription in Germany (Calixto; Ministry of Health; Murray; Taylor; WHO 2005; Winslow & Kroll).

An additional challenge of concern is the availability of herbal products through the Internet. Although the Internet provides many benefits to users, it also produces many challenges for medicinal regulation. One example is that the Internet has "allowed the uncontrolled sale of medicines (including herbal and traditional medicines) across national borders" (WHO 2002, 35). Combine the Internet's ease of use with aggressive marketing by pharmaceutical companies and distributors, such as direct to consumer advertising, and the potential for excessive use of medicines is a real possibility (WHO 2002).

QUESTIONS FOR DISCUSSION

1. Explain two economic and two non-economic reasons that CAM is growing in popularity?
2. If regulation of Internet and mail order sales of herbal products were implemented, which country should regulate the sales; the country of product origin or the country of product receipt? Why?
3. Explain and justify one reason that regulations should be standardized around the world for herbal products. Explain and justify one reason why

regulations may not be appropriate for standardization around the world for herbal products.

4. Explain one of the potential economic impacts of regulation on consumers. Explain one of the potential economic impacts of regulations on the pharmaceutical industry.

5. Explain one of the potential economic impacts of non-regulation on consumers. Explain one of the potential economic impacts of non-regulation on the pharmaceutical industry?

6. Should pharmaceutical companies be allowed to manufacture herbal products for sale in other countries if the sale of that product is restricted in the country of production? Why?

7. What are some ethical questions that should be considered in the manufacture and regulation of herbal products? Why is this a concern?

REFERENCES/BIBLIOGRAPHY

Barnes, P. M., E. Powell-Griner, K. McFann, and R. L. Nahin. *Complementary and alternative medicine use among adults: United States, 2002.* (Publication No. 343). Washington, DC: Department of Health and Human Services, Centers for Disease Control and Prevention, 2004. Retrieved 2 Feb. 2011 from http://www.cdc.gov/nchs/data/ad/ad343.pdf

Blumenthal, M., G. K. L. Ferrier, and C. Cavaliere. "Total Sales of Herbal Supplements in United States Show Steady Growth." *HerbalGram* 71 (2006): 64–66. Retrieved 2 Feb. 2011 from http://cms.herbalgram.org/herbalgram/issue71/article3012.html

Calixto, J. B. "Efficacy, Safety, Quality Control, Marketing and Regulatory Guidelines for Herbal Medicines (Phytotherapeutic Agents)." *Brazilian Journal of Medical and Biological Research* 33 (2000): 179–89.

Cavaliere, C., P. Rea, M. E. Lynch, and M. Blumenthal. "Herbal Supplement Sales Experience Slight Increase in 2008." *HerbalGram* 82 (2009): 58–61. Retrieved 2 Feb. 2011 from http://cms.herbalgram.org/herbalgram/issue82/article3400.html

Cichoke, A. J. *Secrets of Native American Herbal Remedies.* New York: Penguin Putnam, 2001. Print.

Dole, E., R. L. Rhyne, C. A. Zeilmann, et al. "The Influence of Ethnicity on Use of Herbal Remedies in Elderly Hispanics and Non-Hispanic Whites." *Journal of the American Pharmacists Association* 40.3 (2000).

Madsen, H., S. Andersen, R. G. Nielsen, et al. "Use of Complementary/Alternative Medicine among Paediatric Patients." *European Journal of Pediatric* 162 (2003): 334–41.

Mills, S. Y. "Regulation in Complementary and Alternative Medicine." *British Medical Journal* 322 (2001): 158–60.

Ministry of Health. *Ministerial Advisory Committee on Complementary and Alternative Health: Regulation CAM.* Retrieved 2 Feb. 2011 from http://www.newhealth.govt.nz/maccah/regulation.htm

Murray, M., and J. Pizzorno. *Encyclopedia of Natural Medicine*, rev. 2nd ed. New York: Three Rivers P, 1997. Print.

National Institute for Health. *National Center for Complementary and Alternative Medicine: The use of Complementary and Alternative Medicine in the United States.* 2010. Retrieved 2 Feb. 2011 from http://nccam.nih.gov/news/camstats/2007/camsurvey_fs1.htm

Taylor, L. *The Healing Power of Rainforest Herbs.* Garden City Park, NY: Square One, 2005. Print.

Tourism New Zealand. *Rongoa Māori: Traditional Māori Medicine.* Retrieved 2 Feb. 2011 from http://www.newzealand.com/travel/media/features/maori-culture/maori-culture_rongoa-maori-medicine_feature.cfm

U.S. Department of Health and Human Services, National Center for Complementary and Alternative Medicine. *What Is Complimentary and Alternative Medicine?* Retrieved 2 Feb. 2011 from http://nccam.nih.gov/health/whatiscam/D347.pdf

Vocus. "Global Herbal Supplement and Remedies Market to Reach US $93.15 Billion by 2015, According to a New Report by Global Industry Analysts." Retrieved 2 Feb. 2011 from http://www.prweb.com/releases/herbal_-supplements/herbal_remedies_aloe_vera/prweb8058158.htm

Winslow, L. C., and D. J. Kroll. "Herbs as Medicine." *Archives of Internal Medicine* 158.20 (1998): 2192-99.

World Health Organization. "Traditional Chinese Medicine Could Make 'Health for One' True." Retrieved 2 Feb. 2011 from http://www.who.int/intellectualproperty/studies/Jia.pdf

World Health Organization. *The Importance of Pharmacovigilance: Safety Monitoring of Medicinal Product* (2002). Retrieved 2 Feb.2011 from http://apps.who.int/medicinedocs/pdf/s4893e/s4893e.pdf

World Health Organization. *National Policy on Traditional Medicine and Regulation of Herbal Medicines: Report of a WHO Global Survey.* (2005). Retrieved 2 Feb. 2011 from http://whqlibdoc.who.int/publications/2005/9241593237.pdf

World Health Organization. *Traditional Medicine:Fact Sheet 134.* (2008). Retrieved 2 Feb. 2011 from http://www.who.int/mediacentre/fact-sheets/fs134/en/

World Health Organization. *Medicines: WHO Collaborating Centres for Traditional Medicine.* (2011). Retrieved 2 Feb. 2011 from http://www.who.int/medicines/areas/traditional/collabcentres/en/index.html

Human Errors in Inventory Control: Is There a Win-Win Solution?

Varsha Burugula • Graduate Student, Department of Information and Logistics Technology, University of Houston, Houston, TX

Debbie Hughes • Instructional Assistant Professor, Department of Information and Logistics Technology, University of Houston, Houston, TX

Jamison V. Kovach • Assistant Professor, Department of Information and Logistics Technology, University of Houston, Houston, TX

LEARNING OBJECTIVES

After completing this case study, students should be able to do the following:

- *Discuss the purpose of quality improvement tools*
- *Assess methodologies used to investigate/solve problems and develop alternative approaches*
- *Describe strategies to reduce/eliminate human errors*
- *Analyze recommended improvements and discuss the merits of each*
- *Propose control measures to maintain improvements*

This case was prepared for classroom discussion rather than to illustrate either effective or ineffective handling of an administrative, ethical, or legal decision by management. Information was gathered from corporate as well as public sources.

BACKGROUND

It was a typical spring afternoon, and John Mansfield peered out his office window to see the sun coming out from behind the clouds. John knew the comfortable weather wouldn't last long and that he'd better get back to work. John was the vice president for the Houston Division of JDV Pharmaceuticals, Inc., one of the world's leading pharmaceutical distribution companies. He had just finished a conference call with Joseph Short, the regional vice president of

117

JDV, and Tricia Reid, the senior vice president of operations for JDV. As in many similar conversations over the last year, the subject of the Houston Division's high level of inventory discrepancies came up. John had started to dread these discussions. He knew that inventory discrepancies were a problem, but not until that day had he realized the magnitude of the problem and its impact on the division's reputation.

In their previous meeting, Tricia had asked John to send her some data about the Houston Division's recent inventory performance. Using this data, Tricia discovered that over the last five months, gross inventory adjustments (i.e., adjustments made to account for inventory discrepancies) averaged 0.94% for the Houston Division, which was much higher than the benchmark metric (i.e., the company average) of 0.65% year to date. Joseph was quite upset to hear this information because he knew it was likely a symptom of a larger problem—inefficient operations in the division's distribution center. To ease an otherwise tense moment, John assured his senior managers that he would start investigating this problem right away. He explained that he would develop a plan to fix the problem over the course of the next couple of months and make this one of his top priorities.

John had been a valued employee of JDV for over 15 years. He started as the manager of the Houston Division's distribution center and had come to be well-respected among his employees. With all of his experience, he was sure he could solve this problem. As he looked out the window, John thought about how to fix the situation and get his division back on track fast. He immediately recalled that his boss, Ray Shay, was a certified Six Sigma Black Belt and the Six Sigma champion for their division. He quickly headed down the hall to see if Ray was in his office because, perhaps, a structured problem solving methodology like Six Sigma was just what John needed to guide him to a solution.

Ray was happy to hear that John was interested in learning more about Six Sigma. At his previous company, Ray had solved several strategically important problems using Six Sigma and found it to be a valuable approach. As Ray had only been with JDV for six weeks, he listened intently as John explained more about the inventory discrepancy problem. Once John was finished, Ray suggested that he mentor John through his first Six Sigma project, which he suggested that John could complete in conjunction with some formal training at one of the local universities. Before John left Ray's office, Ray reminded him that Six Sigma wouldn't help him just find a solution to this problem; it would help him find the best solution.

COMPANY OPERATIONS

JDV is a pharmaceutical services company based in Chester Brook, Pennsylvania, founded in 2002. It is a market leader in pharmaceutical distribution with over $81 billion in revenue annually. JDV distributes a broad range of pharmaceutical products to customers throughout the United States and Canada, as well as in other select global markets. The company's mission is to deliver products on a just-in-time basis to tens of thousands of healthcare providers, pharmacies, and care facilities. As of 2010, their operations accounted for approximately 25% of all pharmaceuticals sold and distributed in the United States, and they had distribution centers throughout the United States, Puerto Rico, Canada, and the United Kingdom.

The Houston Division of JDV serves the greater Houston metropolitan area, the Gulf Coast region of Texas, and the state of Louisiana. Its 45 employees distribute more than $1.5 billion of pharmaceuticals each year from its 100,000 square foot warehouse facility in northwest Houston. This distribution center operates 24 hours a day, seven days a week.

The operations at the Houston Division's distribution center include receiving, stocking, replenishment, order fulfillment, redistribution, and cycle counting. The SIPOC (Suppliers, Inputs, Process, Outputs, Customers) diagram in Figure 1 provides a brief overview of these operations. The suppliers include the drug manufacturers that provide the products that the company distributes, JDV's customers (i.e., hospitals, pharmacies, and care facilities) that occasionally return products that have to be restocked, and information technology vendors who supply the hardware, software, and other systems that JDV employees use to run the distribution center. The outputs of this work include

a. delivering salable inventory (i.e., inventory that is fit to be sold) to customers

b. maintaining accurate inventory levels in the correct locations

c. sorting inventory on the error resolution pallet to identify whether it is salable or non-salable (i.e., broken or damaged inventory that cannot be sold), and

d. managing non-salable inventory levels.

At this point the company's managers believe that they are succeeding in their mission; however, competitive pressure is growing across the entire pharmaceutical distribution market. Their plan as of 2010 is to improve market share by reducing costs, which requires improving the efficiency of their operations throughout the company.

FIGURE 1

Suppliers	Inputs	Process Steps	Outputs	Customers
Drug Manufacturers	Products	Receiving	Salable Inventory	Hospitals
	Coustomer Returns	Stocking	Accurate Inventory (by location)	Pharmacies
Hospitals/ Pharmacies		Order Fulfillment		Car Facilities
	Hardware/Software	Replenishment	Error Resolution Pallet	
Information Technology Vendors	Warehouse Management System	Redistribution	Non-salable Inventory	
		Cycle Counting	Status Reports	
	Employees			

SIPOC diagram of the operations for the JDV Houston Division's distribution center

PROBLEM INVESTIGATION

The use of a structured problem solving approach, such as Six Sigma, helps companies improve all aspects of their operations in order to better serve their customers and improve competitiveness. The Six Sigma methodology was originally developed by Motorola in the late 1980s as a quality improvement initiative to eliminate defects (errors) through the reduction of variation in manufacturing and business processes (Pande et al.). This approach improves performance by eliminating quality problems before they occur, which saves valuable corporate resources and improves the bottom-line performance of an organization.

To create solutions to eliminate the root cause of performance problems, each Six Sigma project follows a defined sequence of steps known as the DMAIC (Define, Measure, Analyze, Improve, and Control) methodology. In the define phase, the project team is assembled and the mission of the project is identified. The next phase involves verifying the measurement system(s) that will be used throughout the project to collect the data necessary to investigate the problem. In the analyze phase, the data collected are used to identify the root cause(s) of the problem. During the improve phase, the solution(s) to the problem are identified and implemented. Finally, the project team establishes mechanisms in the control phase to ensure that the improvements made through the project will be sustained over the long term, and then they close the project.

Define/Measure

Following the approach John was learning in his training class, he launched his first Six Sigma project by identifying employees from the Houston Division who should participate in the project and by drafting a project charter. The project team consisted of Mike Newell, the operations manager for the Houston Division and Emily Henderson, the inventory manager for the Houston Division along with John and Ray. The charter outlined the mission of the project for the team—to reduce gross inventory adjustments from their current level (0.94%) to at or below the company average (0.65%) by July of that year. The team's next job was to map the entire inventory process. Then, they verified the accuracy of gross inventory adjustment measurements and related work processes (i.e., receiving, order fulfillment, cycle counting, etc.) to provide confidence in the data they would be using to explore this problem in further detail. To begin their investigation, the team collected data about the causes of gross inventory adjustments logged over the past five months in the warehouse management system.

Analyze

To determine the most frequently occurring cause of gross inventory adjustments, the team created a Pareto chart (see Figure 2). In this diagram, the different categories of items that cause gross inventory adjustments are displayed across the x-axis, the frequency of occurrence for each of these causes is shown along the y-axis on left side of the diagram, and the cumulative

FIGURE 2

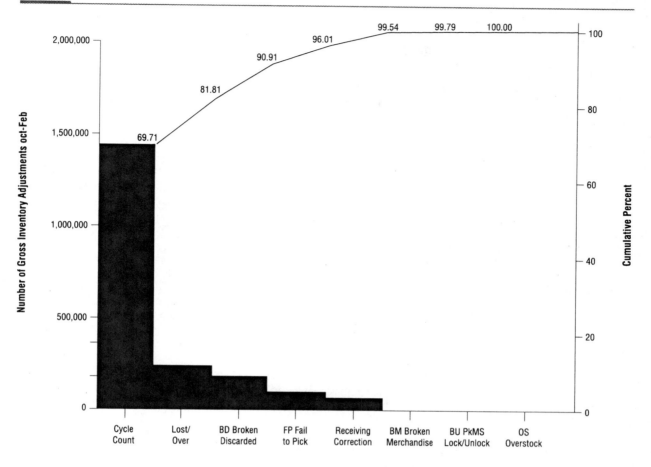

Causes of Gross Inventory Adjustments

Pareto chart for causes of gross inventory adjustments

percentage of occurrences by category is shown on the right y-axis. This type of analysis helped the team to identify the leading cause of gross inventory adjustments—cycle counts, which alone accounted for almost half of the gross inventory adjustments made over the last five months. Since cycle counts are performed as a result of known inventory discrepancies, they almost always result in gross inventory adjustments. After the gross inventory adjustments are made, the physical stock will be placed in the proper storage location and accurately recorded in the warehouse management system. Therefore, the cycle counts are not a root cause but rather a symptom of the true problem.

To further investigate reasons for inventory discrepancies, the team created a cause-and-effect diagram (see Figure 3). This diagram identifies many possible causes for an effect or problem, and it is often used to organize the results of a brainstorming session by sorting ideas into useful categories (Tague). The relevant categories identified in this diagram include receiving, replenishment, order fulfillment, inventory control, and stocking. After reflecting on this information, the team noted the prevalence of operator-related errors identified

FIGURE 3

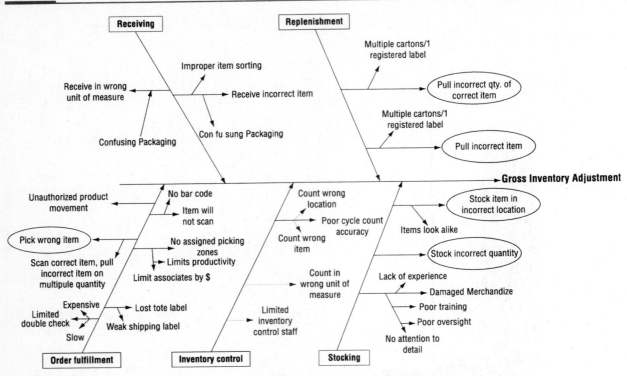

Cause and effect diagram summarizing reasons for gross inventory adjustments

in this analysis (i.e., items circled in Figure 3). These included picking the wrong item, picking the incorrect quantity, stocking items in the incorrect locations, and stocking the incorrect quantity. When John discussed these problems with the operators, a seasoned operator, Albert Rios, complained that the aisles were organized in a different order than the picks forms. Jon Wang, a relatively new operator, agreed and added that sometimes the labeling of the bins was confusing, with the random colors, numbers, and letters.

To better understand the degree of the problem associated with operator errors, the team collected data and created a box plot to analyze error rates by operator (see Figure 4). In this diagram, the bottom and top of the box represents the twenty-fifth and seventy-fifth percentile, respectively (the variation in the data set), and the band near the middle of the box is the fiftieth percentile (the median of the data set) (Tague). Figure 4 indicates that some operators have high error rates and/or a larger amount of variation in their performance as compared to other operators. The operators with the lowest error rates and least amount of variation in their performance are Brasilio Herbert, Peter Yan, and Henry Asbury.

Improve

Based on the information uncovered in the analyze phase, the team turned its attention to developing improvement ideas to reduce operator errors that lead to gross inventory adjustments. Some team members thought that inventory

FIGURE 4

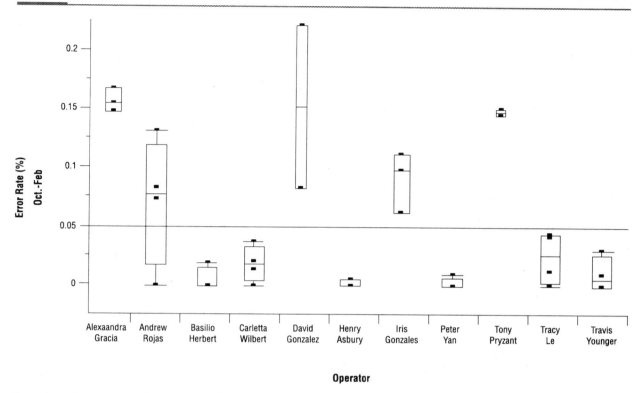

Box plot of error rates by operator

management procedures should be revised based on the practices of those identified as the best operators (i.e., those with the lowest error rates and least amount of variation in their performance). Through discussions with these operators and observations of their practices, the team could write improved standard operating procedures and then retrain all operators to use these new practices.

Other team members thought that the improvements needed to go one step further and address infrastructure-related issues that may be preventing operators from always being able to achieve their best performance. In studying the Six Sigma methodology, John had been introduced to the concept of error proofing (also known as mistake proofing, fool proofing, poka-yoke, etc.). The philosophy behind error proofing is that it's not acceptable to make even a very small number of errors or mistakes, and the only way to make no errors is to put countermeasures in place to prevent the occurrence of errors or mistakes and/or mitigate/detect their occurrence before they cause a negative effect. This approach specifically involves improving the work environment/practices with the aim of preventing problems that may occur as a result of human error (Grout).

CONCLUSION

Over the last three months, John and his team at JDV's Houston Division put in a lot of hard work on their Six Sigma project. They successfully completed the define, measure, and analyze phases of their project, and their next step is to involve selecting and implementing the necessary improvements to drive gross inventory adjustments down to at or below the company average of 0.65%. Team members are confident that they can successfully achieve their goal, but they also want to ensure that the changes they make will result in a positive work environment.

Since the team's investigation uncovered some fairly significant issues related to operator's performance levels, there may be a tendency to place the blame for these issues entirely on the operators themselves. However, this team also recognizes that no matter how hard people try, humans are fallible and prone to making mistakes. As a result they acknowledge managers' responsibility in this situation: They must identify procedures based on best practices and organize work environments in an effort to minimize the potential for error. Because it is impossible for humans to be vigilant about their work absolutely every second, management must support and facilitate the work that employees do to ensure the best possible performance. With this in mind, the team hopes to implement solutions that are beneficial for both operators and management alike—enhance the work environment to facilitate the work that operators are required to do and achieve improved operator performance.

QUESTIONS FOR DISCUSSION

1. Identify two of the quality improvement tools used in the company's investigation and explain their purpose.
2. Evaluate JDV Houston Division's approach to investigating this problem. What, if anything, should the division have done differently?
3. Discuss three error-proofing solutions that could be used to reduce inventory control related human errors.
4. Compare and contrast how each of the improvement ideas developed by the team have the potential to develop a win-win situation for all involved?
5. Develop at least three control measures that the team could use to sustain the improvements that will be achieved as a result of their Six Sigma project?

REFERENCES/BIBLIOGRAPHY

Grout, J. *Mistake-proofing the Design of Health Care Processes.* Rockville, MD: Agency for Healthcare Research and Quality, 2007. Print.

Pande, P. S., R. P. Neumann, and R. R. Cavanagh. *The Six Sigma Way: How GE, Motorola, and Other Top Companies Are Honing Their Performance.* New York: McGraw-Hill, 2000. Print.

Tague, N. R. *The Quality Toolbox.* 2nd ed. Milwaukee, WI: ASQ Quality P, 2005. Print.

The Importance of High Standards of Corporate Governance and Ethics in Business: The Experience of Lebanon

Andrew Ashwin • Content Developer, Biz/ed, Cengage Learning EMEA

LEARNING OBJECTIVES

After reading this case study and completing the questions, students should be able to do the following:

- *Explain the terms* corporate governance *and* business ethics *and outline the key features of each*
- *Explain why sound corporate governance and business ethics are important in promoting economic development in a country*
- *Explain why bureaucratic and prolonged insolvency procedures constrain enterprise*
- *Outline the role of business ethics in promoting economic development*

This case was prepared for classroom discussion rather than to illustrate either effective or ineffective handling of an administrative, ethical, or legal decision by management. Information was gathered from corporate as well as public sources.

INTRODUCTION

The election of General Michel Suleiman as president in November 2008, the appointment of Saad Hariri to the post of prime minister following elections in June 2009, and the subsequent work to establish a unity government created a sense of purpose and renewed optimism in Lebanon. It is hoped that years of conflict and factional strife can be put to one side, and the country can exploit its high literacy rate and traditional mercantile culture to help the economy grow and the country as a whole to become more prosperous. Gaining some element of political stability is an important first step in the process of building the economy of the country, but in the early 2000s, businesses and the government face major challenges in establishing the institutions and the structures to help encourage enterprise both within and from outside the country to help develop commercial activity.

LEGAL LIMITATIONS AND CORPORATE GOVERNANCE AND BUSINESS ETHICS

Key to this institutional structural development is the establishment of sound corporate governance and business ethics. There are a number of reasons why this is important to Lebanon. Lebanon is perceived to have limited legal structures in place relating to business activity. In particular, there are weaknesses in the law relating to insolvency and bankruptcy. In addition, the distinction between foreign and domestic entities, apart from land ownership, is blurred. Bribery and other forms of corruption are also major problems. In a report published in 2004 by Transparency International on Global Corruption, Lebanon was placed seventy-eighth out of a total of 133 countries. A World Bank *Business Environment Snapshot* report suggests that Lebanon falls behind other Middle East and Northern African (MENA) countries on public accountability, quality of administration, and quality of corporate and public governance.

Problems with Legal Structures

What does this mean for business management and economic development in the country? On the domestic front, there are issues for those who want to set up new businesses. Having clear legal structures in place gives a degree of certainty and builds trust in business activity. These structures encourage entrepreneurship and the development of small and medium enterprises (SMEs) that in turn form the basis for further business growth, investment and the creation of jobs, and the generation of economic activity. The support for new businesses is also improved and the risks of failure can be reduced if appropriate structures are in place to help businesses in the early stages of development. An appropriate and predictable legal framework is a prerequisite for successful business growth. It allows businesses to be established more easily and, if they happen to fail, to maintain investor confidence that the exit from the market will be handled quickly and fairly and give those involved the chance to establish new businesses.

In the early 2000s, this structure does not work as well as it could because rules of governance are not clear. A report from the Organisation for Economic Cooperation and Development (OECD) shows that there are problems relating to the way insolvency is handled in Lebanon compared to other nations. For example, it takes an average of 4 years to complete bankruptcy proceedings compared to a regional average of 3.5 years and 1.7 years for the

OECD country average. The costs of entering bankruptcy for all concerned are also higher. In Lebanon 22% of the estate is swallowed up by the procedure compared to 14.1% in the MENA region and 8.4% in the OECD as a whole. Recovery rates are also lower with only 19 cents in the dollar recovered in Lebanon compared to 29.9 cents in the region and 68.6 cents in the OECD as a whole.

Externally, the lack of appropriate legal structures and adherence to sound corporate governance and business ethics means it is less likely that multinational businesses will look to invest in Lebanon, and as a result the country's foreign domestic investment levels are lower. This situation negatively affects levels of economic development. Unemployment and underemployment in the country are estimated to be as high as 25% and the parlous economic condition as of 2010 is leading to a loss of talented workers who are moving to other Gulf States to find employment. The country has a high number of SMEs with 90% being individual or family-owned and 85% of companies having 10 or fewer employees.

The challenge to businesses and the government, therefore, is to establish legal structures that support and encourage good governance and a high standard of business ethics. Business leaders and government officials recognize that there is a need to establish principles and structures that match international standards, particularly in accounting, banking and finance practice, corporate social responsibility, property rights and business ethics. Former minister for economy and vice governor of the Lebanese central bank, Dr. Nasser Saidi, stated that better corporate governance correlated strongly with better operating performance of firms and higher market valuations. "Building institutions—laws, organizations, rules-of-the game, and a framework for economic activity . . . will allow us to have political and economic governance at a par with international codes and standards, allowing us to compete in regional and world markets."

EFFORTS TO BUILD SUPPORTIVE LEGAL STRUCTURES

Given the general agreement that corporate governance and business ethics are important, what is the country doing to build the structures necessary to establish these principles? One of the main ways to accomplish this task is to develop awareness among business leaders and managers of the importance and meaning of corporate governance and business ethics. Measuring the extent to which business leaders and managers are aware of corporate governance and ethical business principles is a first step to identifying the extent of the problem.

In a paper published in 2006, Y. M. Sidani and coauthors stated:

> Corporations have increasingly become more aware of the need to inculcate issues of ethics, corporate social responsibility, and sustainable development in their decision making. Unethical corporate and managerial behaviours and practices are posing serious obstacles in

the move towards development and prosperity. Lebanese respondents displayed mixed responses to various scenarios of unethical behaviours. Such gaps lead to the conclusion that some decision makers may prefer bottom line indicators over issues of transparency, stakeholders' rights, human capital development and similar concerns. Strategies and intervention mechanisms should be implemented to improve the current situation and pave the way towards growth and sustainable development across Lebanon.[1]

This statement suggests the challenges are significant but it perhaps should not be surprising given the turmoil in the country over the past 30 years.

Rima Charbaji, a senior researcher at Charbaji Consultants, points out that corporate social responsibility is "very much in the developing phases in Lebanon." In her study of 99 business managers in Lebanon, only 5.1% said their companies had a mission statement and 11.1% issued a corporate social responsibility report. Charbaji concludes: "It is clear that there is a lack of Social Responsibility consciousness at the corporate level in Lebanon."

Steps to build awareness, therefore, are taking place, and it is hoped that the political stability that has been negotiated will provide the framework for building on these initiatives. One such example is Bicharaf, a non-profit organization whose name translates from the Arabic as *with honor.* Founded by Dr. Tony Feghali at the American University of Beirut, Bischaraf establishes links and partnerships with businesses and educational institutions to promote academic integrity, awareness, and improved business ethics. It also facilitates discussion and debate, inviting in guests from multinational companies to help share their visions and views on corporate governance and business ethics and to look at ways in which these can be developed in Lebanon as a whole. The results of its meetings are published and available to Lebanese businesses throughout the country.

STANDARDIZING LEGAL AND ETHICAL CODES

In 2004, a *Code of Business Ethics* was launched by the Rassemblement de Dirigeants et Chefs d'Entreprises Libanais (RDCL). The code is voluntary and seeks to promote business ethics, transparency, respect for contracts and commitments, and to counter bribery and other forms of corruption. It also encourages the dissemination of information that is important to the smooth running of business and the building of trust.

Other initiatives include the Convention de Diligence, an agreement signed between banks in Lebanon and the Association of Banks which aims to cement the legislation passed to deal with money laundering. Such legislation helps to ensure that an independent banking control commission is set up alongside a special investigation committee to build trust in the governance of the banking sector in Lebanon that leads to deposits and investment from outside the country and enables companies to be listed on international financial markets.

There are also measures in place to bring structure to the many SMEs that exist. One problem regarding the lack of legal structure is that many businesses fail to survive the death of an owner because the separation of ownership and management is not clear. Separation allows firms easier access to capital and specialist knowledge from outside the business, which helps to broaden the management structure and improve the expertise of those in management positions. This arrangement improves efficiency and productivity and also facilitates greater continuity of businesses from one generation to the next. Without a sound legal and corporate governance framework, these steps would not be possible because those involved would not be certain of the risks involved and the effects on them individually if things go wrong.

The fact that legal and voluntary initiatives are being put in place in Lebanon shows that the country is taking the issue of business ethics and corporate governance seriously. Though awareness and understanding may be at an introductory stage, the truth is the cultural and political background of the country has not been conducive to a coordinated and cohesive approach to the issue. The political settlement has provided the backdrop for the changes being introduced and the opportunity for businesses and government to build structures, institutions, and a philosophy that benefits all stakeholders in Lebanon and provides the climate and structure for attracting more foreign direct investment.

Firms investing in Lebanon will bring with them cultures and philosophies relating to business ethics and corporate governance, which will enrich the business environment in the country and bring wider benefits such as lower costs to business, greater efficiency and productivity, a more inviting investment environment, and higher economic growth. Indeed a World Bank report shows that if MENA countries had matched the quality of high achieving Southeast Asian countries such as Singapore, Malaysia, Thailand, and Indonesia with regard to public administration, economic growth would have been an average of 1% higher each year, as Dr. Saidi once stated: "To build a state one needs to know what state to build."

QUESTIONS FOR DISCUSSION

1. State four key features of good corporate governance and explain why these are important in helping to promote economic development in a country such as Lebanon.

2. Explain, using an appropriate example, the meaning of the term *business ethics*.

3. Outline the key steps being taken by the authorities in Lebanon to improve the awareness of and importance of corporate governance and business ethics to the country.

4. Assess the wider benefits to a country such as Lebanon of improving standards of corporate governance and business ethics.

5. What do you think Dr. Saidi meant when he said, "To build a state one needs to know what state to build"? Justify your answer.

NOTES

1. Sidani, Y.M. Imad, J.Z. Zafar, U.A & Moussawer, T.N. Ethical awareness in Lebanon: promoting or hindering business development? *World Review of Entrepreneurship, Management and Sustainable Development* 2.3 (2006): 258–69.

REFERENCES/BIBLIOGRAPHY

Charbaji, Rima. "What New Challenges are Facing the Local Banks in Lebanon." *The International Arab Journal of Information Technology.* 2.3 (2006): 228–33

Hawkamah/World Bank/OECD/INSOL International. *Building Sound Insolvency Systems in the MENA Region.* Web. 27 January 2011. www.oecd.org/dataoecd/11/52/42551472.pdf

Saidi, Nasser. "Corporate Governance and Business Ethics in Lebanon." Speech delivered at the launch of RDCL "Code of Business Ethics". Beirut. 28 Apr. 2008. Retrieved Apr. 2010 at http://www.bcbkuwait.com/english/Articles/ETHICS.pdf

Sidani, Y. M., J. Z. Imad, U. A. Zafar, and T. N. Moussawer, "Ethical Awareness in Lebanon: Promoting or Hindering Business Development?" *World Review of Entrepreneurship, Management and Sustainable Development* 2.3 (2006): 258–69.

Transparency International. *Global Corruption Report 2004: Special Focus: Political Corruption.* London: Pluto Press, 2004.

World Bank. "Lebanon." Web. 27 January 2011. http://web.worldbank.org/WBSITE/EXTERNAL/COUNTRIES/MENAEXT/LEBANONEXTN/0,,menuPK:294909pagePK:141159piPK:141110theSitePK:294904,00.html

Increasing Efficiency across Business Functions: Enterprise Resource Planning Solutions (ERP) and Inventory Management

Andrew Ashwin • Content Developer, Biz/ed, Cengage Learning EMEA

LEARNING OBJECTIVES

After reading this case study and completing the questions, students should be able to do the following:

- *Outline the role of inventory management as part of a business's functions*
- *Outline the nature and purpose of ERP systems*
- *Identify at least three advantages of ERP systems to a business*
- *Recognize some costs and benefits of ERP systems to different types of business*
- *Explain why scale is an important consideration in installing ERP systems*
- *Explain how small firms are increasingly able to benefit from ERP systems*
- *Assess the factors involved in making a decision to implement an ERP system*

This case was prepared for classroom discussion rather than to illustrate either effective or ineffective handling of an administrative, ethical, or legal decision by management. Information was gathered from corporate as well as public sources.

INTRODUCTION

Managing inventory is a demanding task, regardless of the size of a business. The process generates data—often large amounts of it—and efficient inventory management has an impact on many other functions in the business, notably finance, production, and sales. One of the difficulties facing businesses is drawing together data and integrating it across the key functions in order to improve efficiency and productivity. One of the ways of doing this is to invest in an enterprise resource planning solution (ERP). ERP normally consists of software programs designed to bring together various departments and functions across a business within a single computer system that enables the different functions to operate and share information across the organization. The power of information technology and computers now means that much of the data generated can be captured and manipulated to the benefit of a business and its workers.

Most ERP systems are based on databases that collate, organize, and store the data generated by the business. Given the nature of inventory management and the relationship it has with other functions in the business, ERP solutions can be very beneficial. For example, if sales are generated, information can flow to inventory managers to ensure that sufficient products are on hand to meet these sales and if not to coordinate procurement to satisfy the demand. In addition, ERP can communicate with warehousing, distribution, and finance to coordinate the activities in an efficient manner. A good and well understood ERP system can lead to considerable efficiencies, including warehousing costs, taking in inventory, improving warehouse staff productivity and possibly reducing the staffing required, and cutting vital administrative tasks such as invoice generation.

HOW ERP SOLUTIONS WORK

For an example of how ERP solutions can help in inventory management, imagine a publisher who arranges for a print run of LE300,000 worth of a current bestselling novel. Within three months the inventory is run down, and after a simple redesign of the cover and based on forecast figures, the publisher decides to print another LE200,000 worth of the book. However, the forecast sales figures provided by agents on the ground are inaccurate and, in some cases, have only been posted several weeks after the visit to the book seller. As a result, the publisher receives the second batch of LE200,000 of books but then finds that consumer interest has largely evaporated, and the firm is left with LE150,000 worth of books sitting in the warehouse gathering dust.

The firm had discussed the possibility of investing in a tailored ERP system but the initial investment was quoted as LE75,000, and it decided that the cost was too high. What the publisher failed to recognize is that such a system could have logged all orders in almost real time, integrated this data into sales figures and daily reports on order and inventory progress that could have shown the firm that demand for the second batch was waning. Liquidating the unsold inventory costs at least twice as much as the investment in the ERP system.

One of the problems with ERP is that solutions have been generated for larger businesses that have the finance available to benefit from what can be a major investment and so reap the economies of scale that follow, but for small and medium-sized businesses, the cost has been prohibitive. As of 2010, that is changing, and the following examples from the Middle East can serve to highlight this change.

BUSINESS CONSULT

Business Consult, which began in 2001 and is based in Amman, Jordan, was originally part of Saadi Communications Systems. Its aim was to develop and provide software solutions for other businesses and to help them improve operations and operational efficiency. The company was the first one in Jordan to offer ERP solutions based on software developed internationally. Business Consult has established a partnership with Epicor Software Corporation, a U.S.-based software solutions company.

Business Consult specializes in systems that involve inventory management, human resources, business intelligence, and customer relationship management. Between 2001 and late 2010, it built a client list that included companies in Jordan and across the Middle East. In the late 2000s, Business Consult signed a cooperation agreement with Dubai Construction Company (DCC) to implement an ERP solution based on Epicor's iScala software. DCC is based in Dubai but runs projects across the Middle East. In the late 2000s, it completed the JD90 million construction of the Vertex Tower and residencies in Jordan and the Commerce One building as part of the Abdali Urban Regeneration Project. The new building is over 16,744 square yards (14,000 sq. m.) and includes over 3,229 square yards (2,700 sq. m.) for retail use, just under 8,372 square yards (7,000 sq. m.) for offices, and 5,382 square yards (4,500 sq. m.) for parking. The scale of these two projects alone gives some idea of the complex nature of the operations carried out by DCC. As a construction company, its efficient management of inventory, including raw materials, plant, and equipment, is essential to ensure that such developments meet stakeholder needs, within budget.

DCC entered into agreement with Business Consult to use the iScala ERP software mainly because Business Consult could create custom-made financial systems that manage virtually all the company's transactions and help to improve the management of DCC's procurement and inventory. It also allows the company to link different departments in the organization and facilitates monitoring of each. In addition, the system allows DCC to generate profitability reports for each project it is working on, which is vital in successful financial management of large-scale construction projects such as those it has had in Jordan.

PHARMA WORLD HOLDINGS

However, it is not only large businesses such as DCC that benefit from ERP systems. In Egypt, Pharma World Holdings seeks to capture additional market share in the country. Based in Dubai, Pharma is a joint venture between Fund I, Banaja International Group, and Ithmar Capital. It developed Third Party Logistics (3PL), a solution that helps improve efficiency in international trade, warehousing, inventory management, marketing, and distribution. Pharma seeks to expand in Egypt and across the Egyptian Free Zone into countries such as Morocco, Algeria, Libya, and Tunisia.

As understanding, experience, and expertise in ERP has developed, solutions for small and medium-sized firms have become more readily available. In Egypt, a number of firms are developing ERP solutions specifically for small and medium businesses that allow them to implement ERP systems. In some cases, these will be complete solutions. In other cases, firms will use some modules covering key areas of the business and then build on this use by adding in other modules, which may eventually cover the whole organization. This process makes the development of ERP systems for smaller businesses more affordable.

ADVANTAGES AND DISADVANTAGES OF ERP FOR SMALLER COMPANIES

Some of these solutions are based on larger scale ones provided by large companies such as Oracle and SAP. These companies see a market in the Middle East for smaller solutions packages tailored for the smaller business. These are being offered to businesses at lower prices, making them affordable investments for those who previously may have believed that such solutions were beyond their reach. One firm that helps small and medium enterprises (SMEs) benefit from ERP solutions is Gazayerli Group Egypt. Gazayerli advises businesses on solutions that can be developed relatively cheaply using available software, likely to be in existence already in the business such as Microsoft's Access database application. If the business is small and generates relatively small amounts of data that are not time critical then Access may be perfectly suitable for the development of a useful and valuable solution. If more demanding data are generated and need to be maintained and reported in real time, then a firm might invest in a structured query language (SQL) server. SQL is a computer language developed specifically to handle databases. The cost involved may be less than getting a smaller scale solution developed by firms such as Microtech, Oracle, and IBM, which would be the next logical step in the process.

However, there are disadvantages to firms, whatever their size, in implementing ERP solutions. One of the most obvious is the fact that employees have to be prepared and trained for change, which is always difficult to manage. Gazayerli points out that for every LE1,000 spent in investment on the hardware for an ERP solution, a firm needs to set aside from LE3,000 to LE4,000 for associated costs such as the software development training and ongoing support services.

Providers, therefore, encourage firms considering ERP solutions to think carefully about the nature of the business and what the firm wants such a solution to do for the business.

Raya IT, one of Egypt's fastest growing companies, has considerable experience in the development of ERP solutions and is responsible for 80 of the largest implementations in Egypt. Based in Cairo, it began in 1999 when seven existing Egyptian IT companies agreed to merge. As of 2010, it had over 3,000 employees and offices in the Gulf, Saudi Arabia, Algeria, Nigeria, and in the United States.

Working with clients, whatever their size, to establish a clear understanding of the business model and what it needs to achieve is essential to the success of the solution. This means that Raya will spend considerable time quizzing the senior managers to get a full understanding of the business and what its workflows are regardless of whether a function of the business is being included in the solution. This initial planning process makes easier any decision to add modules at a subsequent stage. Raya also points to the importance of managing expectations of management team members to ensure that they are aware of the time that is needed to enable staff to get trained in and used to using and exploiting the new system.

Inventory is a key part of business because minor improvements can lead to significant savings. This principle is true for small and large businesses, given the vital role that inventory management plays in improving efficiency not only in inventory but across related functions. Inventory management systems for businesses of all sizes can benefit from such computer systems as those offered by ERP solutions. A well designed ERP solution can help to answer a large number of the questions that businesses have to ask in relation to inventory management. These questions may concern the following topics:

- The total cost of current inventory policy
- Optimal ordering and associated costs
- Relevance of policy across a number of products
- Accuracy of purchasing and accounting data
- The need to incorporate potential shocks to the system
- The need for an inventory management system that can improve product availability

For large and small businesses, if some or all of these questions can be answered through an appropriate ERP solution, then productivity and efficiency improvements are more likely.

QUESTIONS FOR DISCUSSION

1. Explain why effective inventory management a key element in the success of many businesses?
2. Outline the purpose of an enterprise resource planning (ERP) system?
3. Consider the potential costs and benefits to small business of implementing an ERP system.
4. To what extent is scale important in establishing an effective ERP system?
5. Analyze the key factors that any business needs to take into account in deciding whether to implement an ERP system?

Key Elements in Strategic Planning: Cases from the Middle East

Andrew Ashwin • Content Developer, Biz/ed, Cengage Learning EMEA

LEARNING OBJECTIVES

After reading this case study and completing the questions, students should be able to do the following:

- *Define the essential characteristic of the term strategy*
- *Explain some of the key issues to consider in strategic planning*
- *Explain how short-term investment decisions can help deliver long-term strategic goals*
- *Explain how strategic planning can help generate competitive advantage*

This case was prepared for classroom discussion rather than to illustrate either effective or ineffective handling of an administrative, ethical, or legal decision by management. Information was gathered from corporate as well as public sources.

INTRODUCTION

Strategic planning involves various elements. In many cases, decision-making with regard to strategic planning is not about immediate results to the bottom line; instead, managers may have to consider spending big on investment projects that will build future capacity and flexibility. Doing so requires managers and leaders to see into the future, not an easy task by any means. Some of their decisions are made with the intention of building some competence that will allow the firm to exploit a possible competitive advantage at some point in the future. These decisions may not see bottom-line results for many years, but the skill of the leader is seeing that investment made now can build the potential of the business to better meet the market demands and the needs of its customers and other stakeholders.

This case study presents some examples and attempts to explain the decision-making involved in each. The definition of strategy must be kept at the forefront of the mind as we move through this case study; strategy is a comprehensive plan for accomplishing an organization's goals. The management role is to identify the "alignment between the organization and its environment and the achievement of strategic goals." (Griffin)

ETIHAD AIRWAYS

Etihad Airways, the national airline of the United Arab Emirates (UAE), is an expanding business. The popularity of the UAE with its businesses and tourism industry is set to increase in the coming years, and Etihad is planning on being a major player in this expansion. The chief operations officer of Etihad, Richard Hill, has commented that the company expects its flight numbers to triple in the next ten years, and as a result it has to plan ahead for this anticipated expansion. The anticipated expansion requires Etihad to have sufficient aircraft to handle the increased number of flights and also sufficient staff. Even if planes and staff are in place, other major logistical management issues need to be considered, and investment in such capacity is vital to the long-term success of the airline and its strategic aims.

To help it achieve its aims, Etihad invested in workforce management software. The software was developed by KronosR. Operating an airline requires planes and crew to be available, a major logistical challenge. The airline has to make sure that it has the planes and the crew in the right locations to meet its flight schedules, and management of this process has to be optimized for the company to be efficient, keep costs under control, meet customer needs, and maintain employee morale.

KRONOSR

KronosR provides software that takes into consideration all variables involved in such planning and delivers optimal solutions that meet the aims of the business (i.e., managing costs). The process is automated to make sure that employees are deployed effectively and that they get sufficient periods of rest to recover from the rigors of flying across the globe. Richard Hill has said: "The adoption of the KronosR solutions will enable us to increase operational efficiency and improve our strategic resource planning processes to sustain our long-term business strategies."

Many businesses rely on information as a key part of their business, and in order for information to flow, communication networks have to be in place. Construction planners must ensure that buildings are outfitted with networks for transmitting information. These communication networks have to be capable of carrying increasing amounts of data, including voice, video, and other content, and these have to be carried across both fixed and mobile networks. The services will be used by businesses and individuals and by network providers and carriers; therefore, each system has to be robust and capable of meeting growing needs.

WIRELESS SERVERS

In the UAE, the expansion in construction, especially the growth of high-rise buildings, brought new challenges for meeting communications requirements. To this end, *du*, one of the leading providers of broadband connectivity and fixed and mobile telephony in the UAE, signed an agreement with *iBwave Solutions*, an in-building design and planning software provider, to produce hi-tech indoor wireless networks for high-rise buildings in the Emirates.

Users of these buildings will require fast and reliable data access to support the ever-increasing range of mobile technologies. For both companies, the agreement represented an important step in meeting strategic aims. *du* wanted to become the telecom service of choice in the UAE, and to do this its services had to be efficient and reliable, wherever the customer is. For *iBwave*, forging a link with *du* showed that its services offer value added and that both can share a vision for the future of communications technology. In terms of future growth, this sort of tie-up is important to both businesses. For *iBwave*, the agreement offers an opportunity to expand in the UAE.

Hatem Bamatraf, senior vice president for network development for *du* said:

> du *and* iBwave *share a common goal to provide customers with state-of-the-art wireless mobility services in the UAE. [The new product] will enable us to optimize network efficiency to deliver reliable and innovative services that fulfil our promise to enable better user experience of various services for our customers. We are confident that [the new product] will ensure us long-term sustainability within our operational structure through secured documentation and flexible designs, allowing us to support current and future technologies and deliver on our promise of product and service excellence*

ELECTRONIC PAYMENT NETWORKS

Iraq faced considerable problems in the early 2000s, but as the country emerged from the chaos of war, steps were being taken to return to some sort of normalcy. Part of this process involved developing the systems that are needed to enable ordinary people to go about their business, which includes being able to use credit and debit cards across the country. Visa, one of the major electronic payments networks, announced in 2009 a deal with Al Amwal, an electronic banking services company, a group of 13 Iraqi banks and the Bank of Baghdad, to expand the network of Visa acceptance points in the country. The deal will enable more Iraqis to have and use a Visa card.

The agreement means that many more people and business in Iraq will be able to use the Visa network. Doing so will help speed up payments, encourage spending, make spending more convenient, encourage businesses to expand, and increase the choice of credit and debit cards in the country. It also means that visitors to Iraq, whether on business or as tourists, can use their cards in a wider variety of outlets, which again makes traveling much easier. Hotels, restaurants, travel agencies, and duty-free shops are expected to take advantage of the agreement to provide these services. The move promotes the transition from a cash-based economy, which inherently limits the potential for growth, to a cash-and-credit based one.

This arrangement with Visa is good news for businesses, individuals who use these services, and the economy as a whole. The improvement in payment services encourages additional spending, which in turn helps to provide a boost to the economy as a whole and generates economic growth. Tony Gougassian, Visa's area manager for Iraq, Levant, and Qatar, said:

> We are delighted to extend our global payment services in Iraq and help bring the social and economic benefits which come with electronic payment acceptance. These include stimulating economic growth, promoting transparency and accountability, while also increasing the number of people with access to the formal banking system. Our partnership with Al Amwal and Bank of Baghdad means that Iraqi consumers will be able to take advantage of the increased security, flexibility and convenience that a Visa card offers. Visa debit and credit cards will provide Iraqis and those visiting the country, with a safe and convenient way to shop and access funds, both at home and abroad. (Visa Expands)

For the companies involved, the agreement represents an important opportunity for expanding and providing improved services. As the country rebuilds, services such as banking have to be rebuilt also. Al Amwal has operations in all the Iraqi governorates but wants to expand the number and increase the convenience of its services. As a first step, it hoped to increase the number of point-of-sale (POS) devices in the country from 200 to 400 by the end of 2009, and the link with Visa was anticipated to enable it to meet its strategic aim of increasing the opportunities for Iraqis to make electronic payments.

The Bank of Baghdad aspires to being the leading financial services provider in Iraq. To this end, it aims to make the business and individual customers' experience with the bank much easier and more convenient, and the agreement with Visa will help in this endeavor. The Bank of Baghdad hoped in 2009 to increase the number of its branches from 25 in the middle of 2009 to 35 by the end of that year. In early 2011, it had managed to open 34 branches.

HUMAN RESOURCES MANAGEMENT

Sage Software is a supplier of human resources management (HRM), customer relationship management (CRM), and enterprise resource planning (ERP) software to businesses. ERP allows businesses to plan and manage their resources, both internal and external. These resources might include capital assets and human and financial resources. In seeking out new business, Sage looked for countries where spending on these types of software solutions is increasing, and one market where this is happening is Kuwait, where spending on ERP solutions was forecast to increase by 25% in 2010.

Sage hoped to take advantage of this expansion by working with two partners based in Kuwait to expand its presence in the country. Eastern Solutions and the Arabesque Group launched new products in conjunction with Sage at a February 2010 roadshow held in the JW Marriot Hotel in Kuwait. Users of the software were able to see their cash position easily, monitor cash flow, and enable managers to make decisions faster and more accurately based on reliable information generated from the business, by the software.

Sage and its partners in Kuwait hoped to develop their own businesses but also facilitate the development of other businesses in Kuwait. Those businesses that are using the services provided by Sage and its partners have the opportunity to position themselves favorably for the upturn in the global economy following the recession of 2008 and 2009. These companies have their own individual strategic aims but need the sort of solutions provided by Sage to be better able to meet their goals.

Sage's sales manager for the Gulf region, Reggie Fernandes, summed up the benefits to the group's clients:

> *These new solutions will provide tremendous help to organisations who are seeking to strategically position themselves and gain the lead in the impending upturn. We have packed them with multi-national and multi-company capabilities that will simplify management of data from multiple companies, in addition to technologies to secure business integrity. Our plan is to aggressively address the needs of the Kuwaiti market by developing solutions that will add value to our customers' operations, so that our local clients, which include NBK Capital, Bader Al Sultan, Al Ghanim Industries, Gulf University of Science & Technology, Hits Telecom, Al Fanar Investment Company and Al Manar Financing & Leasing will be the first to benefit from the latest innovations in IT solutions.*

These examples highlight the importance of having the right infrastructure to enable businesses to operate effectively. Strategic aims are not always simply met by increasing sales; gaining competitive advantage may derive from improving the internal operations of the business to enable it to reduce its costs, improve efficiency, and productivity, and thus be in a more competitive position. The complexity of global business requires that more and more companies rely on solutions providers who are specialists in particular fields to give them the edge they need to achieve these aims. The strategy may be, therefore, to improve the inner workings and efficiency of the firm so that it can better compete, and such software solutions can be an important part of this strategy.

QUESTIONS FOR DISCUSSION

1. Using appropriate examples, distinguish between *strategy* and *tactics*.
2. Using an example to provide context, identify and explain three key considerations in formulating any strategic plan.
3. "The adoption of the KronosR solutions will enable us to increase operational efficiency and improve our strategic resource planning processes to sustain our long-term business strategies." What do you think Richard Hill meant by this statement? Explain your answer.

4. Using an example, analyze the importance of having high quality infrastructure in successful strategic planning.

5. To what extent is strategic planning the key to building competitive advantage? Illustrate your answer with examples.

REFERENCES/BIBLIOGRAPHY

"Etihad Airways Selects KronosR to Improve Operational Efficiency" *Al Bawaba*. 18 November 2009. Retrieved Apr. 2010 from http://www1.albawaba.com/en/business/etihad-airways-selects-kronosr-improve-operational-efficiency

Griffin, R.W. *Management (ME Edition)*. Andover, Hampshire: Cengage Learning, 2008. Print.

Ortiz, Victor Philip. "Kuwait Spending on ERP to Increase by 25 per cent in 2010, says Sage Software." *Pcmag-mideast.com*. 14 Feb. 2010. Retrieved Apr. 2010 from http://www.pcmag-mideast.com/2010/02/14/kuwait-spending-on-erp-to-increase-by-25-per-cent-in-2010-says-sage-software/<

"Visa Expands Presence in Iraq." *AMEinfo.com*. 2 Aug. 2009. Retrieved 29 January 2011 from http://www.ameinfo.com/205413.html

Productivity in Palestine: A Better Route to Improving Standards of Living?

Andrew Ashwin • Content Developer, Biz/ed, Cengage Learning EMEA

LEARNING OBJECTIVES

After reading this case study and completing the questions, students should be able to do the following:

- *Give a definition of productivity*
- *State the main definitions of efficiency—productive, technical, allocative, and social*
- *Outline the key drivers of productivity*
- *Outline the main benefits of productivity to a country in both an economic and a wider social and political context*
- *State the main constraints facing the construction and agriculture industries in Palestine*
- *Analyze some of the advantages that Palestine has in helping to improve productivity*
- *Assess the productivity improvements in the construction and agriculture industries in Palestine*

This case was prepared for classroom discussion rather than to illustrate either effective or ineffective handling of an administrative, ethical, or legal decision by management. Information was gathered from corporate as well as public sources.

INTRODUCTION

In any business in any economy, productivity is linked to efficiency and profitability in a firm and in the national economy as a whole. In the region controlled by the Palestinian Authority (PA), productivity takes on a new and perhaps even more important role. In a country ravaged by conflict and subject to severe restrictions on the movement of goods, labor, and capital, the challenges facing managers in trying to improve productivity are especially challenging.

Critical factors that influence levels of productivity in any economy include:

- Skill level of the workers in the industry
- Quality of supervision and management
- Amount, quality, and reliability of equipment and workers' ability to use the equipment
- Quality of workmanship
- Effectiveness of procurement systems
- Skill level of project managers
- Management and leadership skills
- Social and economic climate in which the business operates

At first glance it might seem that efforts to improve productivity in businesses in Palestine are caught in a no-win situation, given the social, economic, and political climate acting against most of these critical factors. However, despite these challenges, improving productivity is key to achieving sustainability and stability in Palestine's economy in general and for the small- to medium-sized businesses, which account for almost 60% of its private sector. Humans are nothing if not creative and resourceful, however, and there is evidence that, despite the odds being stacked against them, managers and businesses in Palestine have found ways to utilize limited resources to bring about improved productivity.

THE CONSTRUCTION INDUSTRY IN PALESTINE

The construction industry in Palestine poses problems for managers committed to improving productivity. Cramped living conditions, the devastation caused by ongoing war with Israel, and internal conflicts among members of the PA fuel a high demand for new construction. Undertaking new construction, however, is hampered by environmental considerations, functionality, and style. While coping with limited resources and a competitive marketplace, managers must strive for good quality in their construction projects. Finding ways to improve productivity, which assumes improvements in quality, is a means to improving performance and competitiveness.

To improve productivity in this industry, managers have to overcome certain pervasive problems. First, at the business level, managers need to find ways to improve monitoring and feedback between themselves the workforce; Palestinian construction businesses must invest in developing project leadership skills. Linked to this effort is the task of improving the information flow between management and workers. Second, according to an United Nations Relief and Works Agency (UNRWA) for Palestinian refugees in the Near East report (UNRWA, 2006) the initial design and drawings used by construction companies can be improved. The difficulty here is that these drawings are frequently revised and amended, which significantly affects the project management process and delays construction.

Palestinian businesses can work on these internal factors to improve productivity, but certain external factors lie outside managers' control. Managers do not always have sufficient access to plants, and equipment is often unavailable or unreliable. Moreover, Israeli restrictions often cause short supply of goods and additional delays. Productivity improvements would increase markedly if such external problems could be overcome.

OTHER PALESTINE-BASED INDUSTRIES

Exploiting the skills Palestinians already have is essential for developing the economy and helping businesses to grow. Nearly half the population of Palestine are under eighteen years of age. Young Palestinians have some facility with information technology despite the infrastructure problems in the country. Given that wages are lower in Palestine than many of its neighbors, multinational companies can be encouraged to outsource work to Palestinian businesses. Managers must find ways to promote the skills that of their businesses to these international companies.

Information Technology

For example, Asal Technologies in Ramallah, which was established in 2000, is involved in software development, outsourcing, and hardware design and testing. Its dynamic approach to building relationships illustrates how companies in Palestine can develop business and improve productivity. The first business in Palestine to receive the ISO9001:2000 certificate in software development, Asal Technologies has developed some impressive clients, including Volvo, Intel, Cisco Systems, Motorola, Greater than Zero (gtz), and Birzeit University, the first higher education institution to be established in Palestine. Asal Technologies has even forged business relationships with companies in Israel: Chip manufacturer Winbond, which is registered on the Taiwanese stock exchange but has a design center in Tel Aviv, has outsourced product development work to Asal, citing advantages in terms of cost, proximity, and sharing the same language and culture. However, Murad Tahboub, managing director of Asal, also recognizes that there are other important factors to winning such business; having workers who can speak English well and high levels of productivity are two important factors that allow Asal to capture clients outside Palestine.

Family-run Businesses and Women in Business

Other factors Palestine has in its favor regarding productivity and improved efficiency include family-run businesses and the contribution of networking women in business. There are a large number of family-run businesses in the country, and research suggests that they have better management performance than non-family firms (Sabri, 2008). Family-run businesses also tend to have higher labor productivity, lower marketing costs through the production of generic product brands, and favorable sales credit policies.

The role of business women is also proving to be a positive factor. In 2006, a group of Palestinian business women formed the Business Women's Forum (BWF) to assist in the development of important skills in women in the business community. Providing networking opportunities, the BWF provides women with a forum in which to share ideas, skills, and management experience, all of which enable women to set up new businesses and develop existing ones. This organization illustrates the benefits of sharing business management ideas and practice. It also provides a collective tool for urging authorities to develop legislation designed to protect the interests of businesswomen. This combined effort can lead to improved relationships and provide a climate for entrepreneurship and improved productivity.

CHALLENGES FACING AGRICULTURE

Agriculture represents around 5.6% of the Palestinian economy according to data from the Palestinian Central Bureau of Statistics. The industry is affected by a number of factors, including the availability of land and water and access to markets. It is also affected by conflicts that destroy land and trees, kill animals, and limit farmers' access their lands. Some farms have even been cut into two by the ongoing conflict. Thus, agriculture faces similar problems to many other industries in Palestine.

Despite these pervasive problems, efforts to improve the management and productivity of agriculture have been made, and there are some signs of success. For example, partnerships with various agencies, such as the Palestinian Agribusiness Partnership Activity (PAPA) and the Palestinian Enterprise Development project, have helped improve the skills of agricultural workers. PAPA has created around 1,400 new jobs in the industry. The Palestinian Enterprise Development project has designated $12.1 million to support the creation of partnerships with over 100 Palestinian industries, including agriculture. These partnerships seek to boost employment, offer training, generate investment, improve quality standards, and increase exports.

Olive Growing and Production

Vital to increasing productivity in agriculture is making better use of available land. Irrigation projects are crucial to this effort. For example, olive trees are suitable for the region because they tolerate poor soil and limited water resources. However, growing olives is not the only way to improve productivity and generate wealth. As with other commodities in agriculture, the real value added occurs in processing commodities. Improving productivity here requires improved access to equipment and machinery designed to help lower costs while improving the quality of production. Aid programs can help in the procurement of pressing and storage equipment and bottling machinery. Olive farmers can also learn new ways to improve harvesting, storage, processing, and distribution. By gaining access to harvesting crates, stainless steel storage tanks, pressing mills and bottling equipment, farmers can dramatically increase productivity.

Negotiations with the Fairtrade Foundation have helped olive growers access international markets and supported the price they receive. Fairtrade olive oil from Palestine appeared on shop shelves in Europe in 2009. The development of cooperatives and the prospect of higher prices for their olives mean that businesses can afford to invest in additional productivity improvements. These include training for farmers on pruning and harvesting techniques, purchasing processing machinery, installing irrigation, constructing communal storage facilities, and strengthening distribution infrastructure.

These examples highlight the key drivers of productivity improvements in three different industries. While specific issues are associated with each industry, there are a number of common factors that managers and authorities have to consider when seeking to boost productivity. Typically, these common factors include the skills of the labor force, the quality and reliability of equipment and machinery, improved access to markets, and, last but certainly not least, the quality of management and leadership in driving projects forward.

This case study has highlighted some key drivers in different contexts. In any situation the challenges are significant, but given its political and social climate, the improvements in Palestine in productivity seen in different industries testify to the determination and skills of those involved to rise above contextual problems and improve their lives.

QUESTIONS FOR DISCUSSION

1. What is productivity and how can it be improved?
2. Discuss the importance of productivity to the development of a country such as Palestine?
3. Consider the similarities and differences in the productivity improvements in the construction and agriculture industries in Palestine?
4. To what extent improvements in productivity help Palestine overcome its political problems?
5. Assess the difficulties face businesses in Palestine in improving productivity?

REFERENCES/BIBLIOGRAPHY

"Cooperation between Israeli and Palestinian Companies Sets the Pace for Building Peace." *Israel Ministry of Foreign Affairs.* 7 July 2008. Retrieved 31 Jan. 2011 from http://www.mfa.gov.il/MFA/Israel+beyond+politics/Cooperation%20between%20Israeli%20and%20Palestinian%20companies%20sets%20the%20pace%20for%20building%20peace%20% 207-Jul-2008

"Palestinian Olive oil to carry the FAIRTRADE Mark in 2009." Fairtrade Foundation. Web. 15 Dec. 2008. Retrieved Apr. 2010 from http://www.fairtrade.org.uk/press_office/press_releases_and_statements/december_2008/palestinian_olive_oil_to_carry_the_fairtrade_mark_in_2009.aspx

Palestinian Central Bureau of Statistics. Web. Retrieved Apr. 2010 from http://www.pcbs.gov.ps

Sabri, Nidal Rashid. "The Palestinian Family Business." Hyderabad: ICFAI University Press, 2008. Web. 28 Feb. 2008. http://ssrn.com/abstract=1097686

Tao, Jingzhou, and Edward Hillier. "A Tale of Two Companies." *China Business Review* May-June 2008. Web. 15 Feb. 2011. http://www.chinabusinessreview.com/public/0805/commentary.html

United Nations Relief and Works Agency for Palestinian refugees in the Near East. Projects completion report, 2006.

Pushing to Make Hyundai a Global Player: Scenes in the Career of Chairman Chung Mong-Koo

Lee W. Lee • Professor, Department of Management and Organization, Central Connecticut State University

LEARNING OBJECTIVES

This case examines moments in the career of Hyundai Motor Company Chairman Chung Mong-Koo (often referred to in South Korean media as "MK"). Episodes in this study are constructed based on stories reported in the South Korean local news media. After reading the case, students should be able to do the following:

- *Apply leadership theories to explain MK's actions and activities in various circumstances in his career*
- *Understand the role of corporate and national culture and its contribution or obstruction to becoming a global competitor*
- *Assess the role of communication in effective leadership*
- *Explore the ethical and social responsibilities of a company and its leadership in the local and global business context*
- *Analyze financial statements for performance management and strategic planning*

This case was prepared for classroom discussion rather than to illustrate either effective or ineffective handling of an administrative, ethical, or legal decision by management. Information was gathered from corporate as well as public sources.

BACKGROUND

Activity at the site of the new Hyundai-Kia plant in West Point, Georgia, was buzzing. Staff members at the plant were finishing preparations for the visit of the company chairman, Chung Mong-Koo (often known as "MK" in the media and within Hyundai Motor Company). It was the last week of

February 2010 and MK was attending the groundbreaking ceremony for a new Kia manufacturing plant. Construction of the plant was due to be completed in Spring 2011, with the capacity to produce more than 300,000 vehicles a year. If sales increase as projected, the plant was expected to operate at its full capacity by 2012 (Tae-gyu).

Everything seemed to be moving as planned. Visiting executives mingled with the hosting management team and workers. Local managers reported that the construction plan had been making steady progress, exactly to plan. There were lively greetings and excited talk about the prospect of construction and production. In the middle of the meeting, in a large conference room, an executive assistant quietly walked in and whispered something into MK's ear. MK turned stiff and mortified. He could not hide the anger and frustration in his face.

It was just one day before Toyota's chairman Akio Toyoda was due to appear in front of the U.S. Congress to apologize for problems that had surfaced with technical aspects of the company's cars. Toyota's sales had dropped as a result. Hyundai had been enjoying historically high sales in 2009 and projections suggested a continuing strong upward trend. It was a great opportunity for Hyundai to win market share from the dominant Toyota Motor Company. Or was it? A problem that bothered the management for a while was becoming an unavoidable reality: a faulty front-door latch in its Hyundai Sonata model. It was bad timing. The issue would cause Hyundai the same kind of bad media that Toyota was receiving in the American news media. MK had to make a decision and had to make it quickly.

MING-KOO TAKES OVER HYUNDAI FROM HIS FATHER

It was a rough beginning for MK, the second son of Chairman Chung Ju-Yung, founder of Hyundai Company. Taking over the motor company was not easy for MK. He had to replace his uncle, Se-Young, who built the company and fiercely resisted MK's attempt to take over the business. It was a tough fight from the outset. Everybody knew Ju-Young had the ultimate authority over the fate of Hyundai. Since Mr. Ju-Yung Chung is the founder of the Hyundai Company and the ultimate patriarch (as father or oldest brother) of Chung family, he commanded unrivaled power and influence over the entire Hyundai chaebol group. As such, he was often called 'King-Chairman.'

Ju-Yung began by selling rice in 1930, but after the Korean civil war in the 1950s, his business grew and he prospered. In the civil war years (1950–1953), the entire Korean peninsula suffered major infrastructure damage. During the following decades of the Cold War, the economy of South Korea improved dramatically. Under the strong leadership of Ju-Yung, Hyundai grew at a remarkable pace. Its presence in various industries grew, and its revenues multiplied. Ju-Yung's businesses ranged from profitable sugar and flour to steel and machinery to ship building. To manage the company's diversified activities, Ju-Yung delegated responsibility; for the motor vehicle manufacturing business, he delegated sole authority to his younger brother, Chung Se-Young.

Nicknamed Pony Chung after his first successful model, the Pony, Chairman and President Chung Se-Young dedicated himself to building the Hyundai Motor Company. Arguably the most successful Korean-made car since the civil war, this car was for many Koreans what the Volkswagen is for Germans: the people's car. Given his illustrious career as Chairman of Hyundai, it was likely a surprise that Se-Young was challenged so aggressively for the company's chairmanship by his nephew, Mong-Koo.

Unlike many other family disputes, this Hyundai family conflict was not so secretive. Pony Chung acquiesced to his big brother Ju-Young's demand, giving up power to MK. The restructuring, announced on 4 December 1997, involved replacing all the people associated with Pony Chung's leadership team. Everybody thought that Pony Chung was finished. At the shareholders meeting on 26 February 1998, however, many attendants were surprised to hear the announcement of four new board members, all from Pony Chung's team. It was clear Pony Chung had fought back. Giving up the company he had built for the past three decades was too much for him to accept.

A debate ensued over whether to separate the car manufacturing from the other Hyundai businesses. MK wanted control of the entire company. After all, Hyundai Motor Company contributed more than 10% of the entire Hyundai group's earnings. That percentage reached around 25% if Hyundai Motor Services were included. MK believed the motor side of the business could not be separated from the group; Pony Chung did not agree. He had a hidden plan, to break the motor company off from the group and put it under his sole control.

There was another complication. MK and his father were preparing to buy Kia Motors Corporation, Hyundai's rival in the Korean domestic market. Kia was financially strapped and available to the highest bidder. MK and his father were involved in the aggressive bidding process. On this move, Pony Chung also disagreed. He believed a merger might jeopardize his chances to take over Hyundai Motor's management. Ultimately, he hoped to separate the motor company from the entire Hyundai group, and was a passive player at best in the bidding process for Kia. Through many small and yet critical management decisions, Pony Chung attempted to stop or minimize his nephew's influence. He made sure that all the board members were on his side in case the internal struggle evolved into a legal battle. Key sales managers and engineers were his loyal subordinates. But all of this effort was ultimately futile. Ju-Yung, the 86-year-old founder of the Hyundai, forced his younger brother to retire, giving up any claim to the Hyundai empire and acknowledging Ju-Yung's son, MK, as its head.

NEW CHALLENGES

Upon taking over the management of Hyundai from his well-respected uncle, MK had to be conscious of much criticism about his management abilities. While he had acquired some management training under his father and managed an automobile services company, he was accused of using vague language in his communications and was often portrayed as unintelligent in the media. No one could doubt, though, that he was determined and single-minded.

MK's first challenge was to show he could do better than his uncle. He put forth his global vision, promising that he would make Hyundai Motors one of the top five auto makers in the global market. Engineers and manufacturing workers were put under extreme pressure to meet this goal. Sales managers were pushed. Employees at all levels experienced pressures and expectations that they had not previously been accustomed to. The existing engineering process and quality improvement expectations did not catch up with demand for production. The continuous push for sales and production generated some serious complaints internally and from consumers. So MK made a tough decision. On January 14, 2000, Hyundai Motors announced a voluntary recall of all minivans for free-inspection and reinstallation of particular parts. The company distributed a press release about its voluntary recall to inspect and replace parts for any defect discovered in its product. The recall was unprecedented in Korea (Weekly Dong-A). Many thought the action unnecessary, given the company's virtual monopoly in Korea. The move, however, was designed to change the international image of Hyundai, demonstrating the company's transparency and quality. There were five recalls in six months. Management dismissed concerns about the frequency of recalls, suggesting that recalls are common even among top global automakers. The demand for cars in the domestic market of Korea practically exploded.

MK's strong leadership helped Hyundai to make great strides in the global automotive market in the late 1990s and early 2000s, but his autocratic style also caused his company and himself controversy and punishment as well. To understand how MK was able to act so decisively, and to understand how this decisiveness nearly led to his downfall, it is necessary to understand the Korean system of chaebol.

KOREAN CULTURE AND CHAEBOL

Korean culture and chaebol are factors in the process and determination of management succession. *Chaebol* is the Korean version of a corporate conglomerate. A chaebol group has many companies under its control. It is similar to Japanese keiretsu (e.g., Mitsubishi or Sumitomo group) and U.S. conglomerates (e.g., Citigroup or GE) but not identical to them. Unlike an American conglomerate, which integrates many companies in related industries, a chaebol extends to any lucrative industries under the ownership of one person or family. The Chaebol Hyundai, for instance, was involved in various related and unrelated industries such as automobile manufacturing, shipping, transportation, electronics, and steel. Although each member company is legally independent and has its own board and chairperson, its strategic decisions and operations are heavily influenced or controlled by the parent company or the group chairperson. Japanese keiretsu stresses the integration of smaller companies, whereas chaebol is managed top-down by a person or family.

In the early period of Korea's economic development, President Park Chung-hee (1917–1973; president of South Korea, 1963-1979) supported a few large companies (e.g., Hyundai, Samsung, and Daewoo) so that each company was large enough to get international funding and to undertake major national building contracts such as the construction of highways and railroads. These selected few companies monopolized the market—domestically at least—and were able to grow into international corporations. Following South Korea's initial nation-building period during the 1960s and 1970s, these few chaebol groups accumulated wealth and exercised considerable political influence. They also had access to virtually limitless finances via the mostly state-run banking system, whereas ordinary citizens had only meager banking resources for financing their homes or small businesses.

Like any industrialized and capitalistic country, the ownership of individual member companies of a chaebol in Korea is broken into millions of shares. However, founders of the chaebol are still perceived to be the owners of these publicly traded companies, wielding complete and unchallenged control of management. Consequently, chaebol founders, including Ju-Yung Chung, built formidable business empires. Ju-Yung's authority over the Hyundai chaebol group was never challenged or threatened by any internal or even external force. This fact reflects the traditional Korean patriarchal system.

In the early 2000s, public pressure to separate chaebol management from business ownership mounted in South Korea. But as of 2010 there was no sign of the owner family system changing or relinquishing power over large companies. Attempts have been made to ease their control over an entire group of companies. The most recent reform allowed a nominal parent company to be set up to manage subordinating companies in exchange for banning their cross-investment back to the parent company. However, controlling shareholders of the parent company can control all the subordinating companies even without owning a single share of them. The net result is not significantly different from the old legal framework.

For many chaebol corporations, a surprisingly small percentage of the total shares is actually owned by the controlling family. The average ownership (shares owned) by the controlling family of 100 chaebol groups is between 4.5% and 5.2%. MK, for instance, owns about 5% of the Hyundai Motor Group, though he has complete and unchallenged control of the business. Because the chaebol groups have significant influence in shaping industrial policy and daily business practices, they also wield financial power via banks and stock markets. They use these financial resources in expanding their businesses. Here is how it works.

Suppose one wealthy person invests $10 million and establishes a parent company. It attracts another $10 million in the stock market (50% minority investment) and 100% in loans from financial institutions. (See Figure 1.) Total assets are now four times the initial investment or $40 million. This parent company reinvests 50% ($20 million) of the total assets and establishes two subordinate companies. Each subordinate company multiplies its assets four times (total assets of $40 million) and reinvests its 50% in another two subordinate companies. In summary, with $10 million investment, the wealthy investor has complete control of five companies with the aggregate total assets of $280 million.

FIGURE 1

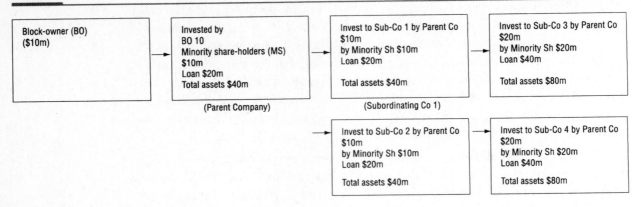

NOTE: *With $10 million investment, a block-owner has a complete and unchallenged control of five companies with total asset of $280 million.*

SOURCE: *Reconstructed based on Kim & Chang Law Offices' presentation slides*

Chaebol Policy and Corporate Governance

CORRUPT PRACTICES FOR INHERITING MANAGEMENT CONTROL

Figure 2 shows a recent partial relationship among owners of Hyundai Motor Company Group. Cross-investment between the parent company and subordinating companies was used both to expand the business and as a tool to pass on ownership and management control to children. A new parent company, Glovis, was created with major shareholder investment by both the

FIGURE 2

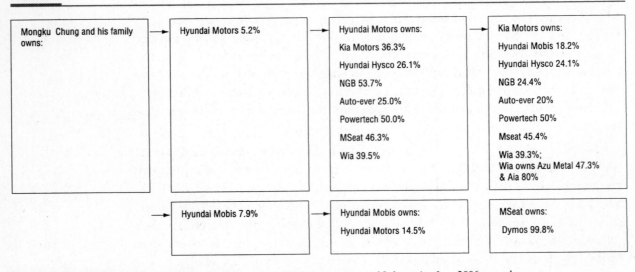

SOURCE: *Constructed based on information provided by Korea Credit Assessment and Information Inc., 2006, posted at http://www.kisinfo.com accessed on June 30, 2010*

Cross-investment of Hyundai Motors Group and Corporate Governance

father (MK) and his son (Chung Eui-Sun), who owned significantly more shares. All businesses (trucking, all completed products, and parts within the group's companies) were directed to this new company. This type of internal transaction is technically illegal, but legality is often determined by how the law is interpreted and on how transactions are written in a contract. After a while, this nominal parent company was enrolled in the stock exchange, and its share price soared quickly. This outcome was predictable. Such stock-market manipulation is designed to pass the fortune from father to son. But due to MK's high profile, the scheme got attention and led to a national policy debate on inheritance of wealth and management, leading to charges being filed against MK and other executives in a South Korean court.

Prosecutor general Choung Snag-Myoung assigned the case to a special team of national prosecutors, who indicted MK for tax evasion, manipulation of the stock market, and other charges. It became clear that he would be convicted and that he would be sentenced to a jail term. MK was arrested in April 2006 and placed in prosecutor's custody until the trial ended. For several weeks, MK's high profile trial fueled a national debate, equally weighted on both sides. The prosecutors asked for a six-year jail term, while MK's defense lawyers called for leniency. In early February 2007, MK was convicted of embezzlement and sentenced to three years in prison, but given a chance to appeal the verdict before having to serve his sentence. After his conviction he was set free by authorities and was left in operational and managerial control of Hyundai. In the end, MK got the leniency his lawyer's requested. Although he was convicted of embezzlement, the appellate court suspended his sentence MK and ordered to pay 1 trillion won (about $1.1 billion USD) to society and 300 hours of community service. The court based its decision upon the possible economic consequences for the country of sending MK to jail. The public was left to reflect on questions of judicial fairness. The outcome seemed the expression of a distorted justice system, in which guilty individuals without money go to jail, but those with money do not. Judge Lee Jae-Hong, who presided over the appellate court panel that suspended MK's jail term, reflected "I am also a citizen of the Republic of Korea. I was unwilling to engage in a gamble that would put the nation's economy at risk" (Associated Press).

CONTINUOUS SUCCESS AMID TURMOIL

Despite all the turmoil and difficulties, Hyundai Motor Company has steadily increased its car sales in the domestic South Korean and global markets. Its presence and sales in the United States market significantly increased between 2000 and 2010 (See Table 1). The company sustained an average 6% annual sales increase between 2001 and 2007. The global economic downturn of 2008 was chaotic for every major corporation, and Hyundai was no exception. In 2009, it rebounded and achieved an 8% sales increase. In 2010, Hyundai achieved 13% increase from the previous sales and far surpassed 2007 sales record.

TABLE 1

Market	Year	2001	2002	2003	2004	2005	2006	2007	2008	2009	Projected* 2010	Jan-April** 2010
Domestic sales (Korea)	PC	344,976	367,014	290,683	250,114	303,983	326,339	356,827	359,435	432,401	394,269	131,423
	RV	155,780	175,579	141,703	141,729	110,391	100,533	101,394	79,240	114,476	108,357	36,119
	CV	233,557	247,411	202,883	159,383	155,347	153,416	166,006	131,441	154,592	167,094	55,698
	Total	734,313	790,004	635,269	551,226	569,721	580,288	624,227	570,116	701,469	669,720	223,240
Sales in the U.S. Market	PC	290,218	296,840	298,943	300,094	325,958	327,316	303,368	292,247	325,667	332,628	110,876
	RV	56,017	78,279	101,278	118,521	129,054	128,204	163,641	109,495	109,397	133,968	44,656
	Total	346,235	375,119	400,221	418,615	455,012	455,520	467,009	401,742	435,064	466,596	155,532
U.S. Industry		17,178,418	16,844,783	16,677,975	16,912,141	16,994,655	16,559,625	16,153,952	13,246,951	10,432,227	10,584,282	3,528,094
Market share		2.02%	2.23%	2.40%	2.48%	2.68%	2.75%	2.89%	3.03%	4.17%	4.41%	4.41%
Export other than U.S.	PC	323,872	349,885	432,919	410,443	300,402	238,810	313,188	375,735	289,768	310,440	103,480
	RV	129,716	157,025	153,764	252,886	308,123	259,456	205,921	196,440	84,038	122,373	40,791
	CV	50,352	47,101	42,590	44,676	67,585	77,028	90,206	124,722	101,655	93,834	31,278
	Total	503,940	554,011	629,273	708,005	676,110	575,294	609,315	696,897	475,461	526,647	175,549
Export Total	PC	614,090	646,725	731,862	710,537	626,360	566,126	616,556	667,982	615,435	643,068	214,356
	RV	185,733	235,304	255,042	371,407	437,177	387,660	369,562	305,935	193,435	256,341	85,447
	CV	50,352	47,101	42,590	44,676	67,585	77,028	90,206	124,722	101,655	93,834	31,278
	Total Export	850,175	929,130	1,029,494	1,126,620	1,131,122	1,030,814	1,076,324	1,098,639	910,525	993,243	331,081
Total Global		1,584,488	1,719,134	1,664,763	1,677,846	1,700,843	1,611,102	1,700,551	1,668,755	1,611,994	1,662,963	554,321

Note: Project* is estimated based on the result of the sales between January and April, 2010. Jan-April** is actual sales figure between January and April, 2010. "PC" refers to passenger cars; RV recreational vehicles; and CV commercial vehicles. Sources: Hyundai's official website (http://worldwide.hyundai.com)

Hyundai Motor Co. Car Sales

Moreover, Hyundai's market share is steadily increasing in the United States: 2.02% in 2001 and 3.03% in 2008. It celebrated the 2.5% market share increase in 2005, which many analysts thought Hyundai Motor Company would never be able to reach in the U.S. market. In fact, between 2008 and 2009, the company showed even stronger market share increase, though total sales volume was hit hard due to the economic downturn in the United States. As of early 2011, Hyundai has well over 4% market share and is forecasting 5%. Even amid the global economic downturn, Hyundai's financial structure is getting stronger (See Table 2). Its revenue increased 14.5% between 2007 and 2008, though its net income shrunk from $1,555,536,000 to $868,828,000.

Behind the steady success was MK's patriarchal leadership and determination. MK made tough decisions, sometimes contrary to the recommendations of his engineering and managerial staff. Confident of quality improvement advances over the past years, Hyundai launched "the industry's best warranty," a 10-year warrantee on all Hyundai cars in the United States No one in the automobile industry at this time had such a long-standing warranty. Responses to this extended warranty in the U.S. market were very positive. Hyundai was becoming competitive with Japanese and European cars.

From the day that MK took over as Chairman, his focus was on the global market. He integrated management control of both Kia and Hyundai Motors and placed the management team in the new head office in Seoul. Both manufacturing plants in India and China were producing to full capacity. The plant in Alabama produced cars for the North American market, while the plant in Brazil manufactured them for South Americans. Kia Motors opened a plant in Zilina, Slovakia, in 2007, and produced more than 200,000 vehicles during the first year, primarily targeting the European market. A plant in Turkey also provided vehicles and parts for the European market. These plants were welcomed by their local communities and supported by the local governments.

RECALL AND VOW FOR CONTINUED QUALITY MANAGEMENT

In West Point, Georgia, MK acted quickly regarding the Sonata faulty front-latch problem: a voluntary recall. In the U.S. Congressional hearings on Toyota's safety defects, United States Secretary of Transportation Ray LaHood accused Toyota of being "safety deaf," and the panel accused Toyota of delaying a recall to fix a mechanical defect in its accelerator pedals. Toyota would be fined $16 million by the U.S. Government, the largest ever levied on a automobile company, and the controversy drastically affected auto sales for Toyota. MK would not allow the same distrust and bad publicity to affect Hyundai. Above all, he wanted Hyundai car buyers to trust that warranty services are not an empty promise; they are a part of any sale of a new Hyundai. In response to the faulty front-latch problem in Korea and elsewhere, MK was quick and decisive in his response, and even at the cost of short-term benefit and profit.

TABLE 2

Balance Sheet Assets	2008	2007
Current assets		
Cash and cash equivalents	4,944,905	3,493,990
Short-term investment	3,526,442	2,772,978
Trade notes and account receivables	6,093,613	5,157,811
Inventories	13,404,372	8,958,317
Other current assets	2,865,171	2,033,833
Total current assets	**30,834,503**	**22,416,929**
Non-current assets		
Long-term investment	865,070	1,191,203
Investment securities for the equity	2,148,975	1,618,352
Property, plant and equipment	22,996,629	20,381,336
Intangibles	2,742,630	2,384,003
Other assets	22,484,386	18,686,130
Total non-current assets	51,237,690	44,261,024
Total Assets	**82,072,193**	**66,677,953**
Liabilities and shareholders equity		
Current libailities		
Short-term borrowings	17,199,286	13,063,277
Current maturities of long-term debt	5,104,068	3,521,386
Trade notes and accounts payable	10,343,951	8,079,762
Acrued warrantees	1,107,443	1,065,819
Other liabilities	4,494,462	3,695,836
Total current liabilities	**38,249,210**	**29,426,080**
Long-term liabilities		
Long-term debt	17,684,223	13,409,763
Accrued severance benefits	890,312	795,377
Long-term accounts payable	185,896	235,451
Other Long-term liabilities	4,901,998	3,953,520
Total long-term liabilities	23,662,429	18,394,111
Total Liabilities	**61,911,639**	**47,820,191**
Shareholder's equity		
Capital stock	1,184,090	1,182,489
Capital surplus	4,644,035	4,574,953
Capital adjustment	(571,956)	(571,296)
Accumulated other comprehensive income	491,697	259,820
Retained earnings	9,416,985	8,938,657
Minority interests	4,995,703	4,473,139
Total shareholder's equity	20,160,554	18,857,762
Total Liabilities and Shareholder's Equity	**82,072,193**	**66,677,953**
Income Statement		
Sales	63,408,629	55,349,118
Cost of sales	49,168,627	44,109,325
Gross profit	14,240,002	11,239,793
Selling and administrative expense	11,797,025	8,974,965
Operating income	2,442,977	2,264,828
Other income (expense)	(1,252,535)	(190,220)
Income before income tax	1,190,442	2,074,608
Income tax expense	**325,979**	**519,072**
Net gain(loss) of newly consolidated subsidiaries before aquisition	4,365	
Net Income	**868,828**	**1,555,536**
Earnings per common share	**$ 1.99**	**$ 4.62**

SOURCE: Summarized from annual reports posted at Hyundai's official website (http://worldwide.hyundai.com)

Consolidated Balance Sheet and Income Statements (U.S. Dollar in thousands)

QUESTIONS FOR DISCUSSION

1. Given the success of Hyundai cars in the U.S. market in recent years, are they going to be another major competitive forces next to Japanese cars that three American automakers must pay attention to?

2. Do you think Chung Mong-Koo is an effective corporate leader? Do you think his leadership would be successful in a corporate structure that is not chaebol? Explain your reasoning.

3. What would you recommend the executives of Hyundai Motor Company for continuous and sustainable success in the U.S. automobile market?

4. What are your attractions to Hyundai vehicles? What are the things you would or would not like in considering to buy a Hyundai vehicle? Visit a Hyundai car dealership in your area and do some research of the car you would like to buy before you answer this question.

5. Would Chaebol contribute positively or negatively to the further economic development and the social justice in Korea? Why do you think so?

6. Would you call Hyundai an ethical company, given these scenes in the career of Chung Monk-Koo? Why or Why not?

REFERENCES/BIBLIOGRAPHY

Barth, Liza. "2011 Hyundai Sonata Recall, Stop Sale." *Consumerreports.org.* 25 Feb. 2010. Web. Retrieved 28 Feb. 2011 from http://blogs.consumerreports.org/cars/2010/02/2011-hyundai-sonata-recall-stop-sale.html

Digital-nail. *Hyundai Motor Company and Global Leadership.* Seoul: Human & Books, 2004. Print.

"Hyundai Chairman's Prison Term Suspended." *Associated Press.* 6 Sept. 2007. Web. Retrieved 28 Feb. 2011 from http://www.msnbc.msn.com/id/20620766/ns/business-world_business/

Kim, Tae-gyu. "Kai Motors Opens Plant in Georgia, US." *Koreatimes.co.kr.* 28 Feb. 2010. Web. Retrieved 28 Feb. 2011 from http://www.koreatimes.co.kr/www/news/biz/2010/05/123_61586.html

Kim, Sunghong, and Sangmin Lee. *Chung Mongku's Challenge: Hyundai-Kia Motors.* Seoul: Gozwin, 2005. Print.

Lee, Hyungken (2010). "Hyundai-Kia Cars Are Better than Toyota's." *Digital Times.* 6 May 2010 (Korea in Korean).

Lee, Imgwang (2007). *Driving Innovation: Mongku Chung and Hyundai-Kia Motor Company.* Seoul: Thinking Map, 2007. Print.

"MK Sentenced to 300 Days Community Service." *YTN News* 3 June 2008. Web. http://www.ytn.co.kr

"Politics of Marketing: Toyota's Crash Leaves Hyundai in Driving Seat." *Marketing Week* 18 Feb 2010: 9. Print.

Ramstad, Evan. "Hyundai Recalls Sonata to Fix Doors." *Wall Street Journal* 24 Feb. 2010. Print.

Shinmoongo (2010). "Chaebol Chairmen Enjoy Great Anger. Characteristics of Korean-style Chaebol system: Big Anger, Great Anger, and High Anger." *Internet News Shinmoongo* 25 Feb. 2010. Web. http://www.shinmoongo. net

Weekly Dong-A. "Dream to Become the World's 5th Largest Automaker? Well..," No. 220, 3 Feb 2000. Print.

Yang, Sangwoo. "Hyundai Kingdom Drowned into the Mud of Internal Struggle for Management Take-Over." *Hankyoreh* 21.248 (11 Mar. 1999). Print.

Yoon, Youngho. "Dream of the World's Top Five Automaker for Hyundai-Kia Motors: Well, I'm not so sure." *Donga Weekly* 3 Feb. 2000. Print.

Searching for Competitive Advantage in the Middle East

Andrew Ashwin • Content Developer, Biz/ed, Cengage Learning EMEA

LEARNING OBJECTIVES

After reading this case study and completing the questions, students should be able to do the following:

- *Explain the meaning of the term 'competitive advantage' and the key determinants of competitive advantage*
- *Identify and explain at least two sources of competitive advantage*
- *Analyze the main sources of competition facing small businesses in international markets*
- *Analyze and evaluate at least two ways in which small businesses can respond to competition from larger rivals*
- *Assess the benefits of generating competitive advantage*

This case was prepared for classroom discussion rather than to illustrate either effective or ineffective handling of an administrative, ethical, or legal decision by management. Information was gathered from corporate as well as public sources.

INTRODUCTION

The trend for markets in the Middle East to become more open presents significant benefits to the region but also major challenges, not least of these for companies located in the region who face competition from new entrants. Many of these new entrants represent strong competition with experience and size on their side. For local firms, responding to such competition is an increasingly important strategic imperative.

CLOTHING RETAILERS IN EGYPT

In Egypt, there have been an increasing number of new clothing retailers taking advantage of the economic growth in the county that has led to a rise in the market segment of young, fashion-conscious, and relatively affluent people looking for new products. Between 2007 and 2010, stores such as *H&M*, *Zara*, *French Connection*, and *Next* established a presence in the country. For local firms such as *Wave*, which has over 15 clothing stores across Egypt, these changes presented particular challenges.

The Predicament for Wave

Zeinab Turma, brand manager for *Wave* saw a 30-40% drop in customer numbers between 2007 and 2010, a trend she puts down to the influx of new labels and brands into Egypt. The influx accelerated after a 2002 lift of a ban on major imports of clothes and other textiles, and the investment in shopping malls has helped to build the critical mass of shoppers required by firms from Western Europe to justify the investment to enter the market.

Wave faces a number of competition elements to which it must respond. First, it has to try to compete with the demand for international brands. These brands bring with them status for the wearer; they advertises that the wearer is part of the wealthy elite in the country. Second, international brands can exploit economies of scale, meaning they can afford to sell at prices that local, smaller firms are unable to match. The benefits of economies of scale are brought into even sharper focus when one considers that international firms have to pay import taxes that push up prices by as much as 30%.

New Strategies for Wave

To respond to this sort of competition, local firms have to adopt different strategies. In some respects, it is not possible for them to compete directly in the same markets. They have the disadvantage of not being able to produce large volumes like their international competitors who are able to exploit mass markets in a number of countries rather than in just one country.

One possible option for firms such as *Wave* is to get out of the top end of the market and focus on the middle to lower end of the market. However, some are not keen to do that because it means effectively giving in to international competition and leaving the market open for high-end brands to exploit. However, as the market expands, there may be enough room to accommodate everyone; the opening up of the economy does not create a zero-sum game. The expansion of shopping malls and the development of mixed-use property and estates means that there are opportunities for local firms to expand their operations and to meet local market needs more directly—at all levels of the market.

ENERGY IN THE GULF REGION

The Gulf Region is traditionally associated with having a comparative advantage in the production of oil. Companies producing oil are able to exploit their position because they have the key components of competitive advantage: Their operations are distinctive and defensible. Energy production is a broad area, and as the Middle East continues to expand and grow, the demand for power will increase. The global concern with the effects of human activity on the environment has encouraged a move toward investing in clean energies, and in Egypt, one firm is heavily involved at the forefront of the growth of wind power. El-Sewedy Cables, a cable and electrical products manufacturing company based in Egypt, employs over 10,000 workers across 23 production facilities in 12 countries around the world. Its operations include involvement in telecoms, energy, turnkey projects (where a project is constructed and handed over to the buyer in a ready-to-use state), electrical products, and wind generation.

El-Sewedy

In October 2008, El-Sewedy bought a 30% stake in a Spanish wind turbine maker and also set up a joint venture called SET with SIAG, a German wind tower manufacturer. The aim of the company is to be the choice of company in Egypt to develop new wind farms. The Egyptian government has stated that it wants 20% of the country's power supplied by renewable sources of energy by the end of 2022. The local advantage is that there is abundant wind in Egypt. The Red Sea and Gulf of Aqaba shorelines have plentiful supplies of wind as do the Eastern and Western Deserts. El-Sewedy, which has positioned itself to exploit the market highlights, illustrates how key elements of competitive advantage can be built.

El-Sewedy's acquisition and joint venture agreement means that the company can supply elements of renewable energy projects and complete solutions, a capability not easy to copy by rivals. It is now able to build towers, turbines, blades and put them all together, which means that buyers can rely on El-Sewedy to carry out all the aspects of developing new wind farms. Its ability to cover all angles means that it is ideally placed to offer its turnkey projects to prospective buyers not only in Egypt but also in the rest of the Middle East. This example shows that if a company can build capacity and expertize that is difficult for a rival to imitate quickly (and that is crucial), it is able to maintain a competitive advantage for some time. The more El-Sewedy is able to maintain this competitive advantage, the more expertize it builds up and the more it is able to secure new contracts because of the reputation it is able to generate.

Egypt Aluminium

The two examples given so far highlight the fact that changing market conditions mean that firms, both large and small, have to be constantly aware of the need to re-position themselves and review their strategy on an on-going basis. However, doing so may be associated with firms in the private sector but not necessarily with those in the public sector. Egypt Aluminium is an example of a firm which has remained state owned since it was first established in 1973 but which has developed a private sector mentality for doing business. Egypt Aluminium has a plant situated at Nag Hammady, some 62 miles (100 km) north from Luxor. The site covers over over 7 million square yards (6 million sq. m.) and produces ingots, slabs, plates, wires, billets (lengths of aluminum with relatively small cross sections) and anode blocks, which are used in the aluminium smelting process.

Much of the success of the company has been based on its exports. It produces around 250,000 tonnes of aluminum per year and exports around 55% of it. This high proportion of exports is largely due to the lack of use of aluminium in Egypt itself, which does not have, for example, an extensive automobile industry that would make use of the sort of products that Egypt Aluminium produces. Given that it has to compete in international markets, therefore, Egypt Aluminium has to exploit any competitive advantage it has.

For Egypt Aluminium the main sources of competitive advantage in comparison to its international rivals lie in its costs. It has lower labor and energy costs and also boasts lower production costs in general. This advantage allows it to compete on price, charging lower prices than some of its rivals. But it does not compromised on quality. Having lower prices is one factor, but lower prices do not gain additional customers if the product quality is poor. The other main source of its competitive advantage, therefore, is quality.

Egypt Aluminium achieves this quality by adopting a quality assurance at every stage of production. The emphasis on quality requires focus of its labor force. Training is seen as essential, and Egypt Aluminium has built a specialized training facility at its Naga Hammadi site to train new entrants and existing staff. More than 170 trainees pass through the facility every year. The vast majority of the recruits to the business have been through high school and become highly skilled technicians.

The focus on keeping costs under control and on quality give Egypt Aluminium two key elements of competitive advantage that rivals find difficult to imitate. Building a reputation for quality takes time and investment in workers and processes; the location of the business in Egypt means that labor and energy costs are low, which rivals in other developed economies of Western Europe cannot copy easily or quickly. Such is the success of the business that it invariably has sales booked well in advance of production and retains significant interest from buyers across the globe.

As with all the markets in this case study, however, Egypt Aluminium knows that it cannot afford to stand still. It knows that there will be competition from new firms from the Gulf region. The UAE, Bahrain, Oman, and Qatar are all developing aluminium production facilities with estimates that output could be as high as 5 million tonnes in subsequent years. These countries have low energy costs and access to raw materials needed for production. Given that the key features of competitive advantage are being distinctive and defensible, if Egypt Aluminium faces competition from firms that are able to compete on cost then this ceases to become defensible (or becomes very expensive to defend). As a result the company has to focus its efforts on the advantage it has built up with its reputation for quality, while it monitors the cost situation in Egypt and abroad to keep some clear distance between itself and its competitors.

The firms in this case study operate in different markets and are different sizes, but the principles of competitive advantage are the same for all. They have to find ways in which they can operate that makes them distinctive from their rivals if they wish to capture market share and improve profitability. In the case of firms such as *Wave*, it may be a case of doing so simply to survive. Being distinctive is only one aspect of competitive advantage; the advantages and the distinctiveness has to be defensible;, that is, not easy for a rival to copy the advantage thus eroding its value.

For smaller firms like *Wave*, this can be very difficult, whereas for larger firms operating in specialist markets the opportunity to defend its advantages can be easier. Large scale operation, niche markets, and high levels of expertise can be used as means of leveraging advantage but as Egypt Aluminium illustrates, any firm that stands still and believes it has cracked the market may quickly find out that its competitive advantage is reduced and other firms take over.

QUESTIONS FOR DISCUSSION

1. Explain why competitive advantage is more than simply having any sort of advantage over rivals.

2. What do you think were the main sources of competition facing small textile businesses in Egypt as a result of the increasing openness of the Egyptian economy.

3. Using examples, explain how small firms such as textile businesses in Egypt might seek to develop competitive advantage over larger rivals.

4. Analyze the sources of competitive advantage for El-Sewedy and Egypt Aluminium.

5. Assess the factors that a firm needs to take into account in maintaining its competitive advantage over rivals. Provide an example you are familiar with or one from the case study to illustrate your answer.

Subway International and the Global Fast Food Industry in the Asia-Pacific and Latin America

Fernando Robles • Professor of International Business and International Affairs, George Washington University
Marilyn Liebrenz-Himes • Associate Professor of Global Marketing, George Washington University

LEARNING OBJECTIVES

The analysis of this case allows the student to be able to do the following:

- *Describe the four factors Subway exploited in order to grow nationally, which the company exploits to grow internationally*
- *Identify and distinguish global and regional drivers of fast food markets*
- *Evaluate competitors' threats from other global, regional, and local fast food companies in a regional market*
- *Formulate recommendations to improve the market position of global companies in regional markets*
- *Recommend adaptations of a global strategy to local market conditions*

This case was prepared for classroom discussion rather than to illustrate either effective or ineffective handling of an administrative, ethical, or legal decision by management. Information was gathered from corporate as well as public sources.

BACKGROUND

Fred DeLuca, president and co-founder of Subway, built his company by setting extremely ambitious goals. He succeeded in making Subway one of the leading sandwich restaurants in the world. Subway's success is attributed to its strong brand based on a unique value proposition aimed at a dissatisfied target segment. Moreover, the company's low-cost franchising strategy has allowed Subway to flourish both domestically and overseas.

In the United States, Subway offers a healthy alternative to the dominant burger fast food restaurants, and overseas, it competes with these major players

TABLE 1

Region	Market US$ mn (2009)	CAGR (2004-2009)	% of Market Share (2009)
World	480,464	5.50%	--
Asia Pacific	139,784	9.86%	29.1
Australasia	10,226	5.31%	2.1
Eastern Europe	10,967	9.67%	2.3
Latin America	31,261	11.94%	6.5
Middle East & Africa	14,851	6.40%	3.1
North America*	199,009	2.69%	41.4
Western Europe	74,367	3.83%	15.5

SOURCE: *Consumer Foodservice: Euromonitor from trade sources/national statistics. US market represents 91 percent of the North American Market*

Global Fast Food Market Size

by having a comparatively low-cost franchise and being able to adapt to foreign cultures.

The question for Subway in the early 2000s is whether the Asian and Latin American emerging markets will adopt North American–style sandwiches. Despite considerable domestic competition and an uncertain global future, Subway pursues its goal to be "ranked the number one restaurant by consumers while serving 30 percent of the population each week in every market that [it] serve[s]" (Mintel Report). This aspiration is rooted in the company's U.S. success story.

The emerging regions of Asia and Latin America offer the best promise for growth. These regional markets are growing at compound annual growth rates (CAGRs) of 10 and 12 percent in the period of 2004 through 2009. The growth potential in emerging markets contrast the tepid growth in the mature markets of North America and Europe, which grew at less than 3% in the same period (see Table 1).

HISTORY

The success story of Subway began in the summer of 1965, when Fred DeLuca looked around for money to pay for his college education. Deluca asked Dr. Peter Buck, an old family friend, for advice. Instead of offering tuition money as DeLuca had expected, Buck advised the seventeen-year-old to open a sandwich store in order to earn more than the current $1.25 per-hour minimum wage. Buck presented DeLuca with $1,000 as an initial investment, and soon after, they partnered in opening the first Subway restaurant in Bridgeport, Connecticut, which was then called Pete's Super Submarines. Even though they were successful in selling 312 sandwiches on their first day, the pair could never have imagined that this small sandwich store would one day grow to compete with fast-food giants such as McDonald's and Burger King.

DeLuca and Buck initially aimed to open 32 sandwich shops in ten years, but by 1974, they had only 16. Buck and DeLuca next developed the idea of franchising their business as a growth strategy. Franchising proved to be enormously successful; it allowed the number of Subway stores to grow exponentially ultimately to total 34,098 restaurants in 95 countries as of January 2011 (Subway.com).

STRATEGY AND COMPETITIVE POSITION

Between 2001 and 2010 Subway was ranked either the number one or two franchise opportunity by *Entrepreneur* magazine. Subway's successful strategy exploited four factors: unique value, an underserved customer segment, an aggressive franchising model, and international growth.

The unique value lay in offering a healthy alternative to the burgers and pizzas that dominated the U.S. fast food market in the 1970s. The emphasis on fresh healthy ingredients assembled in front of the customer contrasted with the standardized, pre-cooked options offered by Subway's competitors.

Subway markets its fresh ingredients with its slogan "Eat Fresh." The company is "committed to customer satisfaction through offering high quality food with exceptional service and good value," according to the Subway.com *Student and Educator Resources Guide*. Subway has the added benefit that its products have a higher perceived value than other fast food options, so the company is able to charge moderately higher prices thus increasing its profit margins. Subway uses freshly baked rolls, and the scent of bread baking fills the stores, appealing to customers and reinforcing the fact that Subway's sandwiches are fresh. Meats and vegetables are displayed behind counters so that customers can customize their made-to-order sandwiches, whereas other fast food restaurants offer only standardized products.

The emphasis on healthiness is one way Subway targets customers who are dissatisfied with the standard fare of the market leaders. Due to a rising concern about obesity levels in many developed countries, fast-food chains are feeling the pressure to provide healthy alternatives to the traditional greasy burger and fries (PR Newswire). Subway has been able to capitalize on this trend by offering an array of sandwiches and salads at "6 grams of fat or less." Benefiting from effective advertising, Subway has also attracted health- and weight-conscious consumers with its campaign featuring Jared Fogle, who lost 245 pounds in one year by eating nothing but meals from Subway (Mintel Report).

While the traditional market leaders focus on the family and convenient drive-thru market segments, Subway appeals to young, urban professionals looking for a healthy lunch option. Its small restaurants with minimal seating encourage take-out business. Without playgrounds for children, Subway appeals to young professionals and other adults who want a quick, healthy meal without the distraction of children playing in the restaurant.

While serving this adult customer base, Subway has catered to the six to 11 year-olds who influence where a family eats an estimated 24% of the time. First, the restaurant developed a hipper look and feel. Then, in July 2006, Subway "eschewed action figures and toys typically found in kids' meals and partnered with such 'lifestyle, appropriate' brands as Vans, a popular footwear brand, to target the highly sought 8-12 demographic" (Hein 15). Vans products were made available to children beginning July 10, 2006, and parents received coupons for back to school shopping. Subway has also partnered with the Discovery Kids channel in order to encourage healthy eating habits among youth and to obtain loyal customers at a younger age. With slogans such as "Play Hard, Eat Fresh," Subway hopes to come off as a hip brand so that young consumers can "find Subway earlier in their lives," Michelle Cordial, director of brand management for the Subway Franchisee Advertising Fund Trust, is quoted as saying (Cebrzynksi).

In the United States, Subway's aggressive franchising model made its expansion possible. Unlike McDonald's and other fast-food chains that have start-up costs ranging from $1,057,200 to $1,885,000 per unit, Subway's per unit opening costs range from $84,300 to $258,300 (Entrepreneur.com). Less expensive equipment and lower real estate costs account for the comparatively lower start-up cost. Subway restaurants require only a counter, a small countertop oven in which bread is baked, a toaster oven, a refrigerator, a freezer, and a microwave, and the small stores require less property. Since the operation of a Subway store is a relatively simple procedure, the company is able to open non-traditional units in areas that its competitors may find difficult and costly (Subway.com).

DEVELOPING SUBWAY'S INTERNATIONAL BUSINESS

Unlike most U.S. fast-food chains and quick service restaurants (QSR's) that typically prefer to expand their businesses first in safe and familiar international locations such as Canada and Mexico, Subway's first overseas store debuted in 1984 in the small Middle-Eastern nation of Bahrain. An Italian businessman presented Subway executives with the opportunity to venture overseas into Bahrain, and doing so proved successful. According to Don Fertman, Subway's director of development, the international expansion approach at the time was, "If you like Subway, you think it's a good thing, and you think it would work in your country, then we'll teach you the concept and how it works and you go make it work in your country" (Chancey). By implementing its franchising strategy, which had succeeded in the United States, Subway was able in to boast that as of January 2011, it had 33,936 restaurants in 95 countries.

In the early 2000s, Subway developed a global strategic plan in order to reap the maximum benefits from its overseas locations. The company decided to focus on high-growth potential markets in which it already operates, such as Australia, New Zealand, the United Kingdom, Spain, Italy, France, Germany, Puerto Rico, Japan, and the Benelux countries (Chancey). High growth potential estimates are based on "population density, political and economic stability, availability of disposable income among targeted demographics, and a willingness to accept quick-service restaurants" (Duecy). Nonetheless, these rankings are not concrete and are revisited on a quarterly basis. As stated by Fertman, "If a market is on the delayed entry list, we say no to having a store there at this point, but we keep looking at these countries with a proprietary rating system. What is a closed country today could be an open country sometime in the future." (History of Subway).

Development Agents

Subway also started to build an international infrastructure to assist in global franchising. Like many companies growing internationally, Subway has begun setting up regional (Europe) and countrywide offices to facilitate rollout by providing training and marketing coordination. However, what really distinguishes Subway's expansion is the use of development agents to push franchisee growth. Development agents are responsible for recruiting franchisees and assisting in their growth. These agents are paid part of the franchise fee and one-third of ongoing royalties to keep their incentives in line with the franchisees. Development agents are independent entrepreneurs, not employees of Subway.

The international expansion of Subway has largely been bottom-up, driven by development agents and local franchisees and not funded at the corporate level. According to Subway, growth in their markets starts slowly and, after reaching a certain level, picks up rapidly. At these tipping points once the brand is known, more franchisees are interested in opening restaurants and restaurant growth increases. Brand awareness grows among customers and per store sales increase and higher advertising contributions from franchisees spur on further growth.

Adapting to Local Markets

At its numerous locations throughout the globe, Subway's core menu is left unchanged except for minor religious and cultural considerations, as the company believes that eventually sandwiches will catch on and overcome cultural barriers. For example, in China where McDonald's offered a spicy chicken burger and KFC replaced coleslaw with more traditional side-dishes such as "shredded carrots, mushrooms, or bamboo shoots," Subway's menu remained the same with the exception of introducing a pork-rib patty with Chinese sauce that "nobody liked" (Adler). In India, where many Hindus and Muslims live, the menu had to be adjusted in order to offer more chicken, lamb, and turkey as substitutes for beef and pork, which attempt to reflect the religious beliefs of Hindus and Muslims.

In addition to local customs, the purchasing power of the overseas nation must be taken into consideration when expanding globally. For example, the number of people per store must be taken into account because in the United States, one Subway can serve 10,000 people and be successful. "An international store might have to serve a much higher number of meals in order to make a profit because only a small percentage of the population can afford to eat out."(Chancey)

Subway's international success consists of offering something that tastes good, is made with fresh ingredients, located in a convenient place, and can be easily adapted to the local taste without departing from its formula of a customized sandwich. Subway's strong brand based on this unique value proposition and its low-cost franchising strategy have allowed it to flourish overseas.

GLOBAL FAST FOOD MARKETS

The global fast-food market is comprised of the sales by chain and independent companies of ready-to-eat foods of all categories. This market is estimated to have a value of $480.4 billion (Euromonitor). Most of the growth will be driven by the expansion in emerging and developing countries—most notably in the Asia-Pacific region. The United States accounts for 38.7% of the market (North America 41.1%), followed by Asia-Pacific with 29.1%, Europe with 17.8%, and Latin America, Middle East, and Africa with the remaining 11.7%. Burger and chicken categories are the bulk of global fast food with a 51.2% share of sales worldwide. As of 2010, due to health concerns, increased obesity, and the avian flu scare, these two categories were on the decline while other categories such as salads and healthy sandwiches were on the increase in most markets.

The global fast food market is dominated by U.S. corporations with McDonald's; YUM! Brands, Inc; and Burger King among the leading competitors. Increasingly, local and regional players are eroding their dominance with fast food options more attuned to local or regional tastes and capitalizing on the backlash against anti-globalization movements. Niche specialists are also eroding the giants' market share with more focused strategies based on health, format, and service. The major players, however, remain formidable as they revise their menu, diversify their businesses, and invest in intensive advertising and promotion.

Subway faces fierce competition by sandwich chains that have replicated and improved upon Subway's model. Subway considers global expansion the key to its sustained success, but it is questionable whether the fastest growing markets elsewhere will adapt to Subway's American-style sandwiches. With considerable domestic competition and an uncertain global future, Subway ponders how to meet its goal to be a leading restaurant in its various international markets.

SUBWAY SEEKS EXPANSION IN LATIN AMERICA

Along with Asia, the emerging Latin America markets offer promise for Subway to expand and grow. With only a 6.5% market share of the global fast food market, the Latin American market contained some of the fastest growing markets in the world with Brazil and Venezuela's markets growing at CAGRs of

TABLE 2

Country	Market Size US $ million in 2009	CAGR (2004-2009)	% of Market Share (2009)
Argentina	2,485	14.73%	8.7
Brazil	17,409	16.41%	61
Chile	686	3.80%	2.4
Colombia	1,119	11.96%	3.9
Mexico	4,215	2.38%	14.8
Peru	n.a.	n.a.	n.a.
Venezuela	2,611	17.35%	9.2

SOURCE: *Consumer Foodservice: Euromonitor*

Latin America Fast Food Market Size

16.5% and 17% (see Table 2). As of 2009, the region represented only 5% of the total restaurants in the Subway network. To make Latin America's presence in this network proportional to its potential, Subway would need to open new restaurants in this region. Should Subway make such a resource commitment to this region? If so, how many and where? These are the challenges that Subway needed to ponder quickly as other restaurant chains moved aggressively to this market.

LATIN AMERICAN MARKET

Latin America's large population of 580 million provides a large customer base for the fast food market. As of 2009, the annual disposable income of an average household in Latin America is $16,428. Seventy percent of the buying power is concentrated in the 10 largest metro markets. According to Euromonitor International Annual Disposable Income figures, the average annual disposable incomes in the top three economies are Venezuela with $30,523, Mexico with $22,046 and Chile with $21,912 (see Table 3) (Euro monitor International, Annual Disposable Income).

TABLE 3

Country	2004	2005	2006	2007	2008	2009	CAGR
Argentina	9,413	10,860	12,086	14,518	17,658	16,507	9.81
Brazil	8,353	10,762	13,099	15,999	18,953	18,588	12.26
Chile	13,840	16,510	18,749	20,734	23,007	21,912	7.96
Mexico	21,074	24,577	26,674	27,648	27,069	22,046	0.75
Peru	7,584	8,142	8,629	9,743	11,700	11,669	7.44
Venezuela	8,939	10,898	13,677	18,606	24,622	30,523	22.71

SOURCE: *Annual Disposable Income: Euromonitor International from National Statistics; ©2011 Euromonitor International*

Household Annual Disposable Income in Selected Latin American Countries in Current Prices

The food consumer market in Latin America has sometimes been referred to an untapped gold mine. Only in the early 2000s have people there shown an interest in eating outside their homes and adopting North American modes of consumption. The population booms of the 1950s and 1960s produced a mass exodus to the cities in search of work, wealth, and success. This change from rural to urban constituted an important turning point for Latin American food consumption. Increased urbanization, changes to the nuclear family with more women entering the work force, the implementation of a five-day work week policy, and shorter lunches increased the demand for eating out (Hernandez).

As the middle class and overall population continue to increase, the market is expected to grow larger. In the years prior to mass urbanization, traditional meals used to be a family-oriented affair. However, with the majority of the population living in urban centers, perpetuating the tradition became increasingly difficult. People found it difficult to return home from work to eat a meal with their families when they work far away from the household. Therefore, people began choosing faster and more convenient ways of eating. This change was a positive sign for fast food expansion in Latin America.

Even though there were emerging trends that pointed toward increasing market share for the fast food industry in Latin America, there were also key threats in the regional market. The first group of threats were the social/political risks characteristic of the region. These risks included the viability of a politically stable society, the prevalence of the unspoken acceptance of corruption through the public and private sectors, and the continued battle against high unemployment levels and poverty (Singh). Although the middle class was growing to become the majority in the more advanced Latin American countries such as Argentina, Chile, Uruguay, and Mexico, other countries were less affluent, and the majority of their people less likely to have the disposable income required for consuming fast food. In addition to challenges, there were also business risks specific to the industry. There is intense competition in the fast food industry and there are low barriers to entry, especially from small local competitors specializing in hamburgers or dishes more common to the region.

EATING OUT IN LATIN AMERICA

Latin American consumers love restaurant chains. The food quality and sanitary conditions maintained by the food chain are very attractive to consumers in the region. Consumers know they can eat at restaurant chains and not get sick, especially given that contracting gastro-intestinal conditions is common in the region. Also the clean, air-conditioned environment can be very relaxing when compared to the polluted, hot, and noisy conditions outside.

The consumer markets in Latin America are mostly in metropolitan cities such as Lima, Buenos Aires, Mexico City, and Sao Paulo. The market is large and as of 2010 was growing by the day. Fast food in Latin America is gaining increased popularity. As Latin America becomes more urbanized, the population's food choices are expected to change.

The fast food industry was considered well positioned to capitalize on the changing regional dynamics. In the early 2000s, it stressed the importance of family-oriented, efficient meals. Another key factor to success in this region is pricing. As seen from local competitors, affordability is a critical element of fast food success in the region.

As the largest economy in Latin America, Brazil offers the greatest market potential. Brazilian expenditures for eating out in all types of outlets grew at 33% in the 2005-2009 period (see Table 3). The fast food market category in 2009 surpassed the US $19 billion mark. The increase was attributed to consistent improvement in disposable income of Brazilians and stable employment conditions. The business lunch remained the most important meal for meeting and socializing. As part of their work benefits, Brazilian companies provide debit cards that can be used to cover meals at lunchtime. Dining out is typically a privilege for upper middle-income households and individuals. In countries such as Mexico, Argentina and Brazil, McDonald's offered a place where children could socialize after school. Due to the industry's variety in meal options, interest in this kind of food increased. Variety was taken as a sign of affluence and gave costumers a sense of being free to choose the restaurant and the meal.

In Mexico, the second largest market, the lunch market is also the most important segment of the country's $4 billion market. Given urban distances and congestion, most Mexicans chose to eat breakfast and dinner at home and eat out at lunchtime. As is traditional in many Latin American countries, breakfast at home consists of coffee and toast. In contrast to other Latin countries, urban commuters grab a quick bite of traditional Mexican cuisine from the many street vendors that concentrate around bus or metro stops. With this supplemental meal, Mexicans can work continuously to past mid-day. It is not uncommon to see Mexicans eating lunch at 2 p.m. For low-paid office workers, affordability and speed are important. Business executives and more affluent families prefer full-service restaurants.

The 2002 collapse of Argentina's economy directly affected how often Argentineans eat out. Perhaps, the most important consideration for Argentineans was the total price of the meal rather than the price of individual items. Many Argentineans had a budget for expenditures, including eating out. Thus, Argentineans tended to prefer the affordable full inclusive meals (menu del día) in restaurants, the self-service foodservice restaurants, and meal packages in fast food restaurants. Full service restaurants suffered a contraction of revenues in this period. By contrast, during the worst period of the economic crisis in February 2002, the number of meals served by the fast food industry in Argentina fell at lower rate than in overall retail and in real GDP (Fizbein).

With the improvement of its economy in the early 2000s, Argentineans returned to their usual busy and intense social lifestyle and spent more on eating out and socializing. As socialization and entertainment are very important in Argentine culture, coffee shops remained a strong category of growth. The coffee culture stems from Argentinean appreciation of European lifestyles. Argentineans enjoy the kind of coffee shop where they can meet friends and family and browse through books, read a newspaper, or enjoy poetry readings. Such an environment is difficult to capture by global coffee chains.

Prepared foods to take out and home delivery constitute another category of growth in Argentina. The diversity and sophistication of prepared take-out foods rival the offerings by full service restaurants. Argentineans rely on these establishments for dinner and snacks during the day. It is not unusual to call for a delivery of an order of empanadas (turnover or filled pastry) in the middle of the day. The cost of the meal is cheap and so is the delivery. Fast food mini-outlets embedded in retail networks are also growing in Argentina. For instance, the giant fuel retailer Repsol-YPF introduced its version of food and convenience stores in its 1,200 nationwide locations.

With a market size equivalent to that of Argentina, Venezuela is another important Latin American market. In contrast to Argentina, the coffee category decreased in the early 2000s in attracting Venezuelans' eating out expenditures. By contrast, expenditures in full-service restaurants increased, representing 58% of total expenditures in 2009. The fast food category remained stable with a 16% share. Whereas the older and mature middle and upper class prefer full-service restaurants, the younger population continued to be attracted to fast-food chains. Eating out in Venezuela can take many hours as socializing and business are usually mixed.

Chile also has a traditional eating-out market. The lunch segment is the most popular and Chileans will look for fast and nutritious options as the one-hour lunch replaces the traditional two-hour lunch break. Socialization with co-workers is important for Chileans; therefore, seating space for groups and sharing the cost of a meal are important considerations. Chileans enjoy various meats, including beef, pork, and chicken, or seafood, which are all staples of their traditional food.

Chile's fast food market is a maturing market growing at a CAGR of 3.8%. With the proliferation of shopping malls and movie theaters with food courts, the fast food industry grew rapidly in the 1990s. Fast food chain sales were $115 million in 1999. In 2005, the fast food market represented 30% of the consumer foodservice sector, and chain operations accounted for 53% of sales. Domestic chains grew between 10-24% in 2006 and at 14-24% in 2007. In 2005, 71% of fast food chains had sales between $100,000 and $500,000, and 21% had sales between $500,000 and $1,000,000.

In the early 2000s, over 75% of Santiago residents eat one or more meals outside the home every day. Lunch is the meal most eaten outside the home and Saturday is the most common day for visiting a fast food establishment. When people eat outside the home, their preference is fast food 73% of the time. Those who do eat fast food prefer to eat at the restaurant, spending an average of 15 to 30 minutes in the restaurant. Many fast food brands accommodate these patrons by providing sit-down areas, which promote socialization and family gatherings (Sloop).

Because more women have joined the workforce, fewer women are home with time to cook; so more people are eating out. Also, with more women working, disposable incomes have risen. Workdays are longer, commutes longer, and lunches shorter, all of which makes fast food sometimes the only option for those who spend much time away from home. With more people working outside the home, the middle class grows, disposable incomes increase, and the demand for convenience grows.

In the early 2000s, younger Chileans tended to embrace U.S. eating habits and people between 15 and 35 years of age made up about 60% of the fast food customer base. Highly consistent quality of product resulted in better presentation of food servings to customers. Fresh foods were also perceived as higher quality, but tended to be more expensive. Competitive pricing remained important to Chilean consumers.

In choosing a fast food establishment, the quality and healthiness of the food are important considerations. Excellent food quality and exceptionally clean conditions are additional factors that consumers consider when choosing where to eat. Quick service, restaurant hygiene, location convenience, and food price (cheap and offering promotions) are also important factors in selecting a fast food chain. Other important attributes are the friendliness of service and restaurant appearance. Reasons for not eating at a particular fast food establishment include unhealthy food choices. Increasing obesity concerns was causing health consciousness among Chileans. This trend toward health awareness and healthier lifestyles resulted in higher consumption of healthier foods. Healthier menu options and innovative menu options were major draws to Chilean consumers.

The best promotions a fast food establishment can offer are a free product with the purchase of another product and product price discounts. Television is the most effective media for advertising. Since lunch is the meal most often eaten away from home, fast food establishments can work with local companies to provide coupons for nearby establishments. Eighty percent of Chilean companies already provide their employees with either a company cafeteria or coupons honored by nearby restaurants.

Chile is not a stranger to the growing fast food industry, and fast food chains and franchises from various parts of the world have managed to find their way into the Chilean economy and culture and have performed well and competed successfully with Chilean brands. American brands have penetrated the Chilean market and have proven successful despite cultural differences and strong loyalty to national brands.

McDonald's and the local Chilean Lomitón chain led the fast food market in the early 2000s. Other chains in Chile include: Schopdog, Doggis, Burger Inn, Burger King, and Kentucky Fried Chicken. Pizza Hut, Telepizza, and Domino's led the market for pizza, though pizza is most frequently ordered by phone. Lomitón led the fast food industry with offering the best sandwiches; McDonald's led with offering the best combos, and Burger King offered the best hamburgers. McDonald's was the choice of children; Lomitón, however, was preferred by adults.

Other Latin American markets of importance are Colombia, Peru, and Central America. As of the early 2000s, eating out in Colombia was mostly restricted to lunch time due to personal security and strong traditional influences to go home for a family meal. This pattern changed with increasing prosperity and lower threat of terrorism. Another enticement was the increasing number of foreign and local restaurants offering fast, healthy, nutritious meals. Many of these food outlets were near large concentrations of office workers. Lower income workers chose lower price options that allow them to consume a full meal at a low price. Upper and middle-income households and people also drive the demand for dining out as low-income workers commute long distances to get back home. Partnerships with banks and credit cards are also popular promotions to stimulate demand during the business week as opposed to the traditional entertainment of going out during the weekend. Eating out in Peru is a gourmet experience. The diversity and quality of Peruvian cuisine has been praised in food gourmet circles, and Peruvians enjoy many high-quality and affordable options every day. As a result, Peruvians eat out frequently during work days and weekends. Peruvians are also very conscious of the health impact of food intake and tend to prefer seafood and vegetarian options. Asian cuisine, especially Japanese, is popular among Peruvians for these reasons. Central American markets are small on a country-by-country basis but, given the similarity of their eating out preferences, consumers in Central America as a whole can be considered as a single-sub-regional market. When they eat out, Central Americans prefer barbecued grilled chicken accompanied with rice and beans and fried cassava or plantains. Such a simple and gratifying meal fills the appetite of a Central America family. In the early 2000s, this style of preparing chicken was exported to nearby countries and far-away markets.

COMPETITION

Subway first entered the Latin Market by opening stores in Puerto Rico. Although Puerto Rico is part of North America's Subway network, it exposed Subway to the Latin consumer culture and represented a major market with 212 stores. Further expansion south of the border continued over the years, reaching as many as 1,736 restaurants in 35 countries in Latin America and the Caribbean. As of 2010, Brazil and Mexico were by far the largest country networks in the region with 550 and 499 restaurants respectively. Venezuela also had a strong Subway presence with 157 outlets. Small countries in Central America and Trinidad and Tobago in the Caribbean were also quite receptive to Subway expansion in the region (see Table 4).

Burger King and McDonald's continued to account for the largest share of fast food in the region, representing about 40 percent of all global fast food sales worth about $113 billion in 2004. As of 2010, Brazil was still an untapped fast food market. Venezuela, by contrast, has been the fastest growing food market, with a compound annual growth rate of 17.355 in the 2004-2009 period (Euromonitor International, Consumer Foodservice). However, in 2010, market shares started to decline slightly in the last two quarters showing an increase in ethnic food, coffee, and salad sectors.

The region witnessed a change to healthier and more innovative food choices. McDonald's launched a series of healthier items, including the Salads Plus range. Starbucks, which already had stores in Peru, Mexico, and

TABLE 4

Country	Locations	Country	Locations
Brazil	550	Curacao	7
Mexico	499	Cayman Islands	5
Puerto Rico	212	Sint Maarten	5
Venezuela	157	Jamaica	3
Panama	38	Uruguay	3
Costa Rica	36	Antigua and Barbuda	2
Trinidad Tobago	36	Dominica	2
Guatemala	35	Ecuador	2
El Salvador	25	Grenada	2
Chile	18	Peru	2
Honduras	18	Saint Lucia	2
Colombia	17	Barbados	1
Argentina	13	Martinique	1
Nicaragua	10	Saint Kitts and Nevis	1
Virgin Islands, U.S.	9	Saint Vincent and Grenadines	1
Bahamas	8	Netherlands Bes Islands	1
Aruba	7	St Martin	1
Bolivia	7	**Total**	**1736**

Number of locations as of January 14, 2011

SOURCE: *http://www.subway.com*

Subway Locations in Latin America and Caribbean

Puerto Rico, expanded its operations in South America. Its international business development strategy was somewhat different, adapting to different markets by addressing local needs and requirements. Mexico provided a good startup investment for Starbucks because of the country's population and large consumption rates supporting 300 stores in 2010.

Street vendors are a favorite choice in many urban centers. In Mexico, a lunchtime favorite is a few soft tacos and a Coke purchased from a street vendor for about $2 (Roig-Franzid). In addition to these street vendors, national champions are formidable competitors of global fast food chains in Latin America. For instance, Habib's, the world's largest fast food chain serving Middle Eastern cuisine, is not in the Middle East, but in Brazil. Habib's is the Brazilian national champion, perhaps because about 7% of Brazilians are of Middle Eastern descent (Plummer). Habib's founder, the Portuguese Alberto Savaiva, recognized the opportunity to cater to this large population and coupled it with pricing the menu items at very low prices, which proved to be a winning strategy in the Brazilian market. As of 2005, with 260 franchise restaurants in Brazil, the restaurant outnumbered foreign rivals Pizza Hut, Burger King, Wendy's, Arby's, and KFC, and came in second only to McDonald's, which had over 1,100 outlets (Plummer). Confident that Habib's could appeal beyond Brazil, the owner inaugurated his first outlet in Mexico City in March 2003 and planned to open Mexico's first Arab-food chain with

220 restaurants in the country's three largest metropolitan areas: Mexico City, Monterrey, and Guadalajara. Habib's hoped as of 2000 to offer its menu of familiar Lebanese dishes in the southwest region of the United States ("Brazil-based Habib's Plans North American Expansion"); however, after the September 11, 2001, attacks on the United States, Habib's cooled on the idea (Plummer). In addition to *esfishas*, the flat bread topped with beef, chicken, or cheese for which the establishment is known, the 56-item Habib's menu includes many other traditional Lebanese-Syrian staples. For the less adventurous, Habib's also offers hamburgers, chicken sandwiches, pizzas, french fries, and ice cream for desert (Habib's Web site). In addition, a low price strategy is possible because the restaurant's menu features foods that are inexpensive to produce. An *esfisha* at Habib's, for example, costs less than one-third as much as an original McDonald's hamburger and less than half as much as either a hot dog or a *pao de quejo* (cheese bread), two popular foods sold by street vendors.

A local competitor in Central America is Pollo Campero. Pollo Campero has 340 locations in 14 different markets, Guatemala, El Salvador, United States, Honduras, Nicaragua, Costa Rica, Ecuador, Mexico, Spain, Andorra, Indonesia, China, Bahrain and India.[i] It serves over 75 million customers each year producing about $390 million in annual sales ("Pollo Campero Expands"). The company is planning a rapid expansion program through both corporate-owned and franchised restaurants. It offers three basic kinds of chicken. Original fried recipe, extra crispy, and rotisserie cooked chicken. All three are flavored with a spice-herb blend. The menu also offers chicken nuggets and strips, chicken burgers and sandwiches, and sides of french fries, mashed potatoes, salads, and desserts (Pollo Campero Web site). Pollo Campero has capitalized on its strengths positioning itself strongly in key Latin American fast food markets. The chain's overall weakness locally as well as nationally is the small marketing budget and their consistent strategy to rely on word of mouth marketing. It has been suggested that the restaurant should work to establish a strong relationship with larger corporate companies in an effort to supplement its relatively low marketing budget with a global or a regional champion that would have synergies with companies such as Pollo Campero. In Guatemala a wave of new investments from KFC and Wendy's is challenging the home-based market of Pollo Campero.

In the hamburger category, another local champion is Peru's Bembos, a restaurant that offers a westernized fast food hamburger outlet with a little spice of Peruvian flair (Bembos Web site). Bembos' patrons enjoy the delicious hamburgers and the wide variety of choices. Its layout is similar to McDonald's offering a playground for kids; lively, light color schemes; and a family-oriented environment. The chain offers a wide variety of burgers with a number of toppings and a large palette of salad choices. Its salads come with meat. The menu also includes kids' meals and desserts. Bembos' market strategy is to stay fairly local and affordable. The chain prides itself on the quality of its burgers and its stores are accessible by allowing customers to order meals online.

Chile's Lomitón had 45 restaurants in 2009. Twenty-seven of Lomitón restaurants were owned and 18 franchised (Sipsa vende Lomiton). Customers preferring Lomitón appreciate Lomitón's tasty food, large portions, and better selection of natural foods. However, prices tend to be high and service slow. Lomitón is preferred by males twice as much than by females, and it is the preferred choice of young people age 15 to 25. Lomitón ranks as the most comfortable eating establishment. Lomitón, like other Chilean chains, has smaller advertising budgets as reflected by its limited success with advertising awareness of only 7% compared to 90% for McDonald's. The Lomitón Chilean chain has recently being sold to a Mexican-Spanish retail group ("Compran Lomitón para potencia cadena de fast food de deportes").

KEEPING THE MARKET PUSH IN LATIN MARKETS

By modifying their menus to local tastes, maintaining high quality, and offering low prices, fast food chains are likely to continue to grow as a sector in Latin America. The success of Subway in Venezuela, KFC in Mexico and the Caribbean, and Starbucks in Mexico and Peru have been nothing short of amazing. Different governments and rules and regulations for opening businesses vary greatly from country to country.

A common mistake of U.S. fast food companies in Latin America is to load the start-up costs onto the local franchise investor. Franchise growth in the United States builds upon the ability of the franchise buyers to fund their investments from personal savings or bank loans. In Latin America, new entrepreneurs can rarely obtain such financing, which means that the franchisers must provide credit in the franchise if the franchise is to have sufficient working capital to withstand the initial market entry. Another mistake is failing to provide local management support. Most franchise agreements oblige new franchisers to purchase inputs from the chain's global supplier network and pay for them in dollars. However, when currency weakens against the dollar thus pushing up import costs, the local franchise chains typically try to avoid failure by allowing the franchisee to find his own local supplier. Most are incapable of developing local supply chains because of lack of knowledge. Successful franchisors establish their own support functions for all of their local franchises, and provide support during currency devaluations that otherwise can ruin years of market buildup.

As for Subway's long-term success, it may rely more on its international presence than its dominance of the U.S. market. In order to maintain international competitiveness, Subway might benefit from greater adaptation to local markets. Increasing menu options of ethnic foods that offer regional or global appeal, such as Mediterranean options may be a strategy worth testing.

The passion for food and the diverse variety of food experiences represent both an opportunity and challenge for global fast food companies. A number of local fast food companies are launching their own regional expansion. Favorable economic conditions are supporting growing emerging modern middle classes in Brazil, Colombia, Chile, and Peru, which favor food consumption. Subway would like to be positioned as one of the preferred options in these growing markets.

Subway has clearly targeted the large markets in Latin America: Brazil, Mexico and Venezuela. In the second tier of markets, Chile, Colombia, and Peru, Subway is underrepresented. However, Subway seems overrepresented in the smaller Central American and Caribbean country markets. Further penetration of the region may require some realignment of resources to the growing middle markets in the region.

EMERGING FAST-FOOD MARKETS IN ASIA

In the early 2000s, emerging markets grew at rates twice as fast as developed economies. Five emerging markets—China, India, Brazil, Mexico, and Indonesia—are among the 12 largest economies in the world, with a combined purchasing power that is already one-half that of the Group of Seven industrial nations (United States, Japan, Britain, France, Germany, Canada, and Italy). These emerging markets are anticipated to completely dominate global markets in the near future.

Many emerging markets have growing numbers of consumers who are or will be target markets for fast food companies. In addition to new consumers, emerging markets also provide new suppliers and competitors. As globalization of business continues to develop, businesses will have to participate in this global marketplace of consumers, suppliers, and competitors. Subway is interested in consolidating its global presence in these foreign markets, one of which is Asia.

THE ASIA-PACIFIC MARKET SIZE AND DRIVERS

The Asia-Pacific region constitutes the largest global market segment, with more than four billion people. More than 60% of the global population of 6.7 billion is largely concentrated in China and India. However, according to a United Nations Economic and Social Commission for Asia and the Pacific report, the region's population growth is slowing since 2000, accompanied by declines in household size and employment. Even though the population growth is waning, discretionary income is rising. The result is a major opportunity for fast food sales.

Asia is a heterogeneous market due to differences in income, age, and levels of urbanization. In developing Asia, which includes the Philippines, Indonesia, Thailand, Malaysia, Vietnam, Pakistan, India, and China, more than half (64 %) of the total population is between 15 and 64 years of age. The proportion of younger individuals (below 15 years of age) is expected to drop from 30 % in 2000 to 19 percent by 2050, while the proportion of seniors (ages 65+) is expected to increase by 314 %, due to increased care and healthier lifestyles (Retherford 83).

In a January 2011 *Financial Times* article titled "Asia: The Rise of the Middle Class," McKinsey retail specialist Ireena Vittal notes that a growing segment of households in India (between 14 to 15 million) will be in the

$7,000-$10,000 income bracket, deriving a standard of living one step below the standard of the living of the middle class in the United States or Europe. This group has traditionally spent a greater proportion of their income on housing, education, health care, clothes, and other amenities, rather than food. But, these circumstances are radically changing.

By contrast, countries in affluent Asia (Japan, Korea, Taiwan, Hong Kong, Singapore, Macau, Australia, and New Zealand) have had an average household income of $51,672. Nearly half of the population is over 40 years of age, and 83% live in urban areas ("Affluent Asia"). Affluent people in Asia has the discretionary income to spend on fast food, and they live in city centers where fast food restaurants are available. Despite the income and appropriate locations, however, the aging of this population has been a challenge for the fast food industry, which typically appeals more to younger people.

The Asia-Pacific fast food market experienced a decelerating effect in recent years as a result of a worldwide economic malaise, which was predicted to continue into 2011. However, according to the *DataMonitor* "Fast-Food in Asia" report, the fast food market continued to grow, up to a value of 471.6 billion in 2009, representing a 5.35% increase ("Fast-Food in Asia"). Further, selected countries within the Asia-Pacific region far outpaced the region's overall growth rate. For example, the Chinese market grew at 12.6% and even the more mature South Korea market grew at 5.5%. Despite its relatively small size, Japan accounted for 4.17% of the Asia-Pacific fast food market value in 2009. Even more importantly, it is predicted that the Asia-Pacific region will increase its transactions up to more than 172.2 billion by 2014, which would make this an increase of 25.8% from 2009. With its stronger growth, Asia-Pacific is expected to catch up with or even surpass the U.S. market, becoming the largest global fast food market in the relatively near future.

Datamonitor also reports that the quick service restaurants (QSRs) dominated the Asian market, accounting for 65.1% in 2009, or a total revenue of $46.6 billion. Meanwhile, the takeaway segment contributed revenue of $13.7 billion, 19.1% of the market, and the remaining two segments, mobile and street vendors, plus leisure locations, together comprised 15.8%, or $11.3 billion.

ADAPTING MENUS TO LOCAL CULTURES

Global fast food chains have learned to adapt their offerings to the various cultures, religions, and languages in the vast Asian market. The fragmented geography, cultures, and religions in Asia require the food industry operating there to be flexible, innovative, and competitive. Given the diversity of markets and cultures, it is a challenge to use a single marketing approach in Asia. Customers' food consumption habits are influenced by the country's level of market development. Fast food markets can be grouped into mature markets and emerging markets. For instance, fast food seems to be more developed in East Asia with Japan and Singapore reaching high levels of penetration, whereas emerging markets such as China and India are less developed but growing at faster rate. Further segmentation of the Asian market suggests four clusters: Northeast Asia, Southeast Asia, India, and China. Each group is influenced by its culture and history. East Asia (plus Singapore) is a mostly Confucian society, with a strong focus on education, and a high regard for the well-known educational institutions of the West. Southeast Asia is characterized by its historical colonization by Portugal, and its people are both Muslims and Christians. India and China are markedly different from their neighbors and individually such important markets that they must be considered separately.

The adaptive approach has been used by KFC and McDonald's successfully in Asia. For instance, KFC has adopted a market-to-market strategy in different Asian segments. Especially in China, variety and localization are characteristics of KFC's business. KFC offers more options for customers than just chicken (Newham). KFC created East Dawning, which is a Chinese-style fast food concept in China, whereas in India, KFC offers vegetarian meals because an estimated 25% of the population is vegetarian. According to an article "12 Interesting Menu Items from McDonald's in Asia," McDonald's offers several variations of its burger in Asia, including the Rendan burger in Malaysia, Kiasu burger in Singapore, Bulgogi burger in Korea, McTeriyaki burger in Japan, and Maharaja Mac in India. Other McDonald's variations include Seasoned Seaweed Fries, McSpaghetti, Filet-o-Shrimp, and a McRice sandwich in Singapore.

CONSUMER CULTURE

Despite the impact of modernization on the lifestyles in Asia, rice and chicken remain the main ingredients of Asian diets. Beyond these two foods, however, it is difficult to find other commonalities because of numerous regional differences and influences.

As for fast food, Asian consumers are not only catching up with the rest of world in embracing fast food as a lifestyle, but they are also becoming connoisseurs of fast food. According to a 2004 AC Nielsen market survey, nine of the top ten world markets for weekly fast food consumption are in Asia. In contrast to the rest of the world, Asian consumers frequent fast food places more often than people living elsewhere in the world. On the average, 28% of Asian consumers visit a fast food restaurant two to three times per month, 26% once a month, and 20% at least once a week. Moreover, the particular level of fast food consumption varies from country to country; 22% of consumers in Hong Kong and 20% in Malaysia visit a fast food restaurant as often as three to six times a week, whereas 92% of Vietnamese consumers have never consumed a fast food meal. In sharp contrast, Hong Kong is the number one market for breakfast take-away. Differences in lifestyles, market penetration, and income may explain such variance in fast food consumption habits.

Many Asian consumers regard fast food not only as a quick and cheap alternative but also as a lifestyle. They have embraced fast food consumption not as an option for a quick meal during a fast-paced workday like in the United States, but as an opportunity to socialize while eating with friends and coworkers. In general, Asian consumers are more likely to visit a fast food restaurant with friends than alone. In such a case, 'fast food' may refer to the speed with which the food is prepared, but the consumption of such food in Asia may last far longer than in the United States (Collins).

Western fast food has enjoyed a high-class reputation throughout Asia. This is especially true in growth and emerging markets. Consumers in these markets regard western fast food as a novelty and enjoy such dining experiences. However, in mature markets, the high-class appeal is fading, and convenience is becoming the major driver. In addition, brand image is a more important factor in many Asian consumers' choices, with Taiwanese consumers paying more attention to brand than any other group.

Asian consumers consider type of cuisine, price, convenience of location, good hygiene practices, and health as their top five factors influencing their choices of fast food restaurants. The relative importance of these factors and other factors vary by country. For instance, in Japan the three top choice factors are good hygiene, type of cuisine, and peer group preference. Korean consumers share some similarities with Japanese and rank type of cuisine, hygiene, and convenience as their three top choices. In contrast, in less affluent countries, consumers are driven by different factors. In India, price, type of cuisine, and service are important. In China, consumers are driven by price, type of cuisine, and location. Also, with the ubiquity of Internet access, Asian consumers prefer to order online versus making the trip to a fast food outlet. For instance, the AC Neilson survey of fast food consumers in Singapore revealed that 61% of consumers prefer to order online and 71% download promotional coupons.

JAPAN

The Japanese fast food market is highly developed, and consumers face many fast food options. Japanese consumers are highly discriminating when making their fast food choices. Without exception, Japanese consumers choose the most superior value, which translates into a balance of cost, quality, and exceptional experience. In determining quality, the Japanese focus on taste, nutrition, and food safety (Barber). Japanese consumers refuse to compromise quality or food safety.

Market trends impact the Japanese fast food market. One is the increasing trend of women working and postponing childbearing, which has created increased numbers of professional consumers who are more interested in their jobs and social lives than in traditional food preparation. Eating in fast food restaurants provides a favorite way to socialize and meet friends. In social gatherings, Japanese also tend to share their fast food.

While restaurant eating in general still has a strong social component, a growing number of fast food diners are catering to customers who come to eat alone, according to The NPD Group, Inc., as reported by *Bloomberg.com*. There are a growing number of individuals living alone in Japan. Japan has the oldest population in Asia, with more than 17% of its current population over 65, and experts forecast this percentage to increase to 29% by 2025 (Retherford). While beef noodle restaurants appear to be the leading fast food restaurant option for single diners, hamburger restaurants were second in popularity. The fast food restaurant category was the only one to expand in Japan in the past five years, possibly as the result of these single customers.

According to Subway.com, there are 221 Subway restaurants in Japan as of early 2011. In a 2007 survey by *Hello-Global.com*, Subway ranked ninth in the list of fast food restaurant preferences, where the local Mos Burger restaurant ranked first, followed by KFC, then McDonald's. In keeping with the Japanese trends for taste and nutrition, one Subway restaurant in Tokyo has taken to growing its own hydroponic lettuce in a garden in the middle of the store. While this lettuce garden can only provide about 5% of the store's daily needs and there is an additional charge for this lettuce, its 'garden area' has been surrounded by chairs for customers, creating a special table centerpiece as well. (Subway Restaurants in Japan).

CHINA

At its current growth rate, China is on course to overtake the United States as the world's largest economy around 2020 ("China Overtakes Japan as World's Second-Biggest Economy"). But within China, economic growth has been inconsistent throughout the country, generally more rapid in coastal provinces than in the interior. As a result, there are large regional disparities in income. China is still considered, overall, a lower middle-income country with more than 130 million Chinese falling below international poverty lines, according to the *CIA Factbook*. A major factor in China's economy is the rapid growth of its middle class, which is anticipated to outnumber the entire U.S. population by 2011.

The sheer size of China's market makes it an attractive prospect for growing businesses, including fast food businesses. China's eat-out market was estimated at $132 billion in 2007 (Bremner). Ninety-seven percent of Chinese consumers dine at fast food restaurants, according to a 2004 AC Nielsen survey. Global fast food companies have been in China since 1987, with KFC of Yum! brands leading the charge, closely followed by McDonald's, which had over 600 outlets in China by 2004 (Goodman). Burger King followed in 2005, renaming its Whopper as the "Emperor Burger," ("Here Comes the Whopper"). Most fast food companies consider China their most important market for global expansion and continued success.

Many urban centers have experienced a sharp increase in demand for fast food as more professional dual-income households with limited time and disposable incomes appear. China's upper class and growing middle class have been the target markets for fast food restaurants. China has 140 to 150 cities with more than one million people, but many of those individuals are too poor to support an American fast-food restaurant. Cost is a major driver for Chinese consumers and fast food restaurants are adapting to offer affordable choices.

U.S. fast food is still a novelty in China. Although KFC entered China in 1987, franchised operations have only been present since 1992 (Yum! China home page) The Chinese view American fast food restaurants as an exotic experience that is still a luxury; as such they are more likely to eat inside the restaurants and stay longer than Western consumers. It is common for groups of teenagers to frequent fast food restaurants, using the location for socializing. Chinese consumers appreciate the quality, cleanliness, choice, service, convenience, and affordability that fast food chains offer.

However, the Chinese have not yet truly adopted Western fast food options and tastes. A favorite choice of the Chinese at lunchtime are dumplings, called Baozi, purchased quickly and cheaply from a street vendor (Cody). The Chinese enjoy deep-fried food, which is one explanation for KFC's major success in China. KFC offers not only its traditional fried chicken, but also a Beijing duck wrap with spring onions and hoisin sauce, as well as bowls of congee (rice gruel) in the mornings. At McDonald's, diners enjoy hamburgers with spicy sauces that are appealing to Chinese tastes and a variety of other choices specific for the Chinese, including green pea pies, rice-burgers, and a mint-flavored soda called Blue Haven.

The changing lifestyle in China encourages more eating out, including fast food restaurants. It has been said that, in addition to the Chinese curiosity about Western food, the cleanliness and safety of the Western fast food restaurants has also been a special appear to Chinese consumers (Scarlatelli). China's fast food market is fragmented with the top fast food restaurants (KFC, Pizza Hut, Taco Bell, and McDonald's) accounting for only 18.1% of the 2003 market share. The largest single player is KFC, and it entered China in 1987, a few years before McDonald's. These companies enjoyed significant first mover advantages, including setting up outlets just off Tiananmen Square. KFC is owned by Yum Brands China (along with Pizza Hut and Taco Bell). KFC is one of the most popular fast food chains in China, with more than 3,100 locations in 650 cities across every Chinese province except Tibet ("KFC Parent Company Gets More Revenue from China than U.S."). Part of the appeal of KFC, in addition to the general appreciation of fried chicken, appears to be its use of both local ingredients and local managers for its restaurants, who have "buil[t] partnerships with local companies and used their expertise to offer an array of regional dishes that appear to domestic tastes" (Mellors).

Far behind KFC is McDonald's, which has been in China since 1990 and, as of 2010, has 760 outlets there. McDonald's plans to open 100 sites a year for the next five years in China. On the difference between McDonald's and KFC in China, Aaron Hotfelder wrote: "Perhaps surprisingly, McDonald's is not nearly as successful, with only about half the number of restaurants. This is the reverse of the situation in the United States, where McDonald's is often considered to be number one while KFC trails behind." Yum! Brands, including Pizza Hut and Taco Bell in addition to KFC, had its 2010 sales in China increase 20%, while sales revenue in the United States dropped 8%. Pizza Hut has been in China since 1990 and is number three with more than 560 outlets. Overall, during the second quarter of 2009, Yum Brands in China generated $139 million in profit (up 33% from $105 million in the same quarter a year earlier). While Yum Brand sales in the United States were still overall higher ($184 million profit in the second quarter of 2009), the profit from the U.S. operations only rose 10% (Rooney).

China also has numerous local fast food establishments. The major Chinese fast food brands include Kungfu, Yonghe King, and De Niang Dumpling. While Western fast food appears to revolve around fried or grilled foods such as hamburgers, chicken (pieces or nuggets), sandwiches, and french fries, usually all accompanied by soft drinks, Chinese fast food has a far broader range of foods and condiments. These foods include rice, noodles, and dumplings, and are prepared various ways, including fried and steamed. Typically the meals include soup and/or soft drinks (Research and Markets).

Subway has a presence in China, but only 197 stores as of 2011 (including both the Chinese mainland and Hong Kong), according to *Subway.com*. This is a not strong showing, given the large population of China and the relatively large number of other fast food franchise outlets in that country. However, not to be deterred, Subway president, Fred DeLuca, announced in 2010, that "China had great growth opportunity and [that Subway intended to create] 500 stores in the next 5 years, with 35-50 set to open in the coming [2011] year." Further, DeLuca noted that Subway intended to localize its menu to suit local palates and that the company was "'testing sandwiches such as Beijing roast duck, and local sauces like 'hot spicy Szechuan sauce'"(Master).

Despite the numerous fast food outlets spreading throughout China, the overall impact is less than might be expected. According to a study by AlixPartners, a global business advisory firm, Chinese consumers spend 22% of total food expenditures in restaurants. In the United States, total food expenditures are as high as 50%. But the group expects the percentage of total food expenditures in China to change since almost half of the surveyed consumers anticipate that they will begin eating out more, as a result of having more disposable income.

Interestingly China's booming consumption of automobiles is having an effect on the fast food industry. Chinese consumers want to drive their new cars through fast food drive-through restaurants. In McDonald's restaurants with drive-through outlets, average sales are 25-50% higher than their restaurants without a drive through. McDonald's is capitalizing on this opportunity by signing a deal with Sinopec, the state-owned petroleum company with 30,000 stations, giving McDonald's first right to build drive-through outlets on those locations (Arndt and Roberts). In general, it is estimated that restaurants in China with drive-through operations post 50-80% higher sales volume than stores without the service. Also interesting is that many patrons who purchase their meals through the drive-through then park their car and eat their meal inside the restaurant. Chinese fast food consumers want the full experience that the restaurants have to offer.

Another cultural nuance is that the Chinese do not touch their food with their hands. They view it as very unsanitary, so they use chopsticks to eat all types of food. McDonald's locations do not offer chopsticks, but they do have hand-sanitizing lotion available. For more particular eaters, plastic gloves are sometimes available.

INDIA

India's population of one billion is the world's fourth largest economy (India Country Overview). The country's population growth provides both problems and opportunities, including the fact that its relatively fast population growth will provide it with the world's largest proportion of working age (15-64) people. It has been noted that "India already has an advantage over more advanced economies. The median age in India in 2000 was 24, compared to 30 in China, 38 in Europe and 41 in creaky old Japan." (Einhorn)

India's impressive macro-economic growth means that its one billion people are experiencing increased income, which in turn causes a growing middle class. Traditionally, Indians prefer home-cooked meals, but that preference has changed in recent years. With more women working and more well-paid young professionals, the perception that eating out is a form of entertainment is more common. Growing urbanization also contributes to more Indians eating out. By one estimate, the fast food market in India has been growing at an annual rate of 25–30%, according to a report published by market research firm RNCOS in September 2010, titled "Indian Fast Food Market Analysis." Another source, the India Brand Equity Foundation, reports that currently the fast food marketplace in India is expanding at 40%, especially since the entrance of multinational fast food companies into India as of 1992. This rapid expansion does not appear to be limited to specific types of fast food. Domino's has indicated that it plans to open 60-65 outlines in India each year from 2010-2012. Likewise, Yum Brands intends to open 1000 of its fast food outlets, under its various brands, by 2015.

The challenge for fast food companies is to adapt their offerings to the Indian palate. With so many regional differences, India is a mosaic of sub-cultures and religions. One way to look at the Indian market is to divide their choice for food in terms of vegetarian and non-vegetarian options. Multiple fast food companies seeking to expand their presence in India have been revising their meat-based menus to include numerous vegetarian offerings. It has been reported that McDonald's, KFC, Pizza Hut and Dominos are obtaining 50% of their sales in India from vegetarian items. This varies substantially from their total global offerings, as overall global sales of non-vegetarian items for Dominos and Pizza Hut is 90% and 70% respectively (Mitra and Maji).

Regional differences complicate the challenge of offering a standardized fast-food menu throughout this country. In the north, the preference is for wheat consumption. In the east and south, rice is more popular. Chicken and lamb are popular in the east, whereas fish is popular in the west. Indian cuisine remains the most popular, followed by Chinese, and finally international. Indians, however, are exploring other ethnic cuisines, and it is not unusual to find Mexican and Italian options. Indians, despite their increasing affluence, are extremely price conscious and are also more demanding in terms of quality, hygiene standards, and atmosphere.

McDonald's restaurants are expanding in India despite its population's vegetarian preferences. McDonald's entered into India in 1996 with one restaurant in Delhi, and now has 211 restaurants, which are divided practically evenly with 105 stores in the North or East and 106 in the South or West, and plans to open 40 more stores in the near future. Pizza Hut is also expanding, and increasing its popularity by creating foods reflecting local preferences, such as spicy items for its northern Indian locations ("Fast Food Industry Booms in India").

As of January 2011, Subway has 197 restaurants in India, according to *Subway.com*. Given its format for creating customized submarine sandwiches, its foods are able to be adapted to a variety of cultural preferences, including vegetarian and non-beef items. Its sandwich format, on the other hand, is not as familiar to those regions of India where rice-based dishes are the norm, and sandwiches are seen as a foreign style of food.

COMPETITION

The major players in the Asian fast food market include global fast food chains as well as several local fast food operations. Global chains such as McDonald's, KFC, Burger King, Hardee's, Wendy's, Popeye's, and Subway have established their presence in Asia, either directly or though such global corporations as Yum Brands or the Minor Food Group. McDonald's is a dominating force except in China where KFC is king.

A global leader of fast food, McDonald's entered the Asian market early on and has a strong presence in many Asian country markets. A savvy marketer, McDonald's continues to target youth and children successfully and was an active sponsor for such sporting events such as 2002 World Cup and the 2008 Beijing Olympic games. Operating a slightly different business model, McDonald's owns its franchise properties, a practice allowing it to collect rent in addition to franchise fees. However, this requires huge capital investments. It also makes the company subject to higher risks due to the unstable and speculative nature of real estate in some markets. Other weaknesses of McDonald's include its less localized menu, the increased health concerns among consumers, and safety issues of beef products in light of such issues as mad cow disease.

KEEPING THE MARKET PUSH IN ASIAN MARKETS

Numerous global companies are also attracted to Asia and are seeking ways to distinguish their fast food offerings from the other global and local competitors. Subway is focusing its efforts in dominating certain Asian market niches with its healthier menu, as well as possible locally adapted offerings, and its customized sandwiches.

Subway's long-term success may rely more on its international presence abroad than its dominance of the U.S. market. In order to maintain international competitiveness, Subway should consider greater adaptation to local markets. Increasing menu options of ethnic foods that offer regional or global appeal, such as Mediterranean options is a strategy worth testing.

Perhaps the most challenging region throughout the world for Subway to penetrate today is Asia. Despite Subway's substantial presence in 96 countries, its involvement in the Asia-Pacific region is relatively low. Subway has a presence in a number of these additional Asian countries, but far less than expected, especially given the populations of such countries as China. With the Asia-Pacific market expected to out-grow all other markets, Subway must learn how to compete with other multinational chains in this region as well as local food chains in order to ensure its continued global growth.

QUESTIONS FOR DISCUSSION

1. How important are the Asia-Pacific and Latin America fast food markets to Subway International?

2. What countries and consumer segments offer the best market opportunities for future growth in the Asia-Pacific and Latin America? Why?

3. What are the market trends and consumption behavior towards fast food in the Asia-Pacific and Latin America?

4. Who are the major competitors for Subway in each region?

5. Which Asia-Pacific and Latin American market opportunities do you think better match the strengths and competencies of Subway International? Justify your answer. Provide a recommendation for markets where Subway should continue pursue continue penetration (has already market presence in the region) and enter (does not have market presence in the region).

6. What recommendations would you provide for improving Subway's market position in either the Asia-Pacific or Latin America? Make sure that you justify your recommendations with evidence of local market conditions.

REFERENCES/BIBLIOGRAPHY

"12 Interesting Menu Items from McDonalds in Asia." 23 Mar. 2010. Web. Retrieved 14 Feb. 2011 from http://www.weirdasianews.com/2010/03/23/blank-interesting-menu-items-mcdonalds-asia/

AC Nielsen. *Consumers in Asia Pacific—Our Fast Food/ Take Away Consumption Habits, 2nd half.* 2004

Adler, Carlye. "How China Eats a Sandwich." *Fortune Small Business* 15.2 (Mar. 2005): 72-76. Available from http://money.cnn.com/magazines/fsb/fsb_archive/2005/03/01/8253829/index.htm

Arndt, Michael and Dexter Roberts. "A Finger-Lickin' Good Time In China." *Bloomburg BusinessWeek.* 30 Oct. 2006. Web. Retrieved 28 Feb. 2011 from http://www.businessweek.com/print/magazine/content/06_44/b4007074.htm?chan=gl

Barber, Terrence. "Convergence of U.S., Japanese Food Trends Spells Opportunity for U.S. Exporters." Web. Retrieved 14 Feb. 2011 from http://www.fas.usda.gov/info/agexporter/1998/February%201998/converge.html

Bembos Web site: Bembos.com.pe/

"Brazil-based Habib's Plans North American Expansion." *Business Publications* 21 Aug. 2000. Web. 21 Feb. 2011. http://findarticles.com/p/articles/mi_m3190/is_34_34/ai_64704025/

Bremner, Brian. "McDonald's Is Loving It in Asia." *Bloomberg Businessweek*. 24 Jan. 2007. Web. Retrieved 14 Feb. 2011 from http://www.businessweek.com/globalbiz/content/jan2007/gb20070124_420131.htm

"By 2011, the Global Fast Food Market Is Forecast to Reach a Value of $125.4 Billion." *Business Wire*. 18 Oct 2007. Web. Retreived 28 Feb. 2011 from http://findarticles.com/p/articles/mi_m0EIN/is_2007_Oct_18/ai_n27410800/

Canono, Joy F. "Philippine Market Blends Eastern Traditions, Western Tastes." *AgExporter*. 6 Sept. 2001. www.fas.usda.gov/info/agexporter/2001/sept/page08-1.pdf

Cebrzynski, Gregg. "Subway Teams with Discovery Kids to Reach Children." *Nation's Restaurant News* 40.2 (9 Jan. 2006).

Chancey, Blair. "How Subway Went Global." *QSR Magazine*, n.d. Retrieved 14 Feb 2011 from http://www.qsrmagazine.com/articles/interview/138/don_fertman-1.phtml

"China Overtakes Japan as World's Second-Biggest Economy." *Bloomberg News*. 16 Aug 2010. Web. Retrieved 14 Feb. 2011 from http://www.bloomberg.com/news/2010-08-16/china-economy-passes-japan-s-in-second-quarter-capping-three-decade-rise.html

CIA. *The World Factbook*. Web. Retrieved 14 Feb. 2011 from https://www.cia.gov/cia/publications/factbook/rankorder/2001rank.html

Cody, Edward. "A Quick Bite Wrapped in Dough." *Washingtonpost.com*. 3 Nov. 2006. Retrieved 28 Feb 2011 from http://www.washingtonpost.com/wp-dyn/content/article/2006/11/02/AR2006110201626.html

Collins, Samuel. "Review of Golden Arches East-McDonald's in East Asia." H-Net, Humanities and Social Sciences Online. Aug. 1998. Web. Retrieved 21 Feb. 2011. http://www.h-net.org/reviews/showrev.php?id=2239

"Compran Lomitón para potencia cadena de fast food de deportes." *Chile-Hoy*. 3 June 2010. Retrieved 28 Feb. 2011 from http://chile-hoy.blogspot.com/2010/06/compran-lomiton-para-potenciar-cadena.html

Datamonitor. *The Global Fast Food Market*. Retrieved 14 Feb. 2011 from http://datamonitor.com

Duecy, Erica. "Global Growth, Urban Sites Speed Subway along Track Toward Overtaking McDonald's" *Nation's Restaurant News* 39.6 (5 Feb. 2005): 4-6.

Einhorn, Bruce. "Can Soaring Population Give India An Edge Over China?" *Bloomburg BusinessWeek*. 19 Sept. 2006. Retrieved 28 Feb. 2011 from http://www.businessweek.com/blogs/eyeonasia/archives/2006/09/can_soaring_population_give_india_an_edge_over_china.html

Entrepreneur Media Inc. *Franchises.* 2011. Retrieved 14 Feb. 2011 from http://www.entrepreneur.com/

Euromonitor International. *Annual Disposable Income from Euromonitor National Statistics,* 2011. Web. 21 Feb. 2011. http://www.euromonitor.com

Euromonitor International. *Consumer Foodservice Statistics.* 2011 Retrieved 14 Feb. 2011 from http://www.euromonitor.com

Euromonitor International. *Consumer Lifestyle Report: Dining Out.* Available from http://www.euromonitor.com

"Fast-Food in Asia-Pacific." *Datamonitor Industry Profiles.* 17 September 2010.

"Fast Food Industry Booms in India." *Rediff Business.* 25 Jan. 2011. Retrieved 28 Feb. 2011 from http://www.rediff.com/business/report/fast-food-industry-booms-in-india/20110125.htm

Fiszbein, Ariel, Paula Inés Giovagnoli, and Isidro Adúriz. "The Argentine Crisis and its Impact on Household Welfare." *Cepal Review.* 79 (April 2003).

"Food Industry." *India Brand Equity Foundation.* Dec. 2010. Web. 14 Feb. 2011. Retrieved 28 Feb. 2011 from http://www.ibef.org/industry/foodindustry.aspx

Goodman, Peter. "Fast Food Takes a Bite Out of Chinese Culture -Consumers Crave Convenience of Western Carryout Choices." *Washington Post Foreign Service.* 26 Dec. 2004; Page A01. Retrieved 27 Feb 2011 from http://www.washingtonpost.com/ac2/wp-dyn/A25868-2004Dec25?

Hein, Kenneth. "Subway Seeks Bigger Taste of Hungry Tween Group." *Brandweek* 47.15 (10 Apr. 2006).

"Here Comes the Whopper: The World's Second Largest Burger Chain is Gearing Up in China." *The Economist.* 23 Oct. 2008. Web. Retrieved 19 Feb. 2011 from http://www.economist.com/node/12488790

Hernandez, L. "Columbia's Consumers Are Ready to Dine." *AG Exporter* 1 July 2001. Web. 15 Feb. 2011. http://www.allbusiness.com/sales/international-trade-exporting/800661-1.html

"History of Subway." *Subway.com.* 2011. Retrieved 14 Feb. 2011 from http://www.subway.com/subwayroot/AboutSubway/history/subwayHistory.aspx

Hotfelder, Aaron. "Why Does China Love KFC More than McDonald's?" *Gadling.com,* 5 June 2010. Web. Retrieved 14 Feb. 2011 from http://www.gadling.com/2010/06/05/why-does-china-love-kfc-more-than-mcdonalds/

Indian Fast Food Market Analysis. *RNCOS Industry Research Solutions.* Sept 2010. Print. Available at http://www.rncos.com/Market-Analysis-Reports/Indian-Fast-Food-Market-Analysis-IM264.htm

International Subway Locations. *Subway.com.* Doctor's Associates, Inc. Retrieved 14 Feb. 2011 from http://www.subway.com/subwayroot/Applications/Reports/CountryCount.aspx

"KFC Parent Company Gets More Revenue from China than U.S." *Manila News.Net.* 24 Jan. 2011. Web. Retrieved 14 Feb. 2011 from http://www.manilanews.net/story/735627

"Korean fast food made bigger, tastier and pricier." *Asianpacificpost.com.* 28 Feb. 2008. Retrieved 28 Feb 2011 from http://www.asianpacificpost.com/portal2/c1ee8c4418586b12011861f77e470174_Korean_fast_food_made_bigger__tastier_and_pricier.do.html

Liszewski, Andrew. "Subway Restaurants In Japan Let You Eat Extra Fresh With Hydroponic Lettuce Grown In The Store." *OhGizmo.com.* 19 July 2010. Web. Retrieved 22 Feb. 2011 at http://www.ohgizmo.com/2010/07/19/subway-restaurants-in-japan-let-you-eat-extra-fresh-with-hydro-ponic-lettuce-grown-in-the-store/

Master, Farah. "Subway Eyes Matching McDonalds in China in 10 years," Reuters. 8 Mar. 2010. Web. Retrieved 14 Feb. 2011 from http://www.reuters.com/article/2010/03/08/us-subway-china-idUS-TRE62723220100308

Mellor, William. "McDonald's No Match for KFC in China as Colonel Rules Fast Food." *Bloomberg.com.* 26 Jan 2011. Web. Retrieved on 28 Feb 2011 http://www.bloomberg.com/news/2011-01-26/mcdonald-s-no-match-for-kfc-in-china-where-colonel-sanders-rules-fast-food.html

Mintel Report. *Sandwiches, Subs and Wraps.* April 2005. Retrieved 14 Feb 2011 from http://oxygen.mintel.com

Mitra, Sreerupa and Jayashree Maji. "America goes vegetarian in India." *Mydigitalfc.com.* 21 Dec 2010. Retrieved 28 Feb. 2011 from http://www.mydigitalfc.com/news/america-goes-vegetarian-india-881

Newham, Fraser. "KFC Marches to a Different Drumstick in China." *Asia Times Online.* 20 Dec. 2005. Retrieved on 27 Feb. 2011 from http://www.atimes.com/atimes/China_Business/GL20Cb01.html

"Physicians Believe Obesity Is America's Most Severe Health Issue; Survey by Epocrates Reveals Individuals and Food Industry Are Most Responsible." *PR Newswire.* 25 Apr. 2007.

Pinto, Veronica. "Chile: Franchise Industry." United States Department of Commerce: U.S. Commercial Service, June 2006. Web. 21 Feb. 2011. www.buyusa.gov/chile/en/franchise/pdf

Plummer, Robert. "Giving Brazil a Taste of Arabia." *BBC News* 11 Dec. 2005. Web. 21 Feb. 2011. http://news.bbc.co.uk/2/hi/business/4468070.stm

Pollo Campero Web site: http://www.campero.com/

"Pollo Campero Expands." *Caribbean Update* June 2010. Web. 21 Feb. 2011. http://www.allbusiness.com/food-beverage/restaurants-food-service/14517268-1.html

Questionnaire Survey on Fast Food Restaurants. *Hello-Global.com.* Tokyo, Japan. Research conducted on April 15–28, 2007. Web. 21 February 2011. http://www.hello-global.com/en/japan/consumer-surveys/question-naire-survey-on-fast-food-restaurants

"Research and Markets: Research Report on China Fast Food Industry 2011-2012: Analysis of the Chinese and Western Brands.". *CNBC.* 31 Jan. 2011. Web. Retrieved 14 Feb. 2011 from http://www.cnbc.com/id/41355437/

Retherford, R.D. "The Future of Population in Asia." Honolulu, HI:East-West Center, 2002. Web. Retrieved 20 February 2011 from http://www.eastwestcenter.org/fileadmin/stored/misc/FuturePop08Aging.pdf

Roig-Franzid, Manuel. "For Real Heat, Hit the Streets." Dumpling, Taco, Borscht, Baguette. *Washington Post* 3 Nov. 2006. Web. 15 Feb. 2011. http://www.washingtonpost.com/wp-dyn/content/article/2006/11/02/AR2006110201625.html

Rooney, Ben. "China: The New Fast Food Nation," *CNNMoney.com.* 14 July 2010. Web. Retrieved 14 Feb. 2011 from http://money.cnn.com/2010/07/13/news/companies/Yum_Brands/index.htm

Scarlatelli, Andrea. "American Junk Food: Why So Popular in China?" *eChinacities.com.* 29 October 2010. Web. Retrieved 28 Feb. 2011 from http://www.echinacities.com/expat-corner/junk-food-in-china-why-so-popular.html

Schoenberger, Chana and Minh Bui. "Japan's Fast-Food Stocks Gain as Diners Eat Alone: Chart of Day." *Bloomberg.com.* Jun 29, 2010. Web. Retrieved 22 Feb. 2011 from http://www.bloomberg.com/news/print/2010-06-30/japan-s-fast-food-stocks-gain-as-51-eat-solo-in-restaurants-chart-of-day.html

Singh, A. "Latin America and the Caribbean: Building a Sustainable Recovery." *Proceedings from 21st Annual Journalists and Editors Workshop on Latin America and the Caribbean.* Miami. 3 May 2003. Paper.

"Sipsa vende Lomiton." *Tormo* 9 Feb. 2009. Web. 21 Feb. 2011. http://www.tormo.cl/actualidad/noticias/noticia.asp?id=610

Sloop, Christine. "Chile: HRI Food Service Sector, Annual 2006, Gain Report Number C16004." Santiago: U.S. Embassy Office of Agricultural Affairs, 27 Feb. 2006. Print.

"Starbucks Opens 300th Store in Mexico." *Starbucks Newsroom.* 20 Dec. 2010. Web. Retrieved 28 Feb. 2011 from http://news.starbucks.com/article_display.cfm?article_id=477

Statistical Yearbook for Asia and the Pacific 2008. United Nations Economic and Social Commission for Asia and the Pacific. Available from http://www.unescap.org/stat/data/syb2008/ESCAP-syb2008.pdf

Subway Student and Educator Resource Guide. 16 Mar. 2006. Retrieved 14 Feb. 2011 from http://www.subway.com/StudentGuide/s_e_welcome.htm

"Tomorrow's Affluent Asia." Global Demographics. 2010. Web. 14 Feb. 2011. www.global-dem.com/Countries/Affluentasia.htm

Waldmeir, Patti. "Fast Food Battle Heats Up in China." *Financial Times.* 1 Feb. 2011. Print.

World Bank. *India Country Overview* September 2010. http://www.world-bank.org.in/WBSITE/EXTERNAL/COUNTRIES/SOUTHASIAEXT/INDIAEXTN/0,,contentMDK:20195738pagePK:141137piPK:141127theSitePK:295584,00.html

Yum! China. Official Webpage. Available at http://www.yum.com/company/china.asp

Zurawicki, Leon and Nestor Braidot. "Consumers During Crisis: Responses from the Middle Class in Argentina." *Journal of Business Research*. 58.8 (2005): 110-1109

Urban Farming: Can It Be Effective in Detroit?

Leslie Karr • Managing Editor, Karr Editorial, LLC

SUGGESTED LEARNING OBJECTIVES

Students should be able to do the following:

- *Identify economic, demographic, and social trends that support or undermine a burgeoning urban agriculture movement*
- *Debate the pros and cons of urban agriculture from a societal, environmental, and economic perspective*
- *Brainstorm ideas for agricultural start-up companies and evaluate the merits of potential new businesses in light of market trends*
- *Develop a SWOT analysis for an entrepreneurial urban farming venture such as Hantz Farms*

This case was prepared for classroom discussion rather than to illustrate either effective or ineffective handling of an administrative, ethical, or legal decision by management. Information was gathered from corporate as well as public sources.

BACKGROUND

During his daily commute from his home in Detroit's historic Indian Village neighborhood to his office in the northern suburb of Southfield, Michigan, John R. Hantz often reflected on the growing problems facing the city of Detroit. Hantz, once a vice president for American Express Financial Advisors, left the company in 1997 to start his own financial consulting and investment firm, Hantz Financial Services, and later Hantz Group, Inc., a full-service financial holding company. As of 2010 Hantz employed over 550 people in 23 offices and managed $1.3 billion of assets (Hantz Group Web site). At age 48 with a net worth exceeding $100 million, this 20-year Detroit resident had become one of the wealthiest men left in the city.

While driving through neighborhood after neighborhood of derelict buildings, abandoned houses, piles of garbage, and overgrown fields of weeds in this once-prosperous city, Hantz would try to convince himself that things were getting better. Many commutes later, he realized that the situation in Detroit was not, in fact, improving, and perhaps he needed to do something about it. Could he use his financial resources to set a direction for the city upon which others would build? Could he implement an idea that would encourage other entrepreneurs to invest in Detroit? Then one day, while stopped at a traffic light, it dawned on him: In order to create value, Detroit needed scarcity. "And that," he told a reporter for Fortune magazine, "is how I got onto this idea of the farm" (Whitford).

INTRODUCING HANTZ FARMS

In 2009 Hantz broadcast his idea: to create the world's largest urban farm, rejuvenating the city through a return to its agrarian roots. "Detroit could be the nation's leading example of urban farming and become a destination for fresh, local and natural foods and become a major part of the green movement," he announced in a press release. "Hantz Farms will transform this area into a viable, beautiful and sustainable area that will serve the community, increase the tax base, create jobs and greatly improve the quality of life in an area that has experienced a severe decline in population" (Bassett). On top of satisfying the increasing consumer demand for locally grown produce, the for-profit venture proposes to answer the call for green-energy-focused operations by harvesting non-polluting solar and wind energy, utilizing geothermal heat, and producing biomass fuel from recycling compost. The development and operation of the farm would create hundreds of green-collar jobs to contribute to a revitalized, postindustrial Detroit economy. Hantz envisioned a twelve-month operation, growing spring vegetables, a variety of summer produce, orchard fruits, pumpkins, and Christmas trees. In addition to providing Detroiters with healthy, safe, homegrown products, the farm would serve as a model for the possibilities of urban agriculture in other postindustrial cities and the capacity of urban farming to transform local economies. Agricultural enthusiasts and tourists would visit the farm to see the latest in farm technology, including compost-heated greenhouses and both hydroponic and aeroponic growing systems that maximize year-round productivity in settings with space constraints.

REGULATORY ROADBLOCKS

The first phase of Hantz's plan called for the utilization of approximately 70 acres of vacant land or abandoned properties on Detroit's lower eastside. Hantz is committed to investing $30 million of his own funds in the project over ten years. From Detroit city officials, he has asked for free tax-delinquent land in conjunction with his own purchases at an average cost of $3,000 per acre, a price comparable to the value of rural farmland in the region. He also has requested a zoning adjustment to recognize agriculture as an approved use of land at a new, lower tax rate. In Hantz's view, he would be alleviating the city of an unmanageable burden by clearing out blight and transforming pockets of the city into bountiful farmland. As a result, the city could consolidate its resources, allowing the fire, police, and public works departments to better serve Detroiters.

Although receptive to Hantz's proposal, the city was not quick to negotiate a deal. As Al Fields, group executive of planning for Detroit, articulated at a "Business of Urban Agriculture" summit hosted by the University of Michigan-Dearborn and Crain's Detroit Business in April 2010: "We're working to integrate [urban farming] into a whole citywide plan. ... We're in the process of looking at the city of Detroit and getting it ready for the future. How do we align our resources, how do we align our land policy, and how do we put those things in place that get us ready when we return from this economic downturn and get into a better position to grow?"

In light of his lack of swift progress with City of Detroit officials, in April 2010 Hantz announced a proposal to create a demonstration farm on 40 acres of state-owned land that formerly served as the site of the Michigan State Fair. Meanwhile, he leaked to the press that he had numerous backup plans, including an undisclosed farm site that he purchased in a nearby suburb. "[I]t got done in two weeks, and it was cheaper than in the city, and everyone was very welcoming," he told the Detroit News (Berman). Clearly attempting to leverage this alternate plan in his negotiations with the city, Hantz argued that the city was overvaluing land, pointing out that the land he sought had no value unless someone was willing to pay for it. Furthermore, he cautioned that the vacant land consumed the city's resources at an unsustainable rate. Hantz's research has indicated that one unused parcel costs the taxpayers $12,000 over a five-year period—significant carrying costs when considering that Detroit has 200,000 parcels of vacant land or derelict properties comprising 30,000 acres (Kaffer).

A SHRINKING DETROIT

Between 1980 and 2010, the City of Detroit has embraced multiple revitalization efforts, including the construction of the Renaissance Center office and retail complex in the 1970s, three downtown casinos in the 1990s, and two new professional sports stadiums in the 2000s. Unfortunately, none of them had the desired impact on peripheral business and residential development. Detroit, which was at one time the fourth-largest city in the United States, has shrunk from a city of two million people to a city comprising 800,000. Experts have estimated that 40 square miles of the city's 139-square-mile footprint are abandoned (Whitford). The vacancies are indeed a burden on city government, which struggles to police the streets, maintain its infrastructure, and provide other necessary services in sparsely populated pockets of Detroit as its tax base dwindles, schools close, and real estate prices plummet.

In the wake of the financial crisis of the late 2000s and the corresponding global recession, the unemployment rate for Detroit was 13.2% as of June 2010 compared to the national unemployment figure of 9.5%. Manufacturing jobs in the state hovered around 460,000 in contrast to 900,000 in the late 1990s (Gallagher, "Unemployment Dips").

DEVELOPING DETROIT'S LOCAL FOOD SYSTEM

Many involved in the local food community believe that urban farming offers an opportunity to re-imagine Detroit, including Dan Carmody, president of Eastern Market Corporation, which manages southeast Michigan's longest-running farmers market and corresponding food district comprising wholesalers, distributors, processors, and retailers.

Carmody has advocated for the growth of a local food system as an economic strategy to provide jobs to people who need them and repurpose underutilized land. At the "Business of Urban Agriculture" conference in April 2010, he posited that shifting 20% of food spending locally to Detroit would lead to 4,700 new jobs and nearly $20 million in local business tax revenue, referring to economist Michael H. Shuman's study "Economic Impact of Localizing Detroit's Food System" (Shuman).

To support his contention that urban farming can be successful, Carmody cited the example of the craft-beer industry, which now comprises 4.3% of the beer market by volume and 6.9% by dollars (Brewers Association Facts). In the 1980s brands such as Budweiser and Miller drove small brewers out of the marketplace, but in the early 2000s microbreweries occupy a modest, but viable market segment, growing from just a handful in the late 1970s to around 1,600 in 2010 (Brewers Association Facts).

Patty Cantrell of the Michigan Land Use Institute has called for creativity and an entrepreneurial spirit to build local and regional links in the current supply chain. "Potato farmers have an easier time sending their potatoes halfway around the country and back as a potato chip than ... sell[ing] potatoes down the road to a school nearby. ... There's an issue in our food system where farmers aren't able to get their products to market and there's people who aren't able to get products they want," she stated (Business of Urban Agriculture Summit). Entrepreneurs in urban agriculture, whether they are growing the food, distributing it, or providing related support services, will help meet the growing consumer demand for fresh, local, and organic foods, she argued. "These are the entrepreneurs that are going to remake our state, not just our city. ... Their innovation, the jobs and businesses that result, the thriving neighborhoods that result, and the creative culture that results, is what will make a world-class place. And that's what Michigan and Detroit needs to keep and attract business and household investment."

DEMAND FOR LOCAL FOOD

Consumer awareness of the importance of eating high-quality food is on the rise, and the U.S. market for organic and local produce, organic dairy products, and pasture-raised meats is thriving as never before. The United States

Department of Agriculture (USDA) reported 6,132 operational farmers markets in August 2010, representing a 16% increase over 2009 when the agency reported 5,274 markets (Wasserman). "Seeing such continued strong growth in the number of U.S. farmers markets indicates that regional food systems can provide great economic, social and health benefits to communities across the country," said Agriculture Secretary Tom Vilsack. "Farmers markets provide fresh, local products to communities across the country while offering economic opportunities for many producers of all sizes" (Wasserman).

According to the USDA, Michigan farmers markets experienced 60% market growth from 2009 to 2010 with a total of 271 in the state. "Detroit is a hotbed of the local-food movement," affirmed Kami Pothukuchi, a Wayne State University professor and founder of SEED Wayne, which started a monthly farmers market on the university's Detroit campus in 2008 (Aguilar). Due to overwhelming demand, it evolved into a weekly market in 2009; in 2010 the organization added a supplemental monthly market on its medical school campus. SEED Wayne also started a pilot program offering delivery service of farmers market produce, demonstrating the organization's growing effort to fill a void in the city's food supply. A 2008 study conducted by the Detroit Fresh Food Access Initiative found that 550,000 Detroiters have to travel twice as far to reach a grocery store as they do a party store, dollar store, gas station, or fast-food establishment (Aguilar). At the grocery stores that do exist, the quality and selection is lacking, and most have an extremely limited variety of unprocessed foods.

Large-scale Midwestern grocers such as Meijer and Kroger have also taken notice of their customers' growing awareness of, and interest in, where food comes from and their desire to keep dollars in the local economy. Both chains have publicized their commitment to buying and selling local produce as part of their marketing campaigns. "With 'just-picked' fruits and vegetables arriving daily to our stores, we like to think that we provide our shoppers with a farmer's market experience," said Meijer produce director Mark Stevenson. "We're not only putting money in local farmers' pockets, but we help bring farm-fresh, local produce straight to the tables of our shoppers. And there's nothing quite like farm-fresh food from the Midwest" (PR Newswire).

Similarly, Grand Rapids-based Sysco, the largest food-service distributor in North America, embarked on a pilot project in 2008 to "source and sell good food" in response to a change in demand on the part of restaurants, hospitals, schools, and other institutions for locally sourced, sustainably produced foods. The project contributed 10% of the firm's total sales volume in 2008, representing $92,000 in incremental sales (Cantrell). The pilot program demonstrated that a new range of customer values—centered on variety, taste, nutrition, and safety—was driving demand for fresh, local food among food-service buyers.

BENEFITS OF LOCAL FOOD SYSTEMS

Advocates of a strong local food system have touted its many benefits. First, a local food system is energy efficient. According to the 2000 study "Life Cycle-Based Sustainability Indicators for Assessment of the U.S. Food System," conducted by the University of Michigan's Center for Sustainable Systems, it takes 7.3 units of energy to produce one unit of food energy in the current U.S. food system; others have estimated it could be up to 10 units of energy inputs for every unit of food energy (Heller and Keoleian). The same study revealed that the average American food product travels approximately 1,500 miles before being consumed. Foods produced, distributed, transported, and consumed locally would cut down dramatically on the amount of fossil fuels used in the supply chain, thereby impacting the nation's heavy reliance on non-renewable energy sources. Indeed, after automobiles, the food system uses more petroleum than any other sector of the U.S. economy.

Second, a decentralized food system improves food security, a concept that encompasses residents' access to safe, nutritious food as well as the city's ability to respond to a food-related emergency such as that caused by a natural disaster or an act of terrorism. Regional food systems are more resilient to a variety of shocks, notably contamination and a lack of immediate availability. As author and local-food advocate Michael Pollan opined in the New York Times, "When a nation loses the ability to substantially feed itself, it is not only at the mercy of global commodity markets but of other governments as well. At issue is not only the availability of food, which may be held hostage by a hostile state, but its safety: as recent scandals in China demonstrate, we have little control over the safety of imported foods" (Pollan).

Third, a local food system promotes healthy eating by increasing awareness of where food comes from and providing access to the types of foods associated with a healthful diet. For example, vine-ripened fruits and locally grown produce—in addition to tasting better—have a higher nutritional profile than their long-distance counterparts because they are fresher and require less processing. According to the USDA, diets rich in a variety of fruits and vegetables reduce the risk of four of the top-10 chronic diseases in the United States today: heart disease, stroke, Type 2 diabetes, and cancer (USDA Web site). Pollan and other activists have argued that a local food supply—though it does not offer as much food as a centralized system in terms of the sheer quantity of calories produced—provides access to higher-quality food and thus produces healthier populations.

A fourth benefit of a vibrant local food system is its ability to transform neighborhoods and build a community, as well as its capacity to simultaneously promote self-determination and social justice. These aspects of urban farming drive a number of nonprofit, grassroots organizations that have been pioneering efforts in Detroit urban agriculture for the past two decades.

THE GRASSROOTS URBAN FARMING MOVEMENT IN DETROIT

Since the early 1990s a number of organizations have been working to promote urban agriculture and food security for the citizens of Detroit. For example, Gerald Hairston, a Southern-born African American, started a neighborhood volunteer group, the Gardening Angels, to plant gardens on vacant lots. His efforts promoted relationships between elders and youth; brought fresh, healthy food to an economically disadvantaged community; and encouraged neighborhood stewardship, which in turn reduced crime in the surrounding area. In 1997, Brother Rick Samyn, a Catholic monk, started EarthWorks Urban Farm, a program of the Capuchin Soup Kitchen. This human services organization feeds Detroit residents and strives to maximize community self-reliance by improving the ability of all community members to obtain safe, nutritious food. Similarly, the Detroit Black Community Food Security Network is committed to developing a food-secure city in which all citizens are free of hunger, healthy, and benefiting from the food systems that impact them. For twenty years, Greening of Detroit has been planting trees, working with schools to build outdoor classrooms, beautifying parks and streetscapes, and organizing community gardens. Numerous other organizations, including extensions of Michigan State University and Wayne State University, have rallied around and aided the vigorous grassroots urban farming movement in Detroit.

In 2003, Greening of Detroit, Detroit Agriculture Network, EarthWorks Urban Farm, and Michigan State University formed the Garden Resource Program Collaborative to provide Detroit residents with the necessary supplies and resources to grow food in the city, including free seeds, transplants, compost, and hands-on education opportunities. The program grew from a network of 80 urban gardens in 2003 to 1,300 gardens in 2010, comprising backyard gardens, community gardens, and school gardens. The 2009 growing season produced 160 tons of fruits and vegetables worth approximately $500,000. In 2009, 23,000 pounds of produce were sold at Eastern Market and other area farmers markets under the Grown in Detroit label, earning $37,750. Some 1,100 pounds of food were donated to the Capuchin Soup Kitchen. The rest of the harvest was consumed by the families and neighbors who worked the land (Urban Agriculture Workgroup).

In 2010 Greening of Detroit began development of a three-acre market garden on the grounds surrounding Eastern Market to serve as a model for a small-scale, production-based, family-run farming operation. The market garden's business plan estimates the production of $100,000 in produce during its first year of operation and a net profit of $40,000, which is higher than the current average Detroit family household income (Growing Sustainable Communities: Urban Farming). The goal of the garden is to serve as a proven model for a Detroit family to operate an economically viable small-scale farm in the city.

URBAN AGRICULTURE POLICY FOR THE CITY OF DETROIT

As of 2010, members of the nonprofit urban farming community were working with a representative of the Detroit City Planning Commission to devise a strategy to guide the expansion of urban agriculture and delineate the codes and ordinances necessary to facilitate agricultural use of Detroit land. Calling themselves the Urban Agriculture Workgroup, these stakeholders have suggested that the policies of Detroit's urban agricultural system should require that farming activities demonstrate the "triple bottom line" of sustainability (environmental, economic, and social/health benefits). They have further requested that large farming operations be required to prove tangible, measurable benefits to the community as a condition of eligibility for a reduced tax rate and land price. In addition, they have suggested that the city limit allowable pesticides, herbicides, and fertilizers through codes and ordinances, require soil testing and soil remediation standards, and permit farmers to raise livestock under specific conditions.

In drafting proposed policies for urban farming, the Urban Agriculture Workgroup has drawn on research conducted by the American Institute of Architects Sustainable Design Assessment Team in its 2008 report "Leaner, Greener Detroit," in which the architects devoted a chapter to the potential of urban agriculture to serve as a vehicle for economic development. The report posited that putting to use the city's vacant land on a commercial scale would create jobs for residents and small business opportunities in food cultivation, processing, and distribution. It also emphasized urban farming's positive impact on the city's overall carbon footprint by increasing consumption of locally produced food. Moreover, the report recognized the benefit of enhanced community cohesion created by the repurposing of vacant land, leading to reduced social and health hazards such as crime and illegal dumping. The report concluded that Detroit was in a unique position to play a pioneering role in the emerging industry of urban agriculture on account of the success of its community garden programs and established network of community leaders in this field, as well as the food-related infrastructure provided by Eastern Market. "While we are not suggesting any specific targets with respect to number of acres or number of jobs created," the assessment team reported, "we believe that within five years Detroit would be able to build an urban agriculture system that would substantially exceed, in both respects, any other system in place in the United States" (American Institute of Architects Sustainable Design Assessment Team). The study's suggested agricultural activities included the cultivation of sunflowers for bio-diesel fuel; bio-intensive agriculture on small plots of one to 10 acres; the use of abandoned warehouses for hydroponics, fish farming, micro greens, and mushrooms; and the development of large-scale composting facilities.

TENSION BETWEEN THE FOR-PROFIT AND NON-PROFIT MODELS

When news broke of John Hantz's plan to develop the world's largest urban farm, many of those working at the grassroots level were skeptical. "I'm concerned about the corporate takeover of the urban agriculture movement in Detroit," stated Malik Yakini, founder of the Detroit Black Community Food Security Network, in Fortune magazine. "At this point the key players with him seem to be all white men in a city that's at least 82% black" (Whitford). Other activists have characterized Hantz's plan as a "land grab," to which he has responded: "It's not profit versus nonprofit, it's profit and nonprofit" (Business of Urban Agriculture Summit). Hantz pointed out that the city needs capital investment, tax dollars, and jobs, and that entrepreneurs are not going to move into Detroit if the only players in the market are nonprofits and foundations. He has emphasized that with 200,000 parcels of unused land, for-profit entrepreneurs and nonprofit groups could coexist. "We must respect the role of each player, though each player does not perfect the outcome," he said. "They work in concert like a community and provide a different service for each part" (Business of Urban Agriculture Summit).

Hantz has called for an urban agriculture policy modeled on the Homestead Act of 1862, which allowed settlers of the American West to earn ownership of public land through work. If the city were to engage individuals in the community to care for one or two acres surrounding their residence, he argued, these individuals could create equity by taking ownership of and responsibility for the land. In Hantz's view, these committed, taxpaying residents would be Detroit's "ultimate anchor" (Business of Urban Agriculture Summit).

The current partnership between the MGM Detroit Grand Casino and the Greening of Detroit to build a 1.8-acre greenhouse and garden on a corporate-owned gravel parking lot demonstrates the potential for nonprofit and for-profit concerns to work collaboratively (Gallagher, "MGM Grand Digs In for Garden Growth"). The project, which broke ground in July 2010, will grow fresh vegetables, fruit, and herbs to supply the casino's restaurants and other dining establishments in the city. The garden also encompasses an educational component to train youth to grow and harvest food, as well as a charitable component to supply a local food bank with city-grown produce.

CRITICS OF URBAN AGRICULTURE

Grassroots food activists are not alone in their criticism of Hantz's plan. Other detractors have expressed skepticism about the very notion of urban farming as a catalyst for regeneration. Civil rights advocate Reverend Jesse Jackson Sr. derided the concept of urban farming in Detroit as "cute, but foolish" in front of the Detroit City Council in September 2010 (Winter), stressing the city's need for investment in "industry, housing and construction" rather than agriculture. Jackson also intimated that large farms could drive more residents out of the city. Likewise, commentator Richard C. Longworth, a senior fellow at the Chicago Council on Global Affairs and the author of Caught in the Middle: America's Heartland in the Age of Globalism, has argued that urban farming is not a panacea for Detroit's ills, which can only be solved, in his view, by jobs and an economic turnaround. A thriving economy, he has contended, will produce a strong housing market and a healthy populace, while a broken economy will ensure poverty and malnutrition. From his perspective, urban farms are "nothing less than a symptom of civic catastrophe, a desperate last measure for people trapped in destitute neighborhoods" (Longworth).

Longworth has pointed out that the urban agriculture movement consists of niche farms that cannot fulfill global demand on account of their limited yields. Furthermore, he has maintained that the higher prices associated with these specialized farms are only accessible to middle- and upper-class urbanites. Other critics of urban agriculture have cautioned that although the local food movement is gaining momentum across the United States, urban farms have not yet proven economic sustainability in the free market economy, having relied thus far on volunteer labor and government grants for their success. Longworth, for one, has advocated for a large-scale solution involving mega-retailer Wal-Mart. He has suggested that the City of Detroit offer incentives for Wal-Mart to open stores—including smaller neighborhood markets that sell fresh produce—within city limits. By offering the corporation free land or pre-existing retail space in exchange for a commitment to stay in the city for a specified length of time, the city might persuade Wal-Mart to open in Detroit.

FROM MOTOWN TO GROWTOWN: A MODEL FOR THE REST OF THE WORLD

In 2010 media outlets on both sides of the Atlantic featured multiple stories on Detroit's urban farming movement, suggesting that the city could lead the country by creating a sustainable agricultural template for other struggling postindustrial areas—as well as thriving cities like New York and Los Angeles—to emulate. The city is already recognized internationally for its community-based responses to vacant land and lack of access to fresh food; large-scale urban farming initiatives like that proposed by Hantz Farms could repurpose a significant portion of underutilized land and potentially become an indispensable part of Detroit's economic and environmental landscape for years to come. As Hantz sees it, Detroit faces both a massive problem and an unprecedented opportunity. Hantz told his audience:

> This is a learning time. This is a gathering knowledge time. This is taking risk time. We are going to fail at some of the ideas we try—so what? But I believe the outcome of those failures will move us down the road to a better place. And we have to be strong enough to take the risk that we don't have to prove perfection. We're not in a perfect situation now, so why does this new idea have to become perfect to get play? . . . It's very entrepreneurial based . . . Where we end up ten years from now will not be anything you heard today; I believe that to be true. And I believe I will be wrong on a hundred things that we're trying to implement. The issue will be is it sustainable and can you work through those and improve that process and continue to survive. (Business of Urban Agriculture Summit)

As the 2010 growing season neared its end, Hantz had yet to break ground on any of his proposed projects within the city limits due to a stalled municipal process. "Right now, there simply aren't the necessary large tracts of contiguous land," said Detroit city planner Kathryn Underwood, who had hoped the code would be in place by the summer of 2010 (Preddy). The city is bogged down by such issues as valuing tax-delinquent land, relocating residents living in nearly abandoned neighborhoods, and creating tax and zoning policy for agricultural land use. "My personal hope," said Underwood, "is that the model that we roll out benefits as many people across the board in a city that really needs people to be employed and engaged in meaningful work" (Runk). Meanwhile, John Hantz waited for a real estate deal. "We could start overnight. We've got the equipment, everything, ready to go," he told the Detroit News (Berman). Despite being mired in bureaucracy, the ambitious business man still believed that Detroit could become a showplace and centerpiece for all growing systems and forward-thinking farming methods through the creative use of multiple agriculture technologies. "We can build a new, green economy in Detroit, and lead the world by example," he proclaimed on the Hantz Farms Web site. "A journey of a thousand miles begins with a single step. Let's take it together, Detroit."

QUESTIONS FOR DISCUSSION

1. What are the threats facing entrepreneurs in urban agriculture in Detroit? What are the opportunities?

2. What are the potential societal, environmental, and economic benefits of a locally grown food system in Detroit? What are the potential detriments of urban farming in Detroit?

3. Conduct a Strengths, Weaknesses, Opportunities, and Threats (SWOT) analysis of Hantz Farms or an entrepreneurial urban farming venture of your choosing.

REFERENCES/BIBLIOGRAPHY

Aguilar, L. (2010, July 13). "Local Food Movement Sprouts in Detroit." Detroit News 13 July 2010. Web. http://detnews.com/article/20100713/BIZ/7130340/Local-food-movement-sprouts-in-Detroit

American Institute of Architects Sustainable Design Assessment Team. "Leaner, Greener Detroit." Washington, DC: American Institute of Architects, 2008. Print.

Bassett, Tina. "Press: Hantz Farm in the News." Hantz Farms: Detroit, 23 Mar. 2009. http://www.hantzfarmsdetroit.com/press.html

Berman, Laura. "Entrepreneur Finds Detroit Farming a Slow Go." Detroit News 6 Apr. 2010. Web. 16 Feb. 2011. http://detnews.com/article/20100406/OPINION03/4060340/Entrepreneur-finds-Detroit-farming-a-slow-go

Brewers Association Facts. 9 Aug. 2010. Web. 16 Feb. 2011. http://www.brewersassociation.org/pages/business-tools/craft-brewing-statistics/facts

Cantrell, Patty. Sysco's Journey from Supply Chain to Value Chain: Results and Lessons Learned from the 2008 National Good Food Network/Sysco Corporation Pilot Project to Source and Sell Good Food. Wallace Center at

Winrock International, 2009. Web. 16 Feb. 2011. http://wallacecenter. org/our-work/Resource-Library/Innovative-Models/NGFN%20Case% 20Study_Syscos%20Journey%20From%20Supply%20Chain%20to%20Value %20Chain.pdf

Detroit Agriculture Network. Garden Resource Program Collaborative. Web. 16 Feb. 2011. http://www.detroitagriculture.org

Detroit Black Community Food Security Network. Detroit Black Community Food Security Network. Web. 16 Feb. 2011. http://detroitblackfoodse-curity.org

EarthWorks Urban Farm. Web. 16 Feb. 2011. http://www.cskdetroit.org/ EWG

Gallagher, John. (2010, July 31). "MGM Grand Digs In for Garden Growth." Detroit Free Press 31 July 2010. http://www.freep.com/article/ 20100731/BUSINESS04/7310323/MGM-Grand-digs-in-for-garden-growth

Gallagher, John. (2010, July 15). "Unemployment Rate in Michigan Dips to 13.2%." Detroit Free Press 15 July 2010. Web. 16 Feb. 2011. http://www. istockanalyst.com/article/viewiStockNews/articleid/4310052

Greening of Detroit. Web. 16 Feb. 2011. http://www.greeningofdetroit.com

Growing Sustainable Communities: Urban Farming. Dearborn: University of Michigan-Dearborn, 23 Feb. 2010. Print.

Hantz Farms. Detroit: http://www.hantzfarmsdetroit.com

Hantz Group: http://www.hantzgroup.com

Heller, Martin C., and Gregory A. Keoleian. Life Cycle-Based Sustainability Indicators for Assessment of the U.S. Food System. Ann Arbor: University of Michigan Center for Sustainable Systems, 2000. Print. Web. 16 Feb. 2011. http://css.snre.umich.edu/css_doc/CSS00-04.pdf

Kaffer, N. "Urban Farming Can Succeed in Detroit, Panelists Say." Crain's Detroit Business 7 Apr. 2010. Web. 16 Feb. 2011. http://www. crainsdetroit.com/article/20100407/FREE/100409916

Longworth, R. "Forget Urban Farms. We Need a Wal-Mart." GOOD 7 Jan. 2011. Web. 16 Feb. 2011. http://www.good.is/post/forget-urban-farms-we-need-a-wal-mart/

"Meijer 'Plants' More than $60 Million into Local Economies by Sourcing Fruits and Vegetables from Area Farmers." PR Newswire 26 July 2010. Web. 16 Feb. 2011. http://www.prnewswire.com/news-releases/meijer-plants-more-than-60-million-into-local-economies-by-sourcing-fruits-and-vegetables-from-area-farmers-99241544.html

Pollan, Michael. "Farmer in Chief." New York Times Magazine 12 Oct. 2008. Web. 16 Feb. 2011. http://michaelpollan.com/articles-archive/farmer-in-chief

Preddy, Melissa. "Orchards, Greenhouses Could Fill Abandoned Streets of Detroit." AFP American Edition 17 May 2010. Web. 16 Feb. 2011. http://www.google.com/hostednews/afp/article/ALeqM5jxbzzBn GZ2ZtA_W9OiD1QymhBq4Q

Runk, D. "Motor City May Provide Model for Urban Agriculture." Salon.com 23 Apr. 2010. Web. 16 Feb. 2011. http://www.salon.com/food/feature/2010/04/23/us_food_and_farm_detroit_farming

SEED Wayne. Web. 16 Feb. 2011. http://www.clas.wayne.edu/seedwayne

Shuman, Michael H. "Economic Impact of Localizinig Detroit's Food System." Ann Arbor, MI: Fair Food Foundation, April 2010. Web 16 Feb. 2011. http://www.fairfoodnetwork.org/sites/default/files/Economic%20Impact%20of%20Localizing%20Detroit%20Food%20System.pdf

The Business of Urban Agriculture Summit. Dearborn: University of Michigan-Dearborn, 7 Apr. 2010. Print.

Urban Agriculture Workgroup. (2010). City Planning Commission Urban Agriculture Draft Policy.

USDA. Web. 16 Feb. 2011. http://www.mypyramid.gov/pyramid/vegetables_why.html

Wasserman, W. "USDA Announces that National Farmers Market Directory Totals 6,132 Farmers Markets." United States Department of Agriculture Agricultural Marketing Service 4 Aug. 2010. Web. 16 Feb. 2011. http://www.ams.usda.gov/AMSv1.0/ams.printData.do?template=printPage&navID=&page=printPage&dDocId=STELPRDC5085966&dID=136193&wf=false&docTitle=USDA+Announces+that+National+Farmers+Market+Directory+Totals+6%2C132++Farmers+Markets

Whitford, D. "Can Farming Save Detroit?" Fortune 29 Dec. 2009. Web. 16 Feb. 2011. http://money.cnn.com/2009/12/29/news/economy/farming_detroit.fortune/index.htm

Winter, Michael. "In Detroit, Jesse Jackson Calls Urban Farming 'Cute but Foolish'." USA Today 7 Sept. 2010. Web. 16 Feb. 2011. http://www.cityfarmer.info/2010/09/07/in-detroit-jesse-jackson-calls-urban-farming-cute-but-foolish/

DATE DUE

DEMCO 25-380